INFORMATION TECHNOLOGIES IN MEDICINE

INFORMATION TECHNOLOGIES IN MEDICINE

VOLUME I: MEDICAL SIMULATION AND EDUCATION

Edited by

Metin Akay
Dartmouth College

Andy Marsh
National Technical University of Athens

A WILEY-INTERSCIENCE PUBLICATION

JOHN WILEY & SONS, INC.

New York · Chichester · Weinheim · Brisbane · Singapore · Toronto

For ordering and customer service, call 1-800-CALL-WILEY.

Library of Congress Cataloging in Publication Data is available.

Akay, Metin
  Information Technologies in Medicine, Volume I: Medical Simulation and Education, edited by Akay, Metin and Marsh, Andy.

ISBN 0-471-38863-7

10 9 8 7 6 5 4 3 2 1

■ CONTRIBUTORS

Ken-ichi Abe, Department of Electrical Engineering, Graduate School of
Engineering, Tohoku University, Aoba-yama 05, Sendai 980-8579, Japan
abe@abe.ecei.tohoku.ac.jp

Metin Akay, Thayer School of Engineering, Dartmouth Collete, Hanover, NH
03755
metin.akay@dartmouth.edu

Robert Curlee, University of California, San Diego School of Medicine, Learning Resources Center, La Jolla, CA 92093

Adrie C. M. Dumay, TNO Physics and Electronics Laboratory, Oude Walls-
dorperweg 63, P.O. Box 96864, 2509 JG The Hague, The Netherlands
dumay@fel.tno.nl

Gabriele Faulkner, University Hospital Benjamin Franklin, Free University of
Berlin, WE12 Department of Medical Informatics, Hindenburgdamm 30,
D-12200 Berlin, Germany
faulkner@medizin.fu-berlin.de

Alicia Fritchle, University of California, San Diego School of Medicine,
Learning Resources Center, La Jolla, CA 92093

Helene Hoffman, University of California, San Diego School of Medicine,
Learning Resources Center, La Jolla, CA 92093
hhoffman@ucsd.edu

Emil Jovanov, University of Alabama in Huntsville, 213 EB, Huntsville, AL
35899
jovanov@ece.uah.edu

Andy Marsh, National Technical University of Athens, Institute of Communication and Computer Systems, Euromed Laboratory Room 21.27, 9 Iron
Polytechiou Str, 15780 Zographou, Athens, Greece
andy@esd.ece.ntua.gr

Margaret Murray, University of California, San Diego School of Medicine,
Learning Resources Center, La Jolla, CA 92093

Shin-ichi Nitta, Department of Medical Electronics and Cardiology, Division
of Organ Pathophysiology, Institute of Development, Aging, and Cancer,
Tohoku University, Seiryo-machi, Sendai 980-8575, Japan

Vlada Radivojevic, Institute of Mental Health, Palmoticeva 37, 1100 Belgrade, Yugoslavia
drvr@infosky.net/drvr@eunet.yu

Richard A. Robb, Director, Biomedical Imaging Resource, Mayo Foundation, 200 First Street SW, Rochester, MN 55905
rar@mayo.edu

Joseph M. Rosen, Dartmouth-Hitchcock Medical Center, 1 Medical Center Drive, Lebanon, NH 03756

Richard M. Satava, Department of Surgery, Yale University School of Medicine, 40 Temple Street, New Haven, CT 06510
richard.satava@yale.edu

Dusan Starcevic, Faculty of Organizational Sciences, University of Belgrade, Jove Ilica 154, 11000 Belgrade, Yugoslavia
starcev@fon.fon.bg.ac.yu

Tomoyuki Yambe, Department of Medical Electronics and Cardiology, Division of Organ Pathophysiology, Institute of Development, Aging, and Cancer, Tohoku University, Seiryo-machi, Sendai 980-8575, Japan

Makoto Yoshizawa, Department of Electrical Engineering, Graduate School of Engineering, Tohoku University, Aoba-yama 05, Sendai 980-8579, Japan
yoshi@abe.ecei.tohoku.ac.jp

![] CONTENTS

The information technologies have made a significant impact in the areas of teaching and training surgeons by improving the physicians training and performance to better understand the human anatomy.

Surgical simulators and artificial environment have been developed to simulate the procedures and model the environments involved in surgery. Through development of optical technologies, rapid development and use of minimally invasive surgery has become widespread and placed new demands on surgical training. Traditionally physicians learn new techniques in surgery by observing procedures performed by experienced surgeons, practicing on cadaverous animal and human, and finally performing the surgery under supervision of the experienced surgeons. Note that, this is an expensive and lengthy training procedure. However, surgical simulators provide an environment for the physician to practice many times before operating on a patient. In addition, virtual reality technologies allow the surgeon in training to learn the details of surgery by providing both visual and tactile feedback to the surgeon working on a computer-generated model of the related organs.

A most important use of virtual environments is the use of the sensory ability to replicate the experience of people with altered body or brain function. This will allow practitioners to better understand their patients and the general public to better understand some medical and psychiatric problems.

In this volume, we will focus on the applications of information technologies in medical simulation and education.

The first chapter by R. Robb discuss the interactive visualization, manipulation, and measurement of multimodality 3-D medical images on computer workstations to evaluate them in several biomedical applications. It gives an extensive overview of virtual reality infrastructure, related methods and algorithms and their medical applications.

The second chapter by A. C. M. Dumay presents the extensive overview of the virtual environments in medicine and the recent medical applications of virtual environments.

The third chapter by A. N. Marsh covers the virtual reality and its integration into a 21st century telemedical information society. It outlines a possible framework for how the information technologies can be incorporated into a general telemedical information society.

The fourth chapter by J. M. Rosen discusses the virtual reality and medicine challenges with the specific emphases on how to improve the human body models for medical training and education. It also discuss the grand challenge in virtual reality and medicine for the pathologic state of tissues and the tissue's response to intervenations.

The fifth chapter by G. Faulkner presents the details of a virtual reality laboratory for medical applications including the technical components of a virtual system, input and output devices.

The sixth chapter by M. Yoshizawa et al. discusses the medical applications of virtual reality in Japan, including the computer aided surgery, applications of virtual reality for medical education, training and rehabilitation.

The seventh chapter by E. Jovanov et al. presents the multimodal interative environment for perceptualization of biomedical data based on the virtual reality modelling language head model with sonification to emphasize temporal dimension of selected visualization scores.

The eight chapter by H. Hoffman discusses a new virtual environment, Anatomic VisualizeR designed to support the teaching and learning of 3-D structures and complex spatial relationships.

The last chapter by R. M. Satava presents extensive reviews of current and emerging medical devices and technologies and major challenges in medicine and surgery in the 21st century.

We thank the authors for their valuable contributions to this volume and George Telecki, the Executive Editor and Shirley Thomas, Senior Associate Managing Editor of John Wiley & Sons, Inc. for their valuable support and encouragement throughout the preparation of this volume.

METIN AKAY

This work was partially supported by a USA NSF grant (IEEE EMBS Workshop on Virtual Reality in Medicine, BES–9725881) made to Professor Metin Akay.

INFORMATION TECHNOLOGIES IN MEDICINE

PART I

ARTIFICIAL ENVIRONMENT AND MEDICAL STIMULATOR/EDUCATION

■■■■■ **CHAPTER 1**

Virtual Reality in Medicine and Biology

RICHARD A. ROBB, PH.D.

Director, Biomedical Imaging Resource
Mayo Foundation
Rochester, Minnesota

Information Technologies in Medicine, Volume I: Medical Simulation and Education, Edited by
Metin Akay and Andy Marsh.
ISBN 0-471-38863-7   © 2001 John Wiley & Sons, Inc.

The practice of medicine and major segments of the biologic sciences have always relied on visualizations of the relationship of anatomic structure to biologic function. Traditionally, these visualizations either have been direct, via vivisection and postmortem examination, or have required extensive mental reconstruction, as in the microscopic examination of serial histologic sections. The revolutionary capabilities of new three-dimensional (3-D) and four-dimensional (4-D) imaging modalities and the new 3-D scanning microscope technologies underscore the vital importance of spatial visualization to these sciences. Computer reconstruction and rendering of multidimensional medical and histologic image data obviate the taxing need for mental reconstruction and provide a powerful new visualization tool for biologists and physicians. Voxel-based computer visualization has a number of important uses in basic research, clinical diagnosis, and treatment or surgery planning; but it is limited by relatively long rendering times and minimal possibilities for image object manipulation.

The use of virtual reality (VR) technology opens new realms in the teaching and practice of medicine and biology by allowing the visualizations to be manipulated with intuitive immediacy similar to that of real objects; by allowing the viewer to enter the visualizations, taking any viewpoint; by allowing the objects to be dynamic, either in response to viewer actions or to illustrate normal or abnormal motion; and by engaging other senses, such as touch and hearing (or even smell) to enrich the visualization. Biologic applications extend across a range of scale from investigating the structure of individual cells through the organization of cells in a tissue to the representation of organs and organ systems, including functional attributes such as electrophysiologic signal distribution on the surface of an organ. They are of use as instructional aids as well as basic science research tools. Medical applications include basic anatomy instruction, surgical simulation for instruction, visualization for diagnosis, and surgical simulation for treatment planning and rehearsal.

Although the greatest potential for revolutionary innovation in the teaching and practice of medicine and biology lies in dynamic, fully immersive, multisensory fusion of real and virtual information data streams, this technology is still under development and not yet generally available to the medical researcher. There are, however, a great many practical applications that require different levels of interactivity and immersion, that can be delivered now, and that will have an immediate effect on medicine and biology. In developing these applications, both hardware and software infrastructure must be adaptable to many different applications operating at different levels of complexity. Interfaces to shared resources must be designed flexibly from the outset and creatively reused to extend the life of each technology and to realize satisfactory return on the investment.

Crucial to all these applications is the facile transformation between an image space organized as a rectilinear N-dimensional grid of multivalued voxels and a model space organized as surfaces approximated by multiple planar tiles. The required degree of integration between these realms ranges between purely educational or instructional applications, which may be best served by a small library of static "normal" anatomical models, and individualized procedure planning, which requires routine rapid conversion of patient image data into possibly dynamic models. The most complex and challenging applications, those that show the greatest promise of significantly changing the practice of medical research or treatment, require an intimate and immediate union of image and model with real-world, real-time data. It may well be that the ultimate value of VR in medicine will derive more from the sensory enhancement of real experience than from the simulation of normally sensed reality.

1.1 INFRASTRUCTURE

Virtual reality deals with the science of perception. A successful virtual environment is one that engages the user, encouraging a willing suspension of disbelief and evoking a feeling of presence and the illusion of reality. Although arcade graphics and helmeted, gloved, and cable-laden users form the popular view of VR, it should not be defined by the tools it uses but rather by the functionality it provides. VR provides the opportunity to create synthetic realities for which there are no real antecedents and brings an intimacy to the data by separating the user from traditional computer interfaces and real-world constraints, allowing the user to interact with the data in a natural fashion.

Interactivity is key. To produce a feeling of immersion or presence (a feeling of being physically present within the synthetic environment) the simulation must be capable of real-time interactivity; technically, a minimum visual update rate of 30 frames per second and a maximum total computational lag time of 100 ms are required (1, 2).

1.1.1 Hardware Platforms

My group's work in VR is done primarily on Silicon Graphics workstations, specifically an Onyx/Reality Engine and an Onyx2/Infinite Reality system. Together with Performer (3), these systems allow us to design visualization software that uses coarse-grained multiprocessing, reduces computational lag time, and improves the visual update rate. These systems were chosen primarily for their graphics performance and our familiarity with other Silicon Graphics hardware.

We support "fish-tank" immersion through the use of Crystal Eyes stereo glasses and fully immersive displays via Cybereye head-mounted displays (HMDs). By displaying interlaced stereo pairs directly on the computer monitor, the stereo glasses provide an inexpensive high-resolution stereo display that can be easily shared by multiple users. Unfortunately, there is a noticeable lack of presence and little separation from the traditional computer interface with this type of display. The HMD provides more intimacy with the data and improves the sense of presence. We chose the Cybereye HMD for our initial work with fully immersive environments on a cost/performance basis. Although it has served adequately for the initial explorations, its lack of resolution and restricted field of view limit its usefulness in serious applications. We are currently evaluating other HMDs and display systems to improve display quality, including the Immersive Workbench (FakeSpace) and the Proview HMD (Kaiser Electro-Optics).

Our primary three space tracking systems are electromagnetic 6 degree of freedom (DOF) systems. Initially, three space tracking was done using Polhemus systems, but we are now using an Ascension MotionStar system to reduce the noise generated by computer monitors and fixed concentrations of ferrous material. In addition to electomagnetic tracking, we support ultrasonic and mechanical tracking systems.

Owing to the nature of many of our simulations, we incorporate haptic feedback using a SensAble Technology's PHANToM. This allows for 3 degrees of force feedback, which we find adequate for simulating most puncture, cutting, and pulling operations.

1.1.2 Network Strategies

VR simulations can run the gamut from single-user static displays to complex dynamic multiuser environments. To accommodate the various levels of complexity while maintaining a suitable degree of interactivity, our simulation infrastructure is based on a series of independent agents spread over a local area network (LAN). Presently, the infrastructure consists of an avatar agent running on one of the primary VR workstations and a series of device daemons running on other workstations on the network. The avatar manages the display tasks for a single user, and the daemon processes manage the various VR input/ output (I/O) devices. The agents communicate via an IP Multicasting protocol. IP multicasting is a means of transmitting IP datagrams to an unlimited number of hosts without duplication. Because each host can receive or ignore these packets at a hardware level simply by informing the network card which multicast channels to access, there is little additional computational load placed on the receiving system (4). This scheme is scalable, allows for efficient use of available resources, and off loads the secondary tasks of tracking and user feedback from the primary display systems.

1.2 METHODS

1.2.1 Image Processing and Segmentation

Image sources for the applications discussed here include spiral CT, both conventional MRI and magnetic resonance (MR) angiography, the digitized macrophotographs of whole-body cryosections supplied by the National Library of medicine (NLM) Visible Human project (5), serial stained microscope slides, and confocal microscope volume images. Many of these images are monochromatic, but others are digitized in full color and have a significant amount of information encoded in the color of individual voxels.

In all cases, the image data must be segmented, i.e., the voxels making up an object of interest must be separated from those not making up the object. Segmentation methods span a continuum between manual editing of serial sections and complete automated segmentation of polychromatic data by a combination of statistical color analysis and shape-based spatial modification.

All methods of automated segmentation that use image voxel values or their higher derivatives to make boundary decisions are negatively affected by spatial inhomogeneity caused by the imaging modality. Preprocessing to correct such inhomogeneity is often crucial to the accuracy of automated segmentation. General linear and nonlinear image filters are often employed to control noise, enhance detail, or smooth object surfaces.

Serial section microscope images must generally be reregistered section to section before segmentation, a process that must be automated as much as possible, although some manual correction is usually required for the best results. In trivial cases (such as the segmentation of bony structures from CT data), the structure of interest may be readily segmented simply by selecting an appropriate grayscale threshold, but such basic automation can at best define a uniform tissue type, and the structure of interest usually consists of only a portion of all similar tissue in the image field. Indeed, most organs have at least one "boundary of convention," i.e., a geometric line or plane separating the organ from other structures that are anatomically separate but physically continuous; thus it is necessary to support interactive manual editing regardless of the sophistication of automated segmentation technologies available.

Multispectral image data, either full-color optical images or spatially coregistered medical volume images in multiple modalities, can often be segmented by use of statistical classification methods (6). We use both supervised and unsupervised automated voxel classification algorithms of several types. These methods are most useful on polychromatically stained serial section micrographs, because the stains have been carefully designed to differentially color structures of interest with strongly contrasting hues. There are, however, startling applications of these methods using medical images, e.g., the use of combined T1 and T2-weighted images to image multiple sclerosis lesions. Color separation also has application in the NLM Visible Human images; but the natural coloration of tissues does not vary as widely as specially designed stains, and differences in coloration do not always correspond to the accepted boundaries of anatomic organs.

Voxel-based segmentation is often incomplete, in that several distinct structures may be represented by identical voxel values. Segmentation of uniform voxel fields into subobjects is often accomplished by logical means (i.e., finding independent connected groups of voxels) or by shape-based decomposition (7).

All the models discussed in this chapter have been processed and segmented using the automated and manual tools in Analyze$_{AVW}$ (8–10), a comprehensive medical imaging workshop developed by the Biomedical Imaging Resource of the Mayo Foundation. Analyze$_{AVW}$ supports the segmentation of volumetric images into multiple object regions by means of a companion image, known as an object map, that stores the object membership information of every voxel in the image. In the case of spatially registered volume images, object maps allow structures segmented from different modalities to be combined with proper spatial relationships.

1.2.2   Tiling Strategies

For the imaging scientist, reality is 80 million polygons per frame (4) and comes at a rate of 30 frames per second (2400 million polygons per second). Unfortunately, current high-end hardware is capable of displaying upward of only 10 million polygons per second. So although currently available rendering algorithms can generate photorealistic images from volumetric data (11–14), they cannot sustain the necessary frame rates. Thus the complexity of the data must be reduced to fit within the limitations of the available hardware.

We have developed a number of algorithms, of which three will be discussed here (15–17), for the production of efficient geometric (polygonal) surfaces from volumetric data. An efficient geometric surface contains a prespecified number of polygons intelligently distributed to accurately reflect the size, shape, and position of the object being modeled while being sufficiently small in number to permit real-time display on a modern workstation. Two of these algorithms use statistical measures to determine an optimal polygonal configuration and the third is a refinement of a simple successive approximation technique.

Our modeling algorithms assume that the generation of polygonal surfaces occurs in four phases: segmentation, surface detection, feature extraction, and polygonization. Of these phases, the modeling algorithms manage the last three. Data segmentation is managed by other tools found in Analyze$_{\text{AVW}}$ and AVW (8–10).

For all the methods, surface detection is based on the binary volume produced by segmentation. The object's surface is the set of voxels in which the change between object and background occurs. For the statically based methods, feature extraction determines the local surface curvature for each voxel in the object's surface. This calculation transforms the binary surface into a set of surface curvature weights and eliminates those surface voxels that are locally flat (15).

Given a binary volume F, the curvature c is calculated by applying the following to all voxels F_{xyz}:

$$c = \sum_{z=-1}^{1} \sum_{y=-1}^{1} \sum_{x=-1}^{1} F_{xyz} \qquad (1.1)$$

Surface voxels are assigned a weight based on their deviation from being flat, which corresponds to a sum of 17. The magnitude of the weight gives an indication of the sharpness of the curvature; and the sign, an indication of the direction of curvature.

1.2.3 Kohonen Shrinking Network

A Kohonen network, or self-organizing map, is a common type of neural network. It maps a set of sample vectors **S** from an N-dimensional space of real numbers R^N onto a lattice of nodes in an M-dimensional array L. Each node in **L** has a N-dimensional position vector **n**. An arbitrary N-dimensional vector **v** is then mapped onto the nearest node in R^N (16, 18). This node is referred to as the best matching unit (*bmu*) and satisfies the condition

$$\|bmu - \mathbf{v}\| = \|\mathbf{n} - \mathbf{v}\| \quad \forall \mathbf{n} \notin \mathbf{S} \tag{1.2}$$

This defines the mapping

$$T: V \rightarrow L, \quad (\mathbf{v} \in V) \rightarrow (T(\mathbf{v}) \in L) \tag{1.3}$$

where

$$T(\mathbf{v} \in V) = bmu \tag{1.4}$$

By applying T to a given set of sample vectors **S**, V is divided into regions with a common nearest position vector. This is known as Voroni tessellation. The usefulness of the network is that the resultant mapping preserves the topology and distribution of the position vectors. That is, adjacent vectors in R^N are mapped to adjacent nodes in L, and adjacent nodes in L will have similar position vectors in R^N. If we let $P(x)$ be an unknown probability distribution on R^N from which any number of sample vectors are drawn, then to preserve distribution, for any sample vector from $P(x)$, each node has an equal probability of being mapped to that vector. This means that the relative density of position vectors approximates $P(x)$.

   To begin tiling the curvature image, an initial surface consisting of a fixed number of quadrilateral tiles is generated, typically a cylinder that encompasses the bounding box of the object. The network then iteratively adapts the polygon vertices to the points, with non-zero weights in the curvature image; greater weight is given to points with greater curvature. Thus as the cylinder "shrinks" toward the object surface, polygon vertex density becomes directly related to local curvature; many vertices are pulled toward surface detail features, leaving flat regions of the surface represented by a few large tiles (Fig. 1.1).

1.2.4 Growing Net

Owing to the nature of the Kohonen network, a surface with a bifurcation or a hole will exhibit distortions as the network struggles to twist a fixed topology to the surface. This problem was observed in an initial Kohonen-based tiling algorithm (15, 19). To correct this, we implemented a second algorithm based on the work of Fritzke (18, 20).

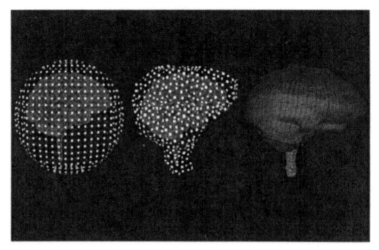

Figure 1.1. Kohonen shrinking network tiler. Reprinted with permission from Ref. 17.

Using competitive Hebbian learning, the network is adapted to the set **S** of sample vectors through the addition and deletion of edges or connections. To define the topologic structure of the network, a set E of unweighted edges is defined, and an edge-aging scheme is used to remove obsolete edges during the adaptation process. The resultant surface is the set of all polygons P where a single polygon P is defined by any three nodes connected by edges.

The network is initialized with three nodes a, b, and c, and their edges, at random positions v_a, v_b, and v_c in R^N, which form a single triangle. A sample signal s is selected from **S** at random, and the nearest node n_1 and the second nearest node n_2 are determined. The age of all edges emanating from n_1 are incremented by adding the squared distance between s and n_1.

$$\Delta\text{err}(n_1) = \|v_n - s\|^2 \tag{1.5}$$

n_1 and its direct topologic neighbors are moved toward s by fractions ε_b and ε_n, respectively, of the total distance

$$\Delta v_{n_1} = \varepsilon_b(s - v_{n_1}) \tag{1.6}$$

$$\Delta v_n = \varepsilon_n(s - v_n) \tag{1.7}$$

$$\forall n \in DTN(n_1) \tag{1.8}$$

If n_1 and n_2 are connected by an edge, that edge's age is set to 0. Otherwise a new edge connecting the nodes is created as well as all possible polygons resulting from this edge. All edges and associated polygons with an age greater than $a_{\max}$ are removed. If this results in orphaned nodes—nodes without any connecting edges—those nodes are removed.

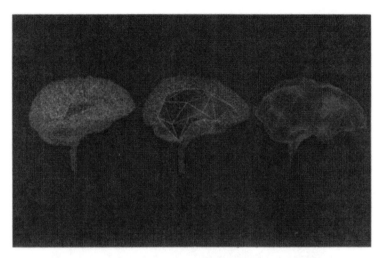

Figure 1.2. The growing cell network tiler. Reprinted with permission from Ref. 17.

If the number of signals s presented to the net is an integer multiple of the frequency of node addition λ, a new node is inserted into the network between the node with the maximum accumulated error q and its direct neighbor with the largest error variable f:

$$v_r = 0.5(v_q + v_f) \tag{1.9}$$

Edges connecting r with q and f are inserted, replacing the original edge between q and f. Additional edges and polygons are added to ensure that the network remains a set of two-dimensional (2-D) simplices (triangles). The error variables for q and f are reduced by multiplying them by a constant α (empirically found to be 0.5 for most cases). The error variable for r is initialized to that of node q. At this point, all error variables are decreased by multiplying them by a constant d (typically a value of 0.995 is adequate for most cases). Figure 1.2 illustrates the growing process.

Because the connections between the nodes are added in an arbitrary fashion, a postprocessing step is required to reorient the polygonal normals. We used a method described by Hoppe (21) with great success (15).

1.2.5 Deformable Adaptive Modeling

Algorithms such as the growing net described above reconstruct a surface by exploring a set of data points and imposing a structure on them by means of some local measure. Although these methods can achieve a high degree of accuracy, they can be adversely affected by noise or other perturbations in the surface data. Deformable mesh-based algorithms, like our Kohonen-based method, are limited to surfaces that are homomorphic to the initial mesh's

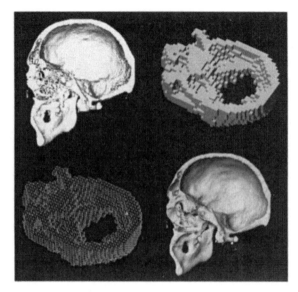

Figure 1.3. Image data and tiled surfaces at different resolution.

topology if they are to successfully reconstruct the surface. Based on the work of Algorri and Schmitt (22), we developed an algorithm that uses a local technique to recover the initial topology of the data points and applies a deformable modeling process to reconstruct the surface.

An initial mesh is created by partitioning the data space into a set of cubes. The size of the cubes determines the resolution of the resultant surface; the smaller the cube the higher the resolution (Fig. 1.3). A cube is labeled as a data element if it contains at least one data point. From the set of labeled cubes, a subset of face cubes is identified. A face cube is any cube that has at least two sides without adjacent neighbors. By systematically triangulating the center points of each face cube, a rough approximation of the surface is generated. This rough model retains the topologic characteristics of the input volume and forms the deformable mesh.

The adaptive step uses a discrete dynamic system constructed from a set of nodal masses, namely the mesh's vertices, that are interconnected by a set of adjustable springs. This system is governed by a set of ordinary differential equations of motion (a discrete Lagrange equation) that allows the system to deform through time.

Given a mass value μ_i, a damping coefficient Υ_i, and the total internal force g_i on node i owing to the spring connections to its neighboring node j then the discrete Lagrange function is defined by

$$f_i = \mu_i \frac{d^2 x_i}{dt^2} + \Upsilon_i \frac{dx_i}{dt} + g_i \qquad g_i = \sum_j s_{ij} \qquad (1.10)$$

Where f_i is the external force applied at node i and serves to couple the mesh to the input data. The total internal force g_i is the sum of the spring forces acting between node i and its neighbor node(s) j. Given two vertex positions x_i and x_j the spring force s_{ij} is determined by

$$s_{ij} = k_j(|x_i - x_j| - l_i)\left(\frac{x_i - x_j}{|x_i - x_j|}\right) \quad (1.11)$$

where k_j is the spring stiffness coefficient, and l_i is the natural spring length.

In our mass spring model, the set of coupled equations is solved iteratively over time using a fourth-order Runge-Kutta method until all masses have reached an equilibrium position. To draw the data toward the data's surface and to recover fine detail, each nodal mass is attached to the surface points by an imaginary spring. The nodal masses react to forces coming from the surface points and from the springs that interconnect them; thus the system moves as a coherent whole. Each nodal mass moves by following the dynamic equation

$$0 = \mu_i \frac{d^2 x_i}{dt^2} + \Upsilon_i \frac{dx_i}{dt} + g_i + k_d(x_i - x_d) \quad (1.12)$$

where k_d is the spring stiffness coefficient of the imaginary spring, and x_d is the position of the surface point in data space. We found that for most datasets, the equations do not converge to a single equilibrium position, rather they tend to oscillate around the surface points. To accommodate this, we terminate the algorithm when an error term, usually a measure of the total force, has been minimized.

1.3   APPLICATIONS

The visualization of microscopic anatomic structures in three dimensions is at once an undemanding application of VR and an example of the greatest potential of the technology. As of yet, the visualization aspect of the task is paramount, little of the interactive nature of VR has been exploited, and screen-based display is generally adequate to the visualization task. However, the reality portrayed is not a simulation of a real-world experience but, in fact, an "enhanced reality," a perceptual state not normally available in the real world.

1.3.1   Prostate Microvessels

New diagnostic tests have increased the percentage of prostate cancers detected, but there is no current method for assessing in vivo the widely varying malignant potential of these tumors. Thus improved diagnosis has led to removing more prostates, rather than the improved specificity of diagnosis that might ultimately lead to fewer surgeries or at least to more precise and morbidity-

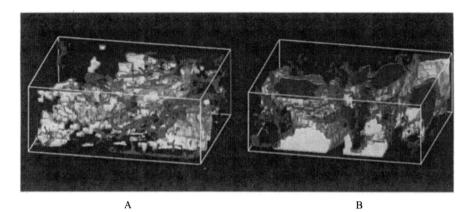

A   B

Figure 1.4. A, Tumor-nourishing neovasculature. **B,** Normal microvessels.

free surgeries. One known histologic indicator of malignancy is the density of microvessels feeding the tumor. This feature could conceivably lead to methods of characterizing malignancy in vivo, but angiogenesis is not fully understood physically or chemically.

In one VR application, several hundred 4-μ-thick serial sections through both normal and cancerous regions of excised tissue after retropubic prostatectomy were differentially stained with antibodies to factor VII–related antigen to isolate the endothelial cells of blood vessels. The sections were digitized through the microscope in color, equalized for variations in tissue handling and microscope parameters, segmented, spatially coregistered section to section, and reconstructed into 3-D views of both normal and tumor-feeding vessel beds.

The two types of vessel trees are visually distinctive; the tumor-associated neovasculature appears much more twisted and tortuous than the normal vessels (Fig. 1.4). Furthermore, measurement of the instantaneous radius of curvature over the entire structure bears out the visual intuition, in that the cancerous neovasculature exhibits a statistically significant larger standard deviation of curvature (i.e., more change in curvature) than the normal vessels (22).

1.3.2   Trabecular Tissue

The trabecular tissue of the eye is a ring of spongy, fluid-filled tissue situated at the junction of the cornea, iris, and sclera. It lies between the anterior chamber of the eye and the canal of Schlemm, which is the conduit for aqueous humor back into the blood supply. Because this tissue lies in the only outflow path for aqueous humor, it has long been implicated in glaucoma, in which the interior ocular pressure rises. Although many investigators have linked changes in this tissue to glaucoma, whether the changes are the cause or a symptom of the pressure rise is not known. The tissue exhibits a resistance to flow much greater than that of a randomly porous material with the same volumetric proportion

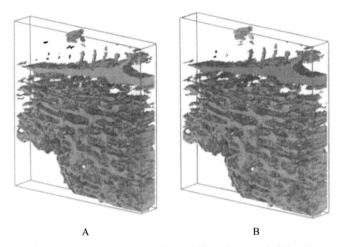

A   B

Figure 1.5. Fluid space in trabecular tissue (**A**) before and (**B**) after morphologic processing. Reprinted with permission from Ref. 24.

of fluid space to matrix, implying there is some sort of funneling or sieving structure in the tissue; but this structure has never been revealed by 2-D analysis.

My group (ZY) digitized and analyzed several hundred 1-μ-thick stained serial sections of trabecular tissue and imaged 60-μ-thick sections of trabecular tissue as volume images, using the confocal microscope, a small-aperture scanning light microscope (SLM) that produces optically thin section images of thick specimens. We found the stained serial sections superior for the extent of automated tissue type segmentation possible (trabecular tissue consists of collagen, cell nuclei, cell protoplasm, and fluid space), although the variations in staining and microscope conditions required significant processing to correct. The confocal images were perfectly acceptable for segmenting fluid space from tissue, however; and their inherent registration and minor section-to-section variation in contrast proved superior for an extended 3-D study.

We found the architecture of the tissue so complex that we abandoned any attempt to unravel the entire tissue and concentrated on the architecture of the connected fluid space. We found the fluid space in all specimens to be continuous from the anterior chamber through the trabecular tissue into Schlemm's canal. However, after a morphometric analysis in which small chambers were successively closed, we found that the interconnection is maintained by small chambers (<3 μ in diameter). There are a large number of these narrowings, and they occur at all regions of the tissue; but all specimens we examined showed disconnection after closing off all the ≤ 3-μ chambers. In Figure 1.5A, before any morphologic processing, all of the lightly shaded fluid space is interconnected, other darker areas illustrate small cul-de-sacs in the remaining fluid space. In Figure 1.5B, after closing all chambers < 2 μ in diameter, shows a loss of connectivity between the anterior chamber and Schlemm's canal. We believe this project helps uncover clues about the normal and abnormal functions of this tissue.

1.3.3   Corneal Cells

The density and arrangement of corneal cells are a known indicators of the general health of the cornea, and they is routinely assessed for donor corneas and potential recipients. The corneal confocal microscope is a reflected-light scanning aperture microscope fitted for direct contact with a living human cornea. The image it captures is a 3-D tomographic optical image of the cornea. The images represent sections about 15 μ thick, and they may be captured at 1-μ intervals through the entire depth of the cornea. This instrument is a potentially valuable new tool for assessing a wide range of corneal diseases.

My group is developing a software system for the automated measurement of local keratocyte nuclear density in the cornea. In addition, we have been producing visualizations of the keratocyte-packing structure in the intact human cornea. Although the images are inherently registered, eye movement tends to corrupt registration, necessitating detection and correction. In-plane inhomogeneity (hot spots) and progressive loss of light intensity with image plane depth are easily corrected. Keratocyte nuclei are automatically detected and counted, size filters reject objects too small to be nuclei and detect oversize objects that are recounted based on area.

We found that both the global and the local automated density counts in rabbit corneas correlate well to those reported by other investigators and to conventional histologic evaluation of cornea tissue from the same rabbits scanned by confocal microscopy. We also discerned a decrease in keratocyte density toward the posterior of the cornea similar to that reported by other investigators. Figure 1.6 shows the stacking pattern of keratocyte nuclei found in a living normal human cornea. Other bright structures too small to be cell nuclei are also shown.

1.3.4   Neurons

The study of neuronal function has advanced to the point that the binding sites for specific neurotransmitters may be visualized as a 3-D distribution on the surface of a single neuron. Visualization of the architectural relationships between neurons is less well advanced. Nerve plexes, in which millions of sensory nerve cells are packed into a few cubic millimeters of tissue offer an opportunity to image a tractable number of cells in situ (25).

In one study, an intact superior mesenteric ganglion from a guinea pig was imaged with confocal microscopy in an 8 × 4 3-D mosaic. Each mosaic tile consisted of a stack of 64 521 × 512 pixel confocal images. In all, 20 complete neurons were located in the mosaic. As each neuron was found, a subvolume containing that neuron was constructed by fusing portions of two or more of

Figure 1.6. Cell nuclei in a confocal volume image of a live human cornea.

the original mosaic subvolumes. Each neuron was converted into a triangularly tiled surface and repositioned globally in virtual space. When completed, the virtual model consisted of 20 discrete neurons in their positions as found in the intact tissue. Figure 1.7 shows the entire field of neurons. The neurons exist in clusters, and most of the scanned volume remains empty. Several different neuronal shapes are seen, and most neurons can be easily grouped by type. Figure 1.8 demonstrates a single neuron with binding sites for specific neurotransmitters shown as objects intersecting the neuron's surface.

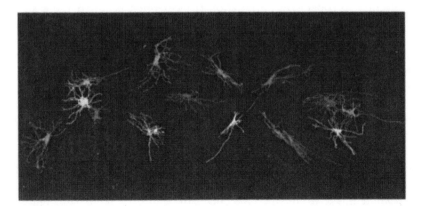

Figure 1.7. Models of 20 neurons in situ from the inferior mesenteric ganglion of a guinea pig.

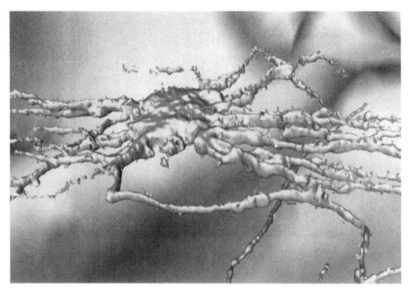

Figure 1.8. Tiled neuron from confocal microscope data showing binding sites for nicotine and VIP.

1.3.5 Surgical Planning

1.3.5.1 Craniofacial Surgery. Craniofacial surgery involves surgery of the facial and cranial skeleton and soft tissues. It is often done in conjunction with plastic surgical techniques to correct congenital deformities or for the treatment of deformities caused by trauma, tumor resection, infection, and other acquired conditions. Craniofacial surgical techniques are often applied to other bony and soft tissue body structures.

Currently, preoperative information is most often acquired using x-ray or CT scanning for the bony structures; MRI is used to visualize the soft internal tissues. Although the information provided by the scanners in useful, preoperative 3-D visualization of the structures involved in the surgery provides additional valuable information (26, 27). Furthermore, 3-D visualization facilitates accurate measurement of structures of interest, allowing for the precise design of surgical procedures. Presurgical planning also minimizes the surgery's duration (28). This minimizes the risk of complications and reduces the cost of the operation.

Figure 1.9 demonstrates the use of 3-D visualization techniques in the planning and quantitative analysis of craniofacial surgery. Data acquired from sequential adjacent scans using conventional x-ray CT technology provides the 3-D volume image from which the bone can be directly rendered. Figure 1.9A shows the usefulness of direct 3-D visualization of skeletal structures for the assessment of defects, in this case the result of an old facial fracture. One approach to planning the surgical correction of such a defect is to manipulate

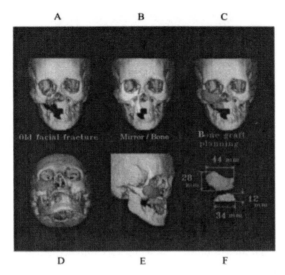

Figure 1.9. Craniofacial surgery planning using volume rendering and segmentation of a 3-D CT scan of the patient. Prosthetic implants can be precisely designed to fill voids or deficits caused by trauma or disease.

the 3-D rendering of the patient's cranium. Using conventional workstation systems, surgeons can move mirror images of the undamaged structures on the side of the face opposite the injury onto the damaged region. This artificial structure can be shaped using visual cutting tools in the 3-D rendering. Such tailored objects can then be used for simulation of direct implantation shown in the different views of the designed implant (Fig. 1.9C–E). Accurate size and dimension measurements, as well as precise contour shapes, can then be made for use in creating the actual implants, often using rapid prototyping machinery to generate the prosthetic implant.

This type of planning and limited simulation is done on standard workstation systems. The need for high-performance computing systems is demonstrated by the advanced capabilities necessary for direct rehearsal of the surgical procedure, computation and manipulation of deformable models (elastic tissue preparation), and the associated application of the rehearsed plan directly during the surgical procedure. The rehearsal of the surgical plan minimizes or eliminates the need to design complex plans in the operating room while the patient is under anesthesia with, perhaps, the cranium open. Further application of the surgical plan directly in the operating room using computer-assisted techniques could dramatically reduce the time of surgery and increase the chances for a successful outcome.

1.3.5.2 Neurosurgery. The most difficult and inaccessible of neurosurgical procedures are further confounded by the variability of pathologic brain anatomy and the difficulty of visualizing the 3-D relationships among structures

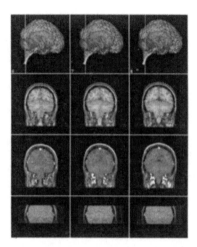

Figure 1.10. Sectional images in three modalities recomputed along the stereotactic line of sight.

from serial MR images. VR techniques hold tremendous potential to reduce operating room time through extended presurgical visualization and rehearsal.

In one project, volumetric MRI scans of patients with particularly inaccessible brain tumors of circulatory anomalies were segmented into the objects of interest. Interactive visualizations of brain structures, arteries, and tumors were made available to the surgeons before surgery. The surgeons in all cases reported insights they had not understood from the serial sections alone; and in some cases, they revised surgical plans based on the visualizations (29). They reported no serious discrepancies between the visualizations and what they found during surgery.

My group has just completed a related project to provide multiplanar and 3-D displays of patient data intraoperatively, with the viewpoint registered to a real-world surgical probe in the patient. Figure 1.10 depicts a screen from that system. Planar images perpendicular to the line of sight of the surgical probe are displayed relative to a 3-D surface model of the brain structures and tumor of a patient.

Figure 1.11 shows an example of augmented or enhanced reality with real-time data fusion for intraoperative image-guided neurosurgery. Real-time video images of the operative site can be registered with preoperative models of the brain anatomy and pathology obtained from patient scans. Using transparency, the surgeon can view an appropriately fused combination of real-time data and preoperative data to "see into the patient," facilitating evaluation of approach, margins, and surgical navigation.

1.5.3.3 Prostate Surgery. The most commonly prescribed treatment for confirmed malignant prostate cancer is complete removal of the prostate. Recent improvements in diagnostic screening procedures have improved prostate

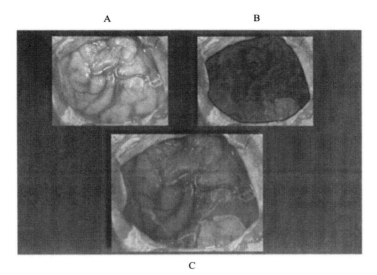

Figure 1.11. Enhanced reality for intraoperative navigation, wherein (**A**) a real-time video of the brain surface and (**B**) anatomic models obtained from a preoperative 3-D scan are (**C**) registered, fused, and displayed with transparency to allow the surgeon to see into the brain and assess tumor location approach, and margins.

cancer diagnoses to the point that radical prostatectomy is the most commonly performed surgical procedure at Mayo-affiliated hospitals (30).The procedure is plagued with significant morbidity in the form of postoperative incontinence and impotence (31). Minimizing these negative affects hinges on taking particular care to completely remove all cancerous prostate tissue while sparing neural and vascular structures that are in close proximity. In a procedure notable for difficulty of access and wide variability of anatomy, routine surgical rehearsal using patient-specific data could have a significant effect on procedural morbidity if the rehearsal accurately portrays what the surgeon will find during the procedure.

In a pilot study (23), presurgical MR volume images of five patients were segmented to identify the prostate, bladder, urethra, vas defrens, external urinary sphincter, seminal vesicles, and the suspected extent of cancerous tissue. The image segments were tiled and reviewed by the surgeons in an interactive on-screen object viewer after performing the prostatectomy. In all cases, the surgeons reported a general agreement between the model anatomy and their surgical experience. This evidence supports the potential value of preoperative 3-D visualization and evaluation of prostate anatomy to enhance surgical precision and reduce the risk of morbidity. Figure 1.12 shows models from three of the patients. Note the wide variability in the shape and size of the normal anatomic structure and the different relationships among the tumors and other structures.

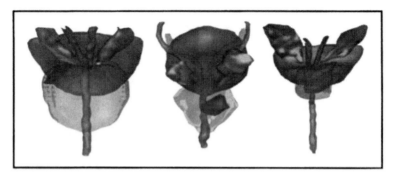

Figure 1.12. Tiled models of the prostate and bladder taken from preoperative MRI scans of three patients.

1.3.6   Virtual Endoscopy

Virtual endoscopy (VE) describes a new method of diagnosis, using computer processing of 3-D image datasets (such as those from CT or MRI scans) to provide simulated visualizations of patient-specific organs, similar or equivalent to those produced by standard endoscopic procedures (32–34). Thousands of endoscopic examinations are performed each year. These procedures are invasive, often uncomfortable, and may cause serious side effects such as perforation, infection, and hemorrhage. VE avoids these risks and when used before a standard endoscopic examination may minimize procedural difficulties, decreasing the morbidity rate. In addition, VE allows for exploration of body regions that are inaccessible or incompatible with standard endoscopic procedures.

The recent availability of the Visual Human Datasets (VHDs) (5), coupled with the development of computer algorithms that accurately and rapidly render high-resolution images in 3-D and perform fly-throughs, provide a rich opportunity to take this new methodology from theory to practice. The VHD is ideally suited for the refinement and validation of VE. My group has been actively engaged in developing and evaluating a variety of visualization methods, including segmentation and modeling of major anatomic structures using the methods described in this chapter, with the VHD (35).

At the center of Figure 1.13 is a transparent rendering of a torso model of the Visible Human Male (VHM). This particular model has been developed to evaluate VE procedures applied to a variety of interparenchymal regions of the body. Surrounding the torso are several VE views (single frames captured from VE sequences) of the stomach, colon, spine, esophagus, airway, and aorta. These views illustrate the intraparenchymal surface detail that can be visualized with VE.

Virtual visualizations of the trachea, esophagus, and colon have been compared to standard endoscopic views by endoscopists, who judged them to be

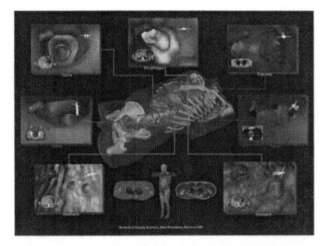

Figure 1.13. Simulated endoscopic views within the Visible Human Male.

realistic and useful. Quantitative measurements of geometric and densitometric information obtained from the VE images (virtual biopsy) are being carried out and compared to direct measures of the original data. Preliminary analysis suggests that VE can provide accurate and reproducible visualizations. Such studies help drive improvements in and lend credibility to VE as a clinical tool.

Figure 1.14 illustrates volume renderings of segmented anatomic structures from a spiral CT scan of a patient with colon cancer and polyps (34). Panel A is a transparent rendering of a portion of the large bowel selected for segmenta-

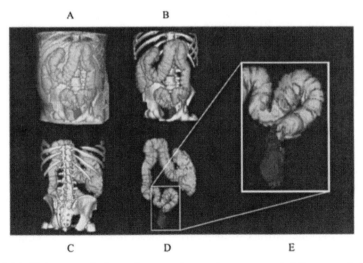

Figure 1.14. Volume renderings of anatomic structures segmented from a spiral CT of patient with colon cancer. Reprinted with permission from Ref. 15.

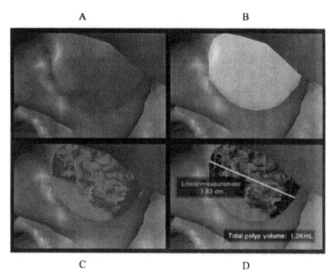

Figure 1.15. Simulated endoscopic view of a polyp showing measurement capability.

tion. Note the large circumferential rectal tumor at the distal end. Panels B and C, reveal the same anatomic segment from different viewpoints after the skin has been removed. Panel D shows a posterior oblique view of the isolated large colon. Note the magnified view of the rectal tumor (panel E); a polyp is also identified, segmented, and rendered in the mid-sigmiodal region.

Figure 1.15 shows virtual biopsy techniques applied to a polyp. Panel A is a texture-mapped view of the polyp at close range, and panel B shows an enhancement of the polyp against the luminal wall. This type of enhancement is possible only with VE, because the polyp can be digitally segmented and processed as a separate object. Panel C is a transparent rendering of the polyp revealing a dense interior region, most likely a denser-than-normal vascular bed. The capability for quantitative biopsy is illustrated in panel D. Both geometric and densitometric measures may be obtained from the segmented data.

1.3.7   4-D Image-Guided Ablation Therapy

There is great potential for the treatment of potentially life-threatening cardiac arrhythmias by minimally invasive procedures whereby an ablation electrode is introduced into the heart through a catheter and used to surgically remove anomalies in the heart's nervous wiring, which cause parts of a chamber to contract prematurely. Before powering the ablation electrode, the electrical activity on the inner surface of the heart chamber must be painstakingly mapped with sensing electrodes to locate the anomaly. To create the map with a single conventional sensing electrode, the cardiologist must manipulate the electrode via the catheter to a point of interest on the chamber wall by means of cine-fluoroscopic and/or real-time ultrasound images. Only after the position of the sensing electrode on the heart wall has been unambiguously identified may the signal from the electrode be analyzed (primarily for the point in the heart cycle at which the signal arrives) and mapped onto a representation of the heart wall. Sensed signals from several dozen locations are needed to create a useful representation of cardiac electrophysiology, each requiring significant time and effort to unambiguously locate and map. The position and extent of the anomaly are immediately obvious when the activation map is visually compared to normal physiology. After careful positioning of the ablation electrode, the ablation takes only a few seconds.

The morbidity associated with this procedure is primarily related to the time required (several hours) and complications associated with extensive arterial catheterization and repeated fluoroscopy. There is significant promise for decreasing the time for and improving the accuracy of the localization of sensing electrodes by automated analysis of real-time intracatheter or transesophageal ultrasound images. Any methodology that can significantly reduce procedure time will reduce associated morbidity; and the improved accuracy of the mapping should lead to more precise ablation and an improved rate of success.

My group is developing a system wherein a static surface model of the target heart chamber is continuously updated from the real-time image stream. A gated 2-D image from an intracatheter, transesophageal, or even hand-held transducer is first spatially registered into its proper position relative to the heart model. The approximate location of the sectional image may be found by spatially tracking the transducer or by assuming it moved very little from its last calculated position. More accurate positional information may be derived by surface-matching contours derived from the image to the 3-D surface of the chamber (36). As patient-specific data are accumulated, the static model is locally deformed to better match the real-time data stream while retaining the global shape features that define the chamber.

Once an individual image has been localized relative to the cardiac anatomy, any electrodes in the image may be easily referenced to the correct position on the chamber model, and data from that electrode can be accumulated into the electrophysiologic mapping. To minimize the need to move sensing electrodes from place to place in the chamber, Mayo cardiologists have developed "basket electrodes," or multi-electrode packages that deploy up to 64 bipolar electrodes on five to eight flexible splines that expand to place the electrodes in contact with the chamber wall when released from their sheathing catheter (37). The unique geometry of these baskets make the approximate positions of the electrodes easy to identify in registered 2-D images that capture simple landmarks from the basket.

When operational, this system will allow mapping of the patient's unique electrophysiology onto a 3-D model of the patient's own heart chamber within a few minutes, rather than several hours. Figure 1.16 illustrates how the chamber model and physiologic data might look to the cardiologist during the procedure.

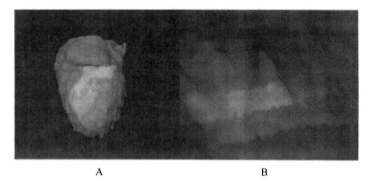

A   B

Figure 1.16. Cardiac electrophysiology displayed on left ventricle viewed from (**A**) outside and (**B**) inside the left ventricle.

1.3.8   Anesthesiology Simulator

Mayo provides training for residents in the medical speciality of anesthesiology. Most of the techniques are used for the management of pain and include deep nerve regional anesthesiology procedures. The process of resident training involves a detailed study of the anatomy associated with the nerve plexus to be anesthesitzed, including cadavaric studies and practice needle insertions in cadavers. Because images in anatomy books are 2-D, only when the resident examines a cadaver do the 3-D anatomic relationships become clear. In addition, practice needle insertions are costly because of the use of cadavers and limited by the lack of physiology. To address these issues, my group has been developing an anesthesiology training system in our laboratory in close cooperation with anesthesiology clinicians (38).

The VHM is the virtual patient for the simulation. A variety of anatomic structures were identified and segmented from CT and cryosection datasets. The segmented structures were subsequently tiled to create models used as the basis of the training system. Because the system was designed with the patient in mind, it is not limited to using the Visible Human Anatomy. Patient scan datasets may be used to provide patient-specific anatomy for the simulation, giving the system a large library of patients, perhaps with different or interesting anatomy useful for training purposes. This capability also has the added benefit of allowing clinicians to plan, rehearse, and practice procedures on difficult or unique anatomy before operating on the patient.

The training system provides several levels of interactivity. At the least complex, the anatomy relevant to anesthesiologic procedures may be studied from a schematic standpoint, i.e., the anatomy may be manipulated to provide different views to facilitate understanding. These views are quite flexible and can be configured to include a variety of anatomical structures; each structure can be presented in any color, with various shading options and with different degrees of transparency. Stereo viewing increases the realism of the display.

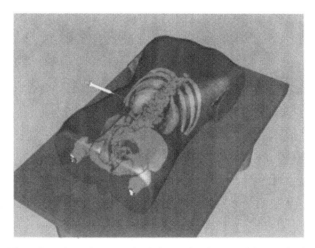

Figure 1.17. Virtual patient for anesthesiology simulator with needle in position for celiac block.

Simulation of a realistic procedure is provided through an immersive environment created through the use of a head-tracking system, HMD, needle tracking system, and haptic feedback. The resident enters an immersive environment that provides sensory input for the visual and tactile systems. As the resident moves around the virtual operating theater, the head-tracking system relays viewing parameters to the graphics computer, which generates the new viewing position to the HMD. The resident may interact with the virtual patient using a flying needle or using a haptic feedback device, which provides the sense of touching the patient's skin and advancing the needle toward the nerve plexus.

Figure 1.17 shows a virtual patient with an anesthesia needle inserted through the back muscle to the site of the celiac plexus. The skin was made partially transparent to illustrate the proper needle path. Figure 1.18 shows a closeup of the model, revealing the celiac plexus target.

1.4 SUMMARY

Interactive visualization, manipulation, and measurement of multimodality 3-D medical images on standard computer workstations have been developed, used and evaluated in a variety of biomedical applications. For more than a decade, these capabilities have provided scientists, physicians, and surgeons with powerful and flexible computational support for basic biologic studies and for medical diagnosis and treatment. My group's comprehensive software systems have been applied to a several biologic, medical, and surgical problems and used on significant numbers of patients at many institutions. This scope of clinical experience has fostered continual refinement of approaches and techniques—especially 3-D volume image segmentation, classification, registration, and

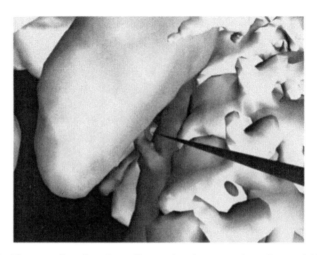

Figure 1.18. Closeup of a virtual needle passing between the spine and kidney to the celiac plexus.

rendering—and has provided information and insights related to the practical clinical usefulness of computer-aided procedures and their effect on medical treatment outcome and cost. This experience led to the design of an advanced approach to computer-aided surgery (CAS) using VR technology. VR offers the promise of highly interactive, natural control of the visualization process, providing realistic simulations of surgery for training, planning, and rehearsal. We developed efficient methods for the production of accurate models of anatomic structures computed from patient-specific volumetric image data (such as CT and MRI). The models can be enhanced with textures mapped from photographic samples of the actual anatomy. VR technology can also be deployed in the operating room to provide the surgeon with on-line, intraoperative access to all preoperative planning data and experience, translated faithfully to the patient on the operating table. In addition, the preoperative data and models can be fused with real-time data in the operating room to provide enhanced reality visualizations during the actual surgical procedures.

VE is a new method of diagnosis using computer processing of 3-D image datasets (such as CT and MRI scans) to provide simulated visualizations of patient-specific organs that are similar or equivalent to those produced by standard endoscopic procedures. Conventional endoscopy is invasive and often uncomfortable for patients. It sometimes has serious side effects, such as perforation, infection, and hemorrhage. VE visualization avoids these risks and can minimize difficulties and decrease morbidity when used before an actual endoscopic procedure. In addition, there are many body regions not compatible with real endoscopy that can be explored via VE. Eventually, VE may replace many forms of real endoscopy.

Other applications of VR technology in medicine that we are developing include anesthesiology training, virtual histology, and virtual biology, all of which provide faithful virtual simulations for training, planning, rehearsing, and/or analyzing using medical and/or biologic image data.

A critical need remains to refine and validate CAS and VR visualizations and simulated procedures before they are acceptable for routine clinical use. We used the VHD from the NLM to develop and test these procedures and to evaluate their use in a variety of clinical applications. We developed specific clinical protocols evaluate virtual surgery in terms of surgical outcomes and to compare VE with real endoscopy. We are developing informative and dynamic on-screen navigation guides to help the surgeon or physician interactively determine body orientation and precise anatomic localization while performing the virtual procedures. In addition, we are evaluating the adjunctive value of full 3-D imaging (e.g., looking outside the normal field of view) during the virtual surgical procedure or endoscopic examination. Quantitative analyses of local geometric and densitometric properties obtained from the virtual procedures (virtual biopsy) are being developed and compared to other direct measures. Preliminary results suggest that these virtual procedures can provide accurate, reproducible, and clinically useful visualizations and measurements. These studies will help drive improvements in and lend credibility to virtual procedures and simulations as routine clinical tools. CAS and VR-assisted diagnostic and treatment systems hold significant promise for optimizing many medical procedures, minimizing patient risk and morbidity, and reducing health-care costs.

ACKNOWLEDGMENTS

I wish to express appreciation to my colleagues in the Biomedical Imaging Resource whose dedicated efforts have made this work possible. Image data were provided by David Bostwick of the Mayo Department of Pathology; William Bourne, Douglas Johnson, and Jay McLaren of the Mayo Department of Ophthalmology; Joe Szurszewski of the Mayo Department of Physiology and Biophysics; Fredric Meyer of the Mayo Department of Neurologic Surgery; Bernard King of the Mayo Department of Radiology; Douglas Packer of the Mayo Department of Cardiology; Ashok Patel of the Mayo Department of Thoracic Surgery; Robert Myers of the Mayo Department of Urology; and Michael Vannier of the University of Iowa Department of Radiology.

REFERENCES

1. K. N. Kaltenborn and O. Reinhoff. Virtual reality in medicine. Meth Inform Med 1993;32:401–417.
2. C. Arthur. Did reality move for you? New Sci 1991;134:22–27.
3. J. Rolhf and J. Helman. IRIS performer: a high performance multiprocessing toolkit for real-time 3D graphics. Paper presented at SIGGRAPH. 1994.
4. M. Zyda, D. R. Pratt, J. S. Falby, et al. The software required for the computer generation of virtual environments. Presence 1994.

5. National Library of Medicine (U.S.) Board of Regents. Electronic imaging: report of the board of regents [Wishful Research NIH Publication 90-2197]. Rockville, MD: U.S. Department of Health and Human Services, Public Health Service, National Institutes of Health, 1990.

6. A. Manduca, J. J. Camp, and E. L. Workman. Interactive multispectral data classification. Paper presented at the 14th annual conference of I.E.E.E. Engineering in Medicine and Biology Society, Paris, France, Oct. 29–Nov. 1.

7. K. H. Hohne and W. A. Hanson. Interactive 3-D segmentation of MRI and CT volumes using morphological operations. J Comput Assist Tomogr 1992;16:284–294.

8. R. A. Robb and D. P. Hanson. A software system for interactive and quantitative analysis of biomedical images. In Hohne et al., eds. 3D imaging in medicine. Vol. F60. NATO ASI Series. 1990:333–361.

9. R. A. Robb and D. P. Hanson. The ANALYZE software system for visualization and analysis in surgery simulation. In Lavalle et al., eds. Computer integrated surgery. Cambridge, MA: MIT Press, 1993.

10. R. A. Robb. Surgery simulation with ANALYZE/AVW: a visualization workshop for 3-D display and analysis of multimodality medical images. Paper presented at Medicine Meets Virtual Reality II. San Diego, CA, 1994.

11. L. L. Fellingham, J. H. Vogel, C. Lau, and P. Dev. Interactive graphics and 3-D modeling for surgery planning and prosthesis and implant design. Paper presented at NCGA. 1986.

12. P. B. Heffernan and R. A. Robb. Display and analysis of 4-D medical images. Paper presented at CAR. 1985.

13. R. Drebin, L. Carpenter, and P. Harrahan. Volume rendering. Paper presented at SIGGRAPH. 1988.

14. K. H. Hohne, M. Bomans, A. Pommert, et al. Rendering tomographic volume data: adequacy of methods for different modalities and organs. In Hohne et al., eds. 3D imaging in medicine. Vol. F 60. NATO ASI Series. 1990:333–361.

15. S. Aharon, B. M. Cameron, and R. A. Robb. Computation of efficient patient specific models from 3-D medical images: use in virtual endoscopy and surgery rehearsal. Paper presented at IPMI. Pittsburgh, PA, 1997.

16. T. Kohonen. Self-organization and associative memory. 3rd ed. Berlin: Springer-Verlag, 1989.

17. R. A. Robb, B. M. Cameron, and S. Aharon. Efficient shape-based algorithms for modeling patient specific anatomy from 3D medical images: applications in virtual endoscopy and surgery. Paper given at the International Conference on Shape Modeling and Applications. Aizu-Wakamatsu, March 3–6, 1997.

18. B. Fritzke. Let it grow—self organizing feature maps with problem dependent cell structures. Paper presented at ICANN-91. Helsinki, 1991.

19. B. M. Cameron, A. Manduca, and R. A. Robb. Patient specific anatomic models: geometric surface generation from 3-dimensional medical images using a specified polygonal budget. In Weghurst et al., eds. Health care in the information age. Vol. 29. IOS Press, 1996.

20. B. Fritzke. A growing neural gas network learns topologies. In Teasauro et al., eds. Advances in neural information processing systems &. Cambridge, MA: MIT Press, 1995.

21. H. Hoppe. Surface reconstruction from unorganized points. Doctoral dissertation, University of Washington, 1994.

22. M. Algorri and F. Schmitt. Reconstructing the surface of unstructured 3D data. Paper presented at Medical Imaging 1995: Image Display. 1995.

23. P. A. Kay, R. A. Robb, D. G. Bostwick, and J. J. Camp. Robust 3-D reconstruction and analysis of microstructures from serial histologic sections, with emphasis on microvessels in prostate cancer. Paper presented at Visualization in Biomedical Computing. Hamburg, Germany, Sept. 1996.

24. J. J. Camp, C. R. Hann, D. H. Johnson, et al. Three-dimensional reconstruction of aqueous channels in human trabecular meshwork using light microscopy and confocal microscopy. Paper presented at SCANNING, 1977.

25. S. M. Miller, M. Hanani, S. M. Kuntz, et al. Light, electron, and confocal microscopic study of the mouse superior mesenteric ganglion. J. Comput Neurol 1996; 365:427–444.

26. U. Bite and I. T. Jackson. The use of three-dimensional CT scanning in planning head and neck reconstruction. Paper presented at the Plastic Surgical Forum of the annual meeting of the American Society of Plastic and Reconstructive Surgeons. Kansas City, MO, 1985.

27. J. L. Marsh, M. W. Vannier, S. J. Bresma, and K. M. Hemmer. Applications of computer graphics in craniofacial surgery. Clin Plastic, Surg 1986;13:441.

28. K. Fukuta, I. T. Jackson, C. N. McEwan, and N. B. Meland. Three-dimensional imaging in craniofacial surgery: a review of the role of mirror image production. Eur J Plastic Surg 1990;13:209–217.

29. F. B. Meyer, R. F. Grady, M. D. Able, et al. Resection of a large temporooccipital parenchymal arteriovenous fistula by using deep hypothermic circulatory bypass. J. Neurosurg 1997;87:934–939.

30. M. B. Garnick. The dilemmas of prostate cancer. Sci 1994.

31. T. A. Starney and J. E. McNeal. Adenosarcoma of the prostate. In Campbell's Urology. Vol. 2. 6th ed.

32. B. Geiger and R. Kikinis. Simulation of endoscopy. Paper presented at Applications of Computer Vision in Medical Images Processing, Stanford University, 1994.

33. G. D. Rubin, C. F. Beaulieu, V. Argiro, et al. Perspective volume rendering of CT and MR images: applications for endoscopic imaging. Radiology 1996;199:321–330.

34. R. M. Stava and R. A. Robb. Virtual endoscopy: application of 3D visualization of medical diagnosis. Presence 1997;6:179–197.

35. R. A. Robb. Virtual endoscopy: evaluation using the visible human datasets and comparison with real endoscopy in patients. Paper presented at Medicine Meets Virtual Reality, 1997.

36. H. J. Jiang, R. A. Robb, and K. S. Holton. A new approach to 3-D registration of multi-modality medical images by surface matching. Paper presented at Visualization in Biomedical Computing, Chapel Hill, NC, Oct. 13–16, 1992.

37. S. B. Johnson and D. L. Packer. Intracardiac ultrasound guidance of multipolar atrial and ventricular mapping basket applications. J Am Col Cardiol 1997;29:202A.

38. D. J. Blezek, R. A. Robb, J. J. Camp, and L. A. Nauss. Anesthesiology training using 3-D imaging and virtual reality. Paper presented at Medical Imaging, 1996.

CHAPTER 2

VEs in Medicine; Medicine in VEs

ADRIE C. M. DUMAY

TNO Physics and Electronics Laboratory
The Hague, The Netherlands

2.1   BACKGROUND

2.1.1   From Wheatstone to VE in Medicine

The first developments in virtual environments (VEs) started in the 2nd century
C.E., when the Greek Galen demonstrated the theory of the spatial perception
of the left and right eye. That theory was a point of departure for the work by
Wheatstone in 1833, to create a breakthrough with his stereoscope. An ingenious system of mirrors presented depth cues to a subject who looked at two
perspective drawings. That was before photography was developed. Yet another breakthrough in the long history of VE technology was the demonstra-
tion of the experience theater called Sensorama by the American Morton Heilig

Information Technologies in Medicine, Volume I: Medical Simulation and Education, Edited by
Metin Akay and Andy Marsh.
ISBN 0-471-38863-7   © 2001 John Wiley & Sons, Inc.

(mid-1950s). Heilig, a photographer and designer of cameras and projectors in Hollywood, devised a machine to stimulate all human senses. The subject in Sensorama experienced the crowd in a street from a motorbike, which could be altered into a helicopter or luxurious car in a split second. Depth cues, sound, motion, and even smell were experienced by the subject. VE techniques were developed worldwide by, among others, Ivan Sutherland and David Evans in the 1960s. Revolutionary developments in computer graphics display hardware and software revolutionized airline safety in the form of real-time interactive flight simulators. The real hype started in 1989, when Jaron Lanier, who is often called the step-father of VEs, generated business from VE technology. Big business. He succeeded at that time in developing and selling sensor technology to interface the subject with the computer in such a way that a nearly natural communication with the system was possible. From that moment, virtual environments were on everyone's mind. The historical experience with interactive flight simulators and their revolutionary effect on airline safety is used today as an argument to proceed with developing simulators for medical training and certification.

2.1.2   From Radon to Medicine in VE

In 1917, Radon discussed the problem of projecting an object in terms of line integrals and reconstructing the object from the set of integrals. He basically created a VE from real objects. His effort led Charles Dotter to start experimenting with threading radio-opaque catheters through blood vessels under fluoroscopic-image guidance in the 1960s. Those experiments were a trigger point for the avalance of minimally invasive imaging procedures emerging today in clinical practice. Dotter was the first to interact and intervene with a patient in an indirect way: He looked at shadow images in stead of the patient. The first step toward medicine in VE was taken.

This chapter advocates the use of VE technologies in the field of medicine to render medical services in a virtual world: to bring medical care to the patient and to improve care by dedicated training and skills building. Therefore, I start with highlighting the technologies involved with VE and how these technologies create benefits for the medical community. The second part of the chapter illustrates that the combined efforts of the medical and computer societies have already created real products. However, there is still a lot of effort needed to revolutionize health care.

2.2   VE IN MEDICINE

2.2.1   Early VE Technologies

Virtual environments are simulation systems in which the subject (user) is to a large extent immersed in the apparent environment of a simulated, multi-dimensional reality (1, 2). VE is the term used by academic researchers to describe the form of computer–human interaction—in which the human is immersed in a world created by the machine, which is usually a computer system (3). The term is derived from virtual reality (VR), which was coined by Jaron Lanier. The term VE emphasizes the immersion of the subject in the virtual environment synthesized by the machine. Other terms are cyberspace, telepresence, mirror world, artificial reality, augmented reality, wraparound compuvision, and synthetic environment.

In principle, all five human senses (sight, hearing, touch, taste, and smell) are involved with the immersion in such a way that there is stimulation by the machine. The human responds to the system by actuating peripheral sensors and absorbs most information by sight. Hearing comes in second place, and touch in third. Motoric activation, speech, and head and eye movements are exploited when the subject responds to the presented information. Response is made by means of advanced computer–human interface techniques. At present, peripheral sensors are based on the DataSuit, DataGlove, SpaceBall and 3-D Mouse; sight and hearing are the most prominent of the senses involved. Stimulating the olfactory and gustatory senses with program-controllable subsystems is still in the laboratory (4).

Contrary to what the popular press wants us to believe, VE technology is not magical but rather a synergy of various technologies that by themselves have been around for some time. VE systems combine human interface technology, graphics technology, sensor and actuator technology, and high-performance computing and networking (HPCN) to allow the subject to explore and interact with computer-animated graphics. Various applications for VE simulations are currently the subject of research and development.

2.2.2 Mature VE Technologies: Potentials and Limitations

A VE system can be broken down into five main subsystems the real environment, the physically modeled environment, the actuator subsystem, the sensor subsystem, and the control subsystem (5). The subject interacts with the real environment and the physically modeled environment, i.e., the subject experiences both environments. The actuator subsystem supports the subject in that experience, and the sensor subsystem enables the subject to interact with the environments. The control subsystem plays a central role in coordinating all tasks of the sensor and actuator subsystems. This concept is the basis of all VE applications (Figure 2.1).

2.2.2.1 The Real Environment. The subject exists physically and is hence part of the real physical environment. The subject stands or walks on a floor, sits in a chair or hardware mock-up, and interacts with that environment through elementary laws of nature (gravity, momentum, etc.). People who share the same real environment are part of the user's environment and so are physically present objects.

2.2.2.2 The Physically Modeled Environment. A physically modeled environment consists of a description of the geometry of objects in the environ-

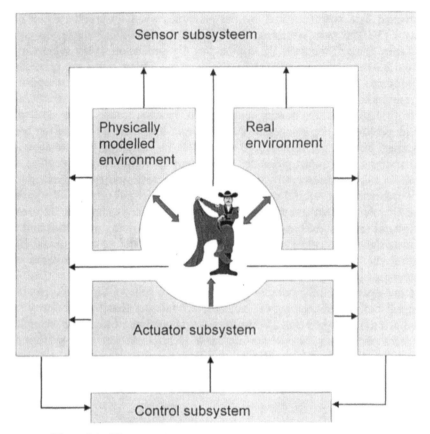

Figure 2.1. The general structure of a virtual environment system.

ment, the behavior of the objects, and the relationships among the objects. In a medical application, the geometry of the objects is determined by human anatomy and pathology, the functions of the objects and their interactions is determined by physiology, and physical deformation is a function attributed to the objects. The objects can also be completely virtual (surgical) instruments or hand-held instruments that are visible in the VE. In the latter case, the objects are part of both the real and the virtual environments.

2.2.2.2.1 Model Extraction and Description. Basically, there are two ways of describing human anatomy. First, a generic description of anatomy can be given, which represents most of the normally functioning people. Generic descriptions can be found in many textbooks, encyclopedias, and other reference materials. Second, a description can be derived from a particular person. The process of constructing an anatomic model from an individual can be broken down into five steps: image acquisition, image reconstruction/restoration, image segmentation/object extraction, object labeling, and polygonal modeling.

At present, the literature provides many methods for each step. Images of CT and MR sections of the body show bone structures, soft tissue, vessels, etc. (6, 7). These images are enhanced by image-processing techniques to show fine details. Individual anatomic structures can be defined at the scan level according to grayscale and/or texture. Once the anatomic structures have been identified, the structures are labeled and polygons are matched against their shape, size, and position. Various levels of detail can be applied, depending on the purpose of visualizing a particular (part of an) object.

Physiology is the field in medicine that describes the functioning of organs and processes. Such processes include cardiovascular physiology and mechanics, cardiomechanics, heart valve dynamics, hemofluid dynamics, respiratory mechanics and lung flow, and kidney and intestinal flow. Ligament modeling is another domain that has to be taken into account for arthroscopy simulation. Textbooks and reference material provide models suitable to surgery simulation. Advanced physiologic models should be pursued to reach a high level of realism in the VE.

Different diseases may cause changes in consistency, elasticity, and other characteristics of a particular organ. Diseases also affect the physiology. Each of these variations should be modeled separately in a VE to allow for a high degree of realism. Photographically extracted textures of, e.g., damaged tissue, scar tissue, tumors, and hemorrhage can be mapped onto anatomic objects to further enhance realism.

2.2.2.2.2 Deformation Modeling. There are two components of the simulation of objects: simulation of the behavior of the objects themselves and simulation of the deformations caused by collision of objects and by simulated surgical instruments. Anatomic models should not only look but also behave as real organs do. As a result of interactive surgical intervention and the laws of physics, soft tissue and objects are deformed. This means the system must produce realistic deformation characteristics as well as feedback and control dynamics that resemble reality.

Despite all the knowledge gained from a physical perspective on the interaction among rigid objects, modeling the interactions among soft objects remains a challenge. At present, there is little known about modeling the stiffness of soft objects, collisions, and contact surfaces between soft objects. Modeling soft and rigid object interaction is also still to be developed.

Modeling soft objects is possible by employing nodal approaches such as finite elements (7) and free-form deformation methods (8). The finite-element method was demonstrated on the biomechanics of muscles (9), and validated against the biomechanics of a human leg (10). A range of free-form deformation methods was initiated by Barr (11), who recognized that a deformation matrix can be altered simultaneously with the application of the matrix to deform a free-form object. Since then, several workers (12–15) have improved the free-form deformation methods. Miller (16) modeled object segments as a mass-spring system and computed for each time interval the spring lengths and spring length velocities to derive at the forces exerted on the masses connected to the springs. The forces, which were corrected for external forces like gravity, were divided by the masses of the elements to yield accelerations. New position points were computed by twice integrating the accelerations with respect to time. Finite element methods and elementary masses methods, however, are computationally expensive and hence limit the frame update rate to levels far below the required level of 30 frames per second. The frame update rate is the number of computer-generated images that appear on the screen each second.

There are also approaches to global transformations. Nonrigid dynamics models have been developed with a relatively few degrees of freedom to allow objects to deform in a geometrically simple but physically correct way (17). Metaxas and Terzopoulos (18) combined locally deformable models with globally deformable models by triangulating the body surface into linear elastic elements to create: dynamically deformable models. These models near the breakthrough required for interactive simulation; however, the models presented cannot be applied to free-form objects and a frame rate of only a few per second can be achieved. Cover et al. (19) started from a physically based paradigm by using deformations on elasticity and combining free-form deformation and energy-minimizing surfaces. Their initial results allow interactive manipulation of a model consisting of about 15,000 polygonal elements. Despite these efforts and improvements, much more research is required before realistic deformation modeling can be applied to advanced surgery simulation.

2.2.2.3 Actuator Subsystem. The actuator subsystem typically includes at least a display device that presents to the operator a computer-generated stereoscopic view of the VE. Hearing comes in second place. Tactile and force feedback give the subject the feeling of really touching objects in the virtual environment.

2.2.2.3.1 Visualization. The visual actuator that stimulates human sight provides a great deal of the situational awareness for the operator in the VE. The VE can be visualized by two types of displays: desktop and immersive. The field of view distinguishes these two displays. Typical desktop displays are monoscopic and stereoscopic. Polarized glasses and shutter glasses deliver the same field of view as the video monitor when the glasses are triggered by electronic means. Head-mounted displays (HMDs), on the other hand, are equipped with optical systems to create a wide field of view (20). A slave headset can be used for slave display purposes to support a tutor or human evaluator of a training session. Advanced optical devices are currently under development for see-through purposes to augment reality in a virtual environment. Such display devices are expected to play a major role in VE applications in medicine. Viewing booms are immersive displays that can be positioned freely in the subject's field of view to deliver a three-dimensional (3-D) scene (21). Other displays are the Cave (22) and Responsive Workbench (23, 24), which are particularly useful when several subjects share the same virtual environment.

Visual depth is perceived from stereo images of objects at small distances (< 10 m). The static phenomena related to sensing visual depth at large distances (> 10 m) are relative position, shading, brightness, size, perspective, and texture gradient; the single important dynamic phenomenon is motional parallax. Not all commercially available displays support the subject well in perceiving depth. There is also a great variety in the resolution provided by the display devices. Present display devices have a resolution in terms of image size that is critical to medical applications. A typical characterization is 748×480 pixels per stereo view. Although there is a lot of dispute about the resolution required for diagnostic purposes, a minimum of 512×512 is required and 1024×1024 should be pursued. Recent advances in 3-D display techniques have been described (25).

2.2.2.3.2 Audio. The ultimate goal of acoustical simulation in virtual environments is the generation and subsequent computation and auralization of sound propagation in real time. When subjects explore and navigate through a VE their current position and orientation should not only affect the presentation of the visual part but also the aural part of the environment (26–28). Present research in the acoustics field focuses on the computation of numerical characteristics such as clarity, early delay time, and steady-state sound pressure level.

2.2.2.3.3 Force and Tactile Feedback. Tactile and force-feedback devices can play important roles in making the operator perceive the virtual environment as valid; but tactile and force feedback are still in the embryonic stages of development. However, haptic feedback in surgical simulation has already been achieved (29). Force and tactile actuators are being developed to subject the user to actual forces, which may be a vital ingredient for sensing reality (30). Worldwide, a lot of effort has been put into realizing such force actuators. An example is described by Bostrom et al. (31), who developed an interactive puncturing device with tactile feedback, allowing the user to feel realistic resistance while inserting a needle into a virtual patient.

2.2.2.4 Sensor Subsystems. The VE sensor subsystem monitors the behavior of the operator. It is a crucial link in the creation of a valid computer-generated experience. The sensor data are used to align the actuator's stimuli with the behavior of the operator: Thus a direct relationship is created between the actions of the operator and his or her experience.

2.2.2.4.1 Position and Orientation Tracking. It is important to make the relationship between the subject's actions and the system's response as intuitive as possible, thereby enabling the operator to gain a large situational awareness. Most often, general position and orientation sensors (based on electromagnetic, mechanical, ultrasonic, or optical techniques) are used to track the head, hand, or other body part of the operator. The DataGlove can be used to measure the position and pose of the hand. Note that the sensor subsystem can also be used to monitor objects in either the real environment or physically modeled environment.

2.2.2.4.2 Interaction Devices. Peripheral feedback sensors are based on, among others, joystick, DataSuit, DataGlove (32), SpaceBall, 3-D Mouse, master arm, and exoskeleton (33). Such electromechanical sensors are interfaced to the computer system. These sensors are usually carried on the human body (34) and used for general and hand- and body-specific positioning. The DataGlove is also suitable for hand-gesture interpretation purposes (35). Glad-in-Art is a glove-like advanced interface for the control of manipulative and exploratory procedures in VEs. A basic characteristic of the Glad-in-Art system is the management of components devoted to replicating kinaesthetic force and internal grasping force feedback to the human hand. Real medical instrumentation (e.g., thermometer, stethoscope, syringe) are designed around these sensors and visualized in the VE, ready for interaction with the casualty. Both prototype and advanced-engineered sensor-based surgical instruments are commercially available.

2.2.2.4.3 Eye Tracking. Eye movements can be followed with an eye movement–tracking system (20) and then interpreted and fed back to the computer control system. This gives the opportunity to adjust the level of detail for displaying information: high-resolution rendering in the field of view and low-resolution rendering outside this field. As a result, computer power can mainly be attributed to visualization in the user's field of view.

2.2.2.5 The Control Subsystem. The control subsystem is used to interpret operator actions registered by the VE sensors, simulation of object behavior, processes, etc. (treated in more detail in later chapters). From these actions, predefined operations within the VE can be started. In principle, an infinite number of interactions can be defined to allow the operator to exchange information with the virtual environment.

2.3 MEDICINE IN VE

2.3.1 Early Medical Applications

VE technology can already be found in training and simulation systems (5). This is by no means surprising, because humans learn best by actively committing themselves to the learning task and involving as many senses as possible. The ability to interact with the virtual environment rather than just with the system makes VE training and simulation systems more appreciated than multimedia systems like interactive CD and interactive video. VE training and simulation systems can give the subject an artificial experience with intrinsic educational benefits. VE applications promise a revolution in medical education (36). Surgeons acquiring a proficiency level of skill may be practicing in a virtual operation theater, alleviating the burden placed on experienced surgeons who are often called out of their own schedules to supervise and train their less experienced colleagues. With a simulated patient, the surgeon has, at least in principle, unlimited ability to remove, reposition and replace tissues and organs. Physiologic models and artificial intelligence control give the surgeon the ability to feel responsible for the life of the virtual patient. The great promise of surgery simulation lies in the fact that the long and expensive training trajectory, starting at textbook studies through animal studies ending at supervised practice on humans, might be shortened.

2.3.2 Recent Medical Applications

Recent innovations in advanced technologies in computing, graphics visualization and simulation, and VEs have progressed to a point that one may seriously consider applying VEs in the following areas: education and training, including education in anatomy, physiology, and pathology, medical emergency-room training, training of ambulance staff, triage training, and minimal access surgery training; conformal radiotherapy planning; rehabilitation, including communication and therapeutic rehabilitation; surgery, including computer-assisted stereotactic neurosurgery and planning of microsurgery and cosmetic surgery; diagnostic radiology; telemedicine for consultation purposes; and for rehabilitation and assisting the elderly and disabled. Currently, the most promising of these areas is education and training, because, at least conceptually, VE technology enables the user to actively engage in a learning task while experiencing multiple computer-generated sensory stimuli.

2.3.2.1 *Learning Anatomy, Physiology, and Pathology.* Learning (human) anatomy and physiology in VE is one educational application. Anatomic models are already available from medical textbooks, and the physiology of the organs is also well documented. Anatomic models are available in electronic format.

A geometrical description of the anatomy and mathematical models of the physiology of body organs are to be stored in a database ready for visual rendering in different levels of detail. More details can be revealed from viewpoints close to the body surfaces, and features that are not visible to the naked eye can be shown. To gain realism, photographs of real textures of the body organs may be mapped onto the virtual organs, again with different levels of detail. This educational aid can be improved by simulating pathologies and giving the subject the ability to take the virtual patient apart and put it together. Optionally, the scoring of individual subjects for an educational program can be recorded.

2.3.2.2 Medical Emergency-Room Training. The emergency room of a hospital is a theater that can function properly only when medical staff are well prepared in and fully informed of procedures and protocols. This requires specialist training, which may be facilitated with a VE system. In such a system, the real emergency room can be modeled, including beds, patient tables, drawers, curtains, surgery facilities, and infusion pumps. The drawers may contain virtual medical aids such as bandages, clamps, and syringes. In principle, a virtual patient can be exposed to any injury. In an interactive VE training session, an injury can be treated following a selected protocol, giving the subject the ability to cure the patient or to inflict even worse injuries. In such a training session, the real atmosphere in an emergency room can be approximated. Even a certain level of stress can be induced by tightening time constraints. Again, the scoring for an educational program can be recorded automatically.

2.3.2.3 Training Ambulance Staff. A relatively simple variation of a medical emergency-room training system is one suitable for the training of ambulance staff. The virtual patient does not need modification, but the virtual interior of the emergency room is replaced with a model of an ambulance interior. A simulator of this type is especially of interest for medical services in countries where ambulance staff need more education beyond acquiring a first aid certificate.

2.3.2.4 Computer-Assisted Surgery. Computer-assisted surgery can be applied in, for example, (stereotactic) neurosurgery after careful planning of the intervention after similar 3-D image-processing methods. Here, VE technology can be applied as an interface to robot-controlled surgery where an extremely high precision is required for micromanipulation. The surgical intervention can be carried out in VE before instructions are sent to the robot for actual intervention in the patient. The feasibility of computer-assisted surgery has already been demonstrated (37, 38).

2.3.2.5 Surgery Planning and Simulation. Microsurgery includes the creation of (small) blood vessels in humans. To study the effect of a surgical intervention, animal studies are often performed before the actual intervention in humans. To lessen the need for animal studies and to improve surgical protocols VE simulation systems can be used to plan a surgical intervention. Cosmetic surgery also requires careful planning and consideration. A graphic model can be derived from scanned patient data, and the effect of surgical interventions can be visualized. Progress and problem areas for craniofacial surgery planning have been reported (39). Surgery planning on scanned patient data in a VE can be facilitated with tools that create corridors through safe areas, without putting the patient at risk. Virtual landmarks can be placed at microvessels, nerves, or other critial locations. Indeed, a whole trajectory can be planned and way points can be recognized even before the patient is in the surgery theater.

2.3.2.6 Endoscopic Surgery Training. Endoscopic surgery is a technique for operating percutaneously in a particular region of interest within the body of a patient with minimal damage to skin, muscle, and surrounding tissue and organs. The minimally invasive nature of endoscopic surgery allows operations to be performed on patients through small incisions, often under local anaesthesia. Patient recovery times and cosmetic detriment are thus greatly reduced, while overall quality of care is improved. These advantages have driven a growth of endoscopic surgery to a wide range of areas of the body (40). Today, endoscopic surgery can be applied to coronary arteries: arteriography (41); the chest: thoracoscopy (42); the abdomen: laparoscopy (43, 44); joints: arthroscopy (45); and the gastrointestinal tract: gastroscopy (46). Conventional surgical instruments can no longer be used. Instead, surgical devices like graspers, scalpels, scissors, staplers, and forceps are customized to allow insertion through long tubes to reach the surgical place. Laser coagulators and electrocoagulators are designed to fit the tube and applied for instant molding of scar tissue. Although the surgeon is physically close to the patient, the surgical environment is effectively remote.

2.3.2.6.1 Vision in Endoscopic Surgery. An endoscope is basically a tubular instrument through which images of the surgical place are transmitted to the surgeon on a video monitor. Basically there are two types of endoscopes: flexible and rigid. A flexible endoscope is designed to extend through twisting paths, as in arteries and the gastrointestinal tract. This type of endoscope conveys images from the surgical place through fiber optics to a video camera at the surgeon's end (47). A video camera is connected to an eyepiece, and images are displayed on a conventional video monitor. Rigid endoscopes with lens optics are used for applications in which the surgical place can be reached easily through the incision. Light is channeled through fiber optics in both flexible and rigid endoscopes from a light source at the surgeons site to the surgical place. Images acquired from the surgical place are continuous in tone and in full color, providing the surgeon additional clues to fine textures of pathologic tissue. The images can be displayed on standard CRT monitors, and straightforward VCR recording can be carried out for documentation and study purposes.

The monoscopic viewing conditions of endoscopes limit the surgeon in gaining insight in distances, and the limited field of view constrains the creation of 3-D mental images of the surgical place. The field of view, which is typically 30°, is narrow compared to the wide field of view of the human eyes. Another limitation of monoscopic viewing can be found in missing depth cues. This limitation is often met by applying camera zoom. However, zoom control forces the surgeon to release the surgical instruments, and then grab the optical control of the endoscope. Hence, the surgeon looses contact with the surgical instruments. Another way of acquiring depth cues is moving the endoscope forward and backward. By doing this, brightness cues with respect to reflections on objects near the tip of the light-channeling tube are acquired from which depth cues can be derived. This method is also often used to estimate apparent sizes of objects. The importance of assessing distances and sizes becomes apparent when andoscopy is combined with surgery. The significance of missing depth cues was investigated and reported by Tendick et al. (48).

Stereo endoscopy provides, at least in principle, the ability to gain depth-disparity information by stereopsis. A stereo-endoscope makes use of two separate optical channels, each with its own lens optics, framed in a single tube. The distance between the axes of the optical systems is critical to reach stereopsis. McLaurin et al. (49) computed that the minimal separation between optic axes is 1.5 mm for achieving a stereoscopic effect on regions < 60 mm from the tip of the endoscope. Basically, a stereo-optical system requires doubling the hardware to record and process the endoscopic images. McLaurin et al. (49) and Mochuzuki and Kobayashi (50), however, demonstrated the use of a single camera system to obtain a 3-D view of the surgical place. This is considered a breakthrough in stereo endoscopy, because a major reduction in hardware equipment can be achieved. High-definition television (HDTV) has also found application in stereo endoscopy (50). Dedicated optics and electronics make a wide field of view feasible. Clinical use of stereo-endoscopic surgery, however, has not yet found widespread acceptance. The cost of equipment is only one factor leading to this marginal acceptance. The difficulty in viewing 3-D images is considered a stronger influence.

Beside limitations owing to the nature of monoscopic viewing, vision control is limited. This is a result of the lack of freedom to manipulate the endoscope. Both the endoscope and the surgical instruments are directed toward the same surgical place, and both can rotate freely about their long axes and about their points of incision. They can also translate along their long axes. The instruments may enter the field of view from any direction and with any angle, introducing a high degree of foreshortening. Hence, there is no single reference with respect to position and orientation between manipulation of the instruments and the image of the instruments on the monitor.

2.3.2.6.2 Manipulation in Endoscopic Surgery. Surgical manipulations (e.g., excision, ablation, cauterization, cutting, grasping, clamping, and suturing) need precision movements, force control, various levels of power, and high dexterity. Instruments used today in open surgery have evolved over centuries to make fine manipulation possible, taking advantage of the many delicate properties of the human hand. Precision force control is a major issue in nearly all surgical procedures and especially when it comes down to ablation, suturing, and testing the elasticity of tissue. Tactile sensation is sensed through the surgeon's hand, and conventional instruments are devised in such a way that the sensations are transmitted with minimal loss. The instruments are available in a variety of sizes and shapes, all adapted to particular surgical maneuvers. In general, the surgeon is not hindered severely in manipulating the instruments.

Endoscopic surgical manipulation, however, is hindered by both mechanical and tactile constraints. Arbitrary rotation and translation of instruments are not possible, because the endoscope and surgical instruments can rotate about and translate along only their long axes and rotate about the incision points. Although there is a wide range of endoscopic surgical instruments available, instruments dedicated to specific maneuvers are yet expected. Present-day endoscopic surgical instruments poorly convey the sensations from the tip to the surgeon's hand. This reduces tactile and force feedback to a minimum. All these mechanical and tactile limitations have a strong effect on surgical procedures and techniques, which is a domain to be explored further.

Performing endoscopic surgery is a complex task involving independent visual and manual skills and combined psychomotor skills. Vision is limited by the narrow monoscopic field of view of the endoscope and by the transmission and video presentation of the endoscope image, whereas tactile and force feedback are significantly hampered as a result of the length of the instruments and the lack of necessary degrees of freedom to allow complex motions.

2.3.2.6.3 Present Training Trajectory. Studies on the time required to gain a proficiency level of skill required for operations on patients report a range of 3 months to 2 years (51, 52). Such a level of proficiency is reached when about 25 supervised procedures have been performed (53). Presently, surgeons are trained to perform endosurgical procedures in a number of ways: practicing with surgical training devices, using animal models, and assisting experienced surgeons. Training under the supervision of experienced surgeons is time-consuming and expensive. In addition, many animals must be sacrificed during the course of surgical skills acquisition, and the surgical equipment industry is playing a leading role in creating and maintaining large-scale training centers where surgeons can work with the latest devices and new techniques. Because no standardized method exists for teaching skills, each subspeciality has developed its own way of assessing a physician's competency. Besides, no single measure for quality exists (54).

There is a high level of proficiency needed in vision, vision control, and manipulation before a surgeon may operate on a patient. These skills, however, cannot be acquired without training and practice. Training facilities are needed to prepare surgeons for those tasks. Today, the first endoscopic surgery simulators are already available (55–58).

2.3.2.7 Triage Training. Triage is the assessment of physical conditions of casualties with limited support of staff and equipment under tight time constraints (59). The treatment of selected casualties who stand a chance to survive their inflictions aims at maintaining at least a minimal functionality of vital organs. At the same time, a limited number of time-consuming surgical interventions should be weighted against the maintenance of vital life functions among a larger number of casualties. In these situations, damage to the internal organs can usually not be rated by diagnostic x-ray screening. The tools for triage and surgery vary throughout the military echelons in combat situations. The critical problem in handling a mass-casualty situation is time. Gaining experience in real-life situations is of utmost importance in medicine. There is a need to know anatomy and physiology, skills in life-saving treatment, and intervention techniques such as surgery. The assessment of the patient condition in trauma situations requires specialized medical knowledge. This is especially true in crisis or combat situations where a great number of casualties may be delivered for triage in a short period of time. Mass-casualty situations occur at major traffic disasters, airplane crashes, earthquakes, etc.

2.3.2.7.1 Triage in Combat and Peace-Keeping Situations. Military distinguish two lines of medical care. First-line medical care (echelons 1 and 2) aims at life- and limb-saving operations, including first aid, emergency medical dental care, stress management, simple emergency surgery without the need of anaesthesia, and preventive health. This care is delivered at dressing and clearing stations, where there is also room for minor surgery under local anaesthesia (like tracheal intubation). Second-line medical care (echelons 3 and higher) is place for full surgery. This care is performed in the Mobile Army Surgical Hospital (MASH) unit, evacuation hospital, combat-support hospital (60, 61), or civil hospital. Each echelon deals with specific types of casualties who may be delivered in a short period of time. At each echelon, triage is carried out, starting with the soldier and ending possibly with a specialist surgeon. The possibilities of being inflicted by high-velocity projectiles or nuclear, biologic, or chemical (NBC) attacks make triage a real challenge, demanding a thorough education and training. Scenarios should be developed, tested, and trained for sudden deployment in polar, tropical, desert, or other area. This applies to soldiers, officers, military ambulance staff, nurses, combat lifesavers, and surgeons. Training medics requires focused learning objectives and diverse trajectories to reach the objectives. The subjects are soldiers without medical background, noncommissioned officers and medical staff, and physicians and surgeons. Obviously, there is a need to flexible training equipment with sufficient realism to emphasize triage.

2.3.2.7.2 Triage-Training Facilities. Education and training of triage protocols can be facilitated with computer-based training facilities, like interactive video (62). Vossen (63) was the first to report such a system and demonstrate its potential to education. However, interactive video does not support sensing the real atmosphere of a mass casualty in a combat situation. It does not support user feedback other than selecting icons: The ability to interact physically with a patient is not present.

Bajura et al. (64) developed a VE system by which live ultrasound images of a fetus inside a pregnant woman are visualized via a see-through HMD. Such VE display devices are currently under development (65, 66). In the next generation of triage-training systems, a hardware dummy of the human anatomy could be seen through a VE display device. This type of augmented reality in medicine can be applied to see a patient (either human or dummy) through an advanced optical display device while internal structures and/or surface injuries are projected onto the patient. In this way, a variety of (changing) textures of injuries can be projected onto the hardware dummy for triage-training purposes. The hardware dummy can be employed for tactile and force feedback. In real-life triage sessions scanned patient data (volume data rather than polygonal data) can also be projected onto such a dummy. Kerlin and Johnson (60) recommend that soldiers to carry their own medical records in opto-electronic format for diagnostic purposes. With this so-called image-save-and-carry (ISAC) philosophy, the scanned images can be projected onto the casualty in second-line medical care and perhaps even in first-line medical care. Optionally, triage support can be delivered by an expert located in one of the higher echelons, who can be consulted through teletriage and VE technology supporting computer–human interfacing.

2.3.2.8 Radiotherapy Planning. Diagnostics and interventional therapy are two steps in the treatment of malignant tumor cells and rely heavily on decisions made by the physician on the basis of visual impressions. One of the most important treatment methods is conformation radiotherapy of tumors, i.e., exposing tumors to radiation.

The close vicinity to the target area of radiosensitive organs, such as the optic nerves, the spinal cord, and the brainstem, often means that conventional radiotherapy cannot administer a sufficiently high dose to the tumor without inducing serious damage to the surrounding healthy tissue. With conformal precision radiotherapy planning, the target area is delineated in scanned patient data and visually presented to the operator. Optimal directions for irradiation can be computed from a desired dose distribution (67). Such therapy planning can be carried out in VE in which the patient can be modeled and the planning results can be shown. Faulkner (68) applied VE technologies to hyperthermia treatment planning.

2.3.2.9 Communication. Disabled individuals lack the ability to fully participate in a society. In a graphic environment, however, there are essentially no constraints imposed to the handicapped. With a focus on the movements of hands, fingers, shoulders, and face, VE technology can be applied as a means of communication with the computer system and the person's environment. VE technologies have the potential to interface a disabled person to computer systems, giving the person access to the wide area of the information society, including electronic network services. A special type of communication can be found in sign language. Interactive learning of sign language can be facilitated with a VE simulation system. Legal signs modeled by hands attributed with DataGloves can be automatically interpreted by the computer system, and incomplete signs can be shown correctly (69). Illegal signs would be ignored. Such a system can keep track of the score of an individual user, who might find this talking mirror interesting and encouraging to use.

2.3.2.10 Therapeutic Rehabilitation. VE technology can also be used in the rehabilitation of muscles and the nervous system after surgery or accidental damage. Conventional rehabilitation sessions are often experienced as dull, and VE technology may give rehabilitation a new dimension. A patient may be motivated in therapeutic rehabilitation via interaction with a playful or even competitive VE simulation. Motor functions can be stimulated by playing with virtual objects with a minimum of energy or effort. An additional advantage of such an approach to rehabilitation is that the patient's performance can be registered and therapy sessions be adjusted accordingly. Diseases may be recognized from response times and finger movements of a patient wearing a DataGlove, and dysfunctions at a perceptive level can be concluded from a patient who senses a growing conflict of sensory input. Also the relationship between the electroencephalogram (EEG) and specific cognitive activities in VE can be investigated in a therapeutic session. Biocontrollers required for this purpose are readily available (70).

2.3.2.11   Diagnostic Radiology. Visualization and interpretation are the main topics in diagnostic radiology. Traditionally, the radiologist interprets 2-D x-ray images of the patient to support medical decision making. Since the introduction of CT to the field of diagnostic imaging, radiologists have gained experience in interpreting 3-D x-ray, nuclear, and MR images. These 3-D images, however, are often visualized on a slice-by-slice basis rather than in 3-D, although fully 3-D applications have already been introduced.

VE technology may provide a whole new repertoire of applications to diagnostic radiology. All applications should depart from scanned patient data from which computer models are extracted and represented in VE. The main advantage of moderating patient data to the physician through graphic models may be that this type of representation is closer to looking at real body organs than are gray-level images. At the same time, however, this is also the main disadvantage. Physicians have become familiar with screening gray-tone images for faint flaws in structures, symmetry, brightness, etc., taking into account the nature of the physical phenomenon underlying the imaging. A functional design of this type of environment was described (71). The radiologists can be supported via metaphors and 3-D widgets in the VE. These tools allow them to interactively put markers at locations of interest without wasting the original patient data.

2.3.2.12   Telepresence Medicine. Telemedicine is the area in which telecommunication meets medicine. Obviously, where telecommunication is applied, some kind of human–system interface is needed, of which VE should be considered. Telemedicine can be applied for remote consultation (physician–physician and patient–physician). Remote diagnosis and surgery can be carried out by a specialist giving assistance to a nonspecialist in, e.g., a hazardous or inaccessible environment during actual procedures.

2.3.2.12.1   Teletriage. Teletriage is defined as a special type of teleconsultation, aiming at supporting the military physician in a war or crisis situation with on-line help from a remote medical expert. Although the military physician is examining a casualty, he or she can report the findings to a remote medical expert by voice. The medical expert, or a team of experts, can respond by projecting instructions through VE technology onto the eye of the military physician, freeing his or her hands. The physician is able to receive being instruction from specialists without having to be a specialist himself or herself.

Linking the VE triage support system to electronic triage systems (ETS) based on picture archiving and communication systems (PACS) is yet another possibility (72). The need of advanced imaging tools in combat situations has already been reported (73). Eventually, remote surgery in a combat situation will be controlled by a surgeon in one of the higher echelons through teletriage support systems. Robotics surgery has been demonstrated (38).

2.3.2.12.2 Telediagnostics and Telesurgery. Instructions from the specialist can be sent to the consulting physician through VE. The local and remote physicians can share the same virtual space in which the patient is present. In this way, the normal and pathologic anatomy can be projected onto the eye of the consulting physician while examining the patient. The same can be done for surgical instructions. Hazardous environments can be found in war situations, and submarines and other navy vessels in full operation are considered to be inaccessible environments. Telemedicine can be particularly interesting helpful in peace-keeping missions of the United Nations in politically unstable areas with a poor medical infrastructures. The 1996 Olympic Games in Atlanta served as a test for instant access to an individual's home country for crossing language barriers (74).

2.3.2.13 Biomechanics. VEs can also be useful in biomechanics. Relatively simple sensor systems can be applied for human posture recognition, which, in turn, can be applied to interactive posture correction. A help-yourself posture correction session can help the disabled, althletes, and physically active individuals, and can be integrated in the process of designing optimal equipment. For example, seats for cars, cockpits, military tanks, etc. could be developed in this manner.

From a pragmatic point of view, the great promise of VE lies in the fact that a long, complicated, and expensive training—involving textbook studies, laboratory practice on animals, and eventually supervized practice on human subjects—might be shortened, be carried out at a lower risk, and require far less involvement of scarce expert supervisors. Of particular concern in medical applications are issues related to verity, fidelity, and validity.

2.4 VE FIDELITY AND VALIDITY

A simulation that faithfully, yet quickly, mimics the real operating environment brings the desired effect. Only VEs that offer sufficient realism and fidelity constitute viable alternatives to cadavers, animals, and patients for training purposes. Several issues determine the level of fidelity. First, most simulators were developed by computer graphics engineers who focused on rendering human anatomy. Physiologic and pathologic modeling are often neglected in these simulators. However a well-matched level of fidelity of anatomic, physiologic, and pathologic models is a key criterion for achieving a valid simulation. A second key criterion for evaluating fidelity is the synchronization of simulation processes. Within interframe time intervals, anatomic, physiologic, and pathologic models must be updated according to actual status information extracted from all sensors. At present, simulations are typically limited to synchronizing deformation computations, resulting from user manipulation of one or more objects, with the visualization process. Synchronization with the physiologic simulation process is often neglected owing to limited computational power. A third criterion for evaluating fidelity and/or validity can be found in spatial calibration of manipulation devices. Each device is featured with its own spatial resolution, mechanical constraints, and read-out complexity. Integrating these devices into an overall simulation requires the registration of all of these devices to a single spatial reference frame to avoid mismatch of position and orientation. As far as the computational aspects of medical VE applications are concerned, note that distributed multiprocessor architectures may provide a solution to the computational requirements made by the fidelity and validity demands. Last, but certainly not least, human factors issues must be taken into account in the first stages of the design of any medical VE application.

2.5 DISCUSSION AND CONCLUSIONS

The VE in medicine and medicine in VE examples lead us to the key question: Can medicine and health care benefit from virtual environments? VE technology is available; However, key technologies such as tactile and force feedback may require another decade of development before they will have reached the level of maturity required for surgery simulation. Display technology also needs to be improved before high-resolution easy-to-use devices can be made. Present display devices have a resolution in terms of image size that is below the critical threshold for many medical applications. Solutions to these problems are expected to be available within 3 to 5 years. The first developments of surgical simulators have clearly demonstrated the great potential of VE technology for training purposes. In addition, this potential is not limited to medical applications but extends to almost any domain. Surgerical and endoscopic simulations need advanced tactile and force feedback technology, high-resolution display devices, and affordable super computing power. All three technologies are currently under development by both national and transnational research programs.

Vanms applications of VE technology in medicine were identified. The literature provides further VE applications for the delivery room of the future (75), human developmental anatomy (76), design purposes for domains outside of medicine (77), eye surgery (78), and the successful treatment of Parkinson disease akinesa (79).

The most promising of these areas is in education and training, because VE technology allows users to actively committing themselves to a learning task with as many senses as possible. The great promise of VE lies in the fact that the long and expensive training trajectory might be shortened.

At present, there are a number of commercially available simulators. There is a great variety in the level of realism reached within this first-generation of surgery simulators, and there are several issues at stake. First, most simulators were brought about by computer graphics engineers who focused on rendering human anatomy and often neglected physiologic and pathological modeling. Second, is the synchronization of processes. Third, is the spatial calibration of manipulation devices. Last, human factors must be taken into account before any surgical simulator is designed.

These considerations bring us back to the key question: Can medicine and health care benefit from virtual environments? VE technology is presently available, but many areas are still being developed. Advances by the U.S. military are reported by Satava (80).

Future developments should be directed towards virtual environments for clinical practice. However, clinical applications are subject to a conglomerate of standards, and their acceptance depend strongly on safety, reliability, precision, and financial issues. Fornage et al. (81) demonstrated the positioning of a needle for the biopsy of a suspected breast tumor by combining VE technology and ultrasound techniques. Applications like this one clearly demonstrate that VE can assist physicians, provided that they are open to new ways of using existing techniques. Augmented reality, metaphors and 3-D widgets, and functional augmented reality create new ways of treating patients. The virtual environment then becomes a dialogue tool between patient and physician on the one hand and between physician and nurses on the other. Virtual corridors can be projected onto the body of the patient to support the surgeon who remains with safe areas, without risking the patient's life. The potential of situational awareness to remote sites make VE technology suitable for remote consultation. A local physician and a remote consultant may share the same virtual space and may come interactively to a single conclusion about their subject. Remote surgery based on VE technology has also been demonstrated (81).

Despite its current limitations, VE will introduce a whole new generation of applications for medicine and medical training.

REFERENCES

1. H. Rheingold. Virtual reality. Summit Books, New York, 1991.
2. K. Pimentel and K. Texeira. Virtual reality: through the new looking glass. McGraw-Hill, New York, 1993.

3. W. Bricken. Formal foundation for cyberspace. In SK Helsel, ed. Beyond the vision. The technology, research, and business of virtual reality. 1992.

4. D. Varner. Contribution of audition and olfaction to immersion in a virtual environment. Paper presented at ICAT/VET, 1993.

5. G. J. Jense and F. Kuijper. Virtual environments for adapted trainers and simulators. Paper presented at the International Training Equipment Conference. 1993.

6. M. J. Ackerman. The Visible Human Project. Paper presented at Medicine Meets Virtual Reality II. San Diego, CA, 1994.

7. K.-J. Bathe. Finite element procedures in engineering analysis, Engle Wood Cliffs, NJ: Prentice-Hall, 1982.

8. M. P. Gascuel. An implicit formulation for precise contact modeling between flexible solids. Paper presented at SIGGRAPH. 1993.

9. D. T. Chen and D. Zeltzer. Pump it up: computer animation of a biomechanically based model of muscle using the finite element method. Paper presented at SIGGRAPH. 1992.

10. S. Pieper, S. Delp, J. Rosen, and S. Fisher. A virtual environment system for simulation of leg surgery. Paper presented at Stereoscopic Displays and Applications Bellingham, WA, 1991.

11. A. Barr. Global and local deformations of solid primitives. Comput Graph 1998; 18:21–30.

12. T. Sederberg and S. Parry. Free-form deformation of solid geometric models. Comput Graph 1986;20:151–160.

13. D. Terzopoulos and K. Fleischer. Modeling inelastic deformation: viscoelasticity, placticity, fracture. Comput Graph 1988;22:269–278.

14. S. Coquillart. Extended free-form deformation: a sculpturing tool for 3D geometric modeling. Comput Graph 1991;25:187–196.

15. W. Hsu, J. Hughes, and H. Kaufman. Direct manipulation of free-form deformation. Comput Graph 1992;26:177–184.

16. G. S. P. Miller. The motion dynamics of snakes and worms. Comput Graph 1990;22:169–178.

17. A. Witkin and W. Welch. Fast animation and control of nonrigid structures. Comput Graph 1990;24:243–252.

18. D. Metaxas and D. Terzopoulos. Dynamic deformation of solid primitives with contraints. Comput Graph 1992;26:309–312.

19. S. A. Cover, N. F. Ezquerra, and J. F. O'Brien. Interactively deformable models for surgery simulation. IEEE Comput Graph Appl. 1993.

20. M. Starks. Stereoscopic video and the quest for virtual reality: an annotated bibliography of selected topics. Stereoscopic Displays and Applications II. 1991.

21. M. Bolas. Head-coupled computer graphics display devices. Paper presented at Medicine meets Virtual Reality. San Diego, CA, 1994.

22. C. Crus-Neira, D. J. Sandin, and T. A. DeFanti. Surrounding-screen projection-based virtual reality: the design and implementation of the CAVE. Paper presented at SIGGRAPH. 1993.

23. B. Froehlich. The responsive workbench: a virtual working environment for architects, designers, physicians, and scientists. Paper presented at SIGGRAPH. 1994.

24. W. Krueger and B. Froehlich. The responsive workbench. IEEE Comput Graph Appl 1994.

25. D. P. Huijsmans and G. J. Jense. Recent advances in 3D display. Adv Elec Electron Physics 1993;85:77–229.

26. P. Astheimer. What you see is what you hear. Acoustics applied in virtual worlds. Paper presented at the IEEE Virtual Reality Annual International Symposium. 1993.

27. E. M. Wenzel, F. L. Wightman, and D. J. Kistler. Localization of non-individualized virtual acoustic display cues. Paper presented at Computer Human Interaction. 1991.

28. D. R. Begault. 3-D Sound for virtual reality and multimedia. Boston: Academic Press, 1994.

29. B. Marcus. Hands on: haptic feedback in surgical simulation. Paper presented at Medicine Meets Virtual Reality. San Diego, CA, 1994.

30. G. Burdea, E. Roskos, D. Silver, et al. A distributed virtual environment with dextrous force feedback. Paper presented at Informatique: Interface to Real and Virtual Worlds. 1992.

31. M. Bostrom, S. K. Singh, and C. W. Wiley. Design of an interactive lumbar puncture simulator with tactile feedback. Paper presented at IEEE Virtual Reality Annual International Symposium. 1993.

32. W. J. Greenleaf. The DataGlove and DataSuit technology for medical applications. Paper presented at Medicine Meets Virtual Reality II. San Diego, CA, 1994.

33. A. Buckert-Donelson. Profile of Beth Marcus of Exos Corp. Virtual Reality World 1994.

34. R. Stone. New developments in telepresence. Paper presented at the second annual conference on Virtual Reality International. 1992.

35. U. Bröckl-Fox, K. Hartenstein, L. Kettner, et al. Using three dimensional hand-gesture recognition as a new 3D input device. Paper presented at the First Eurographics Workshop on Virtual Environments. 1993.

36. J. R. Merril. VR for medical training and trade show "fly-paper." Virtual Reality World 1994:53.

37. W. S. Ng, B. L. Davies, R. D. Hibberd, and R. D. Timoney. Robotic surgery. IEEE Eng Med Biol. 1993:120–125.

38. B. Preising, T. C. Hsia, and B. Mittelstadt. (June). A literature review: robots in medicine. IEEE Eng Med Biol 1991:13–22

39. C. McEwan, R. Robb, and I. Jackson. Craniofacial surgery planning and simulation: current progress and problem areas. Paper presented at the International Symposium on CAR. 1989.

40. A. C. M. Dumay. Endoscopic surgery simulation in a virtual environment. Comput Biol Med in press.

41. G. White and R. White. Angioscopy: vascular and coronary applications. Chicago: Year Book, 1989.

42. C. Boutin, J. Viallat, and Y. Aelony. Practical thoracoscopy. New York: Springer-Verlag, 1991.

43. J. Saleh. Laparoscopy. Philadelphia: Saunders, 1988.

44. P. Testas and B. Delaitre. Chirurgie digestive par voie coelioscopique. Paris: Éditions Maloine, 1991.

45. J. Parisien. Arthroscopic surgery. New York: McGraw-Hill, 1988.

46. R. Pearl. Gastrointestinal surgery for surgeons. Boston: Little, Brown, 1984.

47. K. Knyrim, H. Seidlitz, N. Vakil, and M. Classen. Perspectives in electronic endoscopy: past, present and future of fibres and CCDs in medical endoscopes. Endoscopy 1990;22 (Suppl 1):2–8.

48. F. Tendick, R. W. Jennings, G. Tharp, and L. Stark. Sensing and manipulation problems in endoscopic surgery: experiment, analysis, and observation. Presence 1993;2:66–81.

49. A. P. McLaurin, E. R. Jones, and J. L. Mason Jr. Three-dimensional endoscopy through alternating-frame technology. Paper presented at Stereoscopic Displays and Applications 1–256, Bellingham, WA, 1990.

50. R. Mochizuka and S. Kobayashi. HDTV single camera 3D system and its application in microsurgery. Paper presented at Stereoscopic Displays and Virtual Reality Systems 2177. Bellingham, WA, 1994.

51. Health and Public Policy Committee of the American College of Physicians. Clinical competence in diagnostic esophagogastroduodendoscopy. Ann Intern Med 1987;107:937.

52. Health and Public Policy Committee of the American College of Physicians. Clinical competence in endoscopic retrogade cholangiopancreatography. Ann Intern Med 1987;107:142.

53. R. Hawes, G. Lehman, and J. Hast. Training resident physicians in fibreoptic sigmoidoscopy: how many supervised examinations are required to achieve competence? Am J Med 1986;9B:465.

54. C. Dommaraju, D. Kruss, and F. Iber. Evluation of trainee-performed colonoscopy using depth of insertion (DOI) as a quality assurance (QA) indicator. Am J Gastroentr. 1990;85:1292.

55. K. T. McGovern and L. T. McGovern. Virtual clinic. Virtual Reality World 1994.

56. S. Pieper, M. McKenna, D. Chen, and I. McDowall. Computer animation for minimally invasive surgery: computer system requirements and preferred implementations. Paper presented at Stereoscopic Displays and Virtual Reality Systems 2177. Bellingham, WA, 1994.

57. D. Hon. Ixion's realistic medical simulations. Virtual Reality World. 1994.

58. U. G. Kühnapfel. Realtime graphical computer simulation for endoscopic surgery. Paper presented at Medicine Meets Virtual Reality II. San Diego, CA, 1991.

59. A. C. M. Dumay. On a virtual environment for traige training. Paper presented at International Training and Equipment Conference and Exhibition. Arlington, VA, 1994.

60. B. D. Kerlin and W. P. Johnson. The pros and cons of various optical media for the soldier's interfacility radiographic record (SIRR) in the combat casualty care system. Paper presented at Medical Imaging III. 1989.

61. L. D. Nadel, M. A. Forrester, M. E. Glenn, et al. Prototype system for digital image management in combat casualty care. Paper presented at Medical Imaging III. 1989.

62. J. Parikh and J. Rakinic. Applications of CD-interactive technology in health care. Paper presented at Medicine Meets Virtual Reality. San Diego, CA, 1994.

63. P. Vossen. Computer based training: as a case of flexible automation. Paper presented at the International Training Equipment Conference. 1993.

64. M. Bajura, H. Fuchs, and R. Ohbuchi. Merging virtual objects with the real world: seeing ultrasound imagery within the patient. 1992;26:203–210.

65. E. K. Edwards, J. P. Rolland, and K. P. Keller. Video see-through design for merging of real and virtual environments. IEEE Virtual Reality Annual International Symposium. 1993.

66. P. K. Manhart, R. J. Malcolm, and J. G. Frazee. Augeye. IEEE Virtual Reality Annual International Symposium. 1993.

67. S. Webb. Optimisation of conformal radiotherapy dose distributions by simulated annealing. Phys Med Biol 1989;34:1349–1370.

68. G. Faulkner. A first approach to virtual reality for interactive volume rendering and hyperthermia treatment planning. Paper presented at Medicine Meets Virtual Reality. San Diego, CA, 1994.

69. L. Koenen, T. Bloem, and R. Janssen. Gebarentaal. De taal van doven in Nederland [Sign language. The language of the deaf in the Netherlands]. Amsterdam: Nijgh & Van Ditmar, 1993.

70. R. B. Knapp and H. S. Lusted. Biocontrollers for the physically disabled: a direct link from nervous system to computer. Paper presented at Virtual Reality and Persons with Disabilities. Northridge, CA, 1993.

71. I. Hunter, M. Sagar, L. Jones, et al. Teleoperated microsurgical robot and associated virtual environment. Paper presented at Medicine Meets Virtual Reality. San Diego, CA, 1994.

72. G. H. B. Devey and M. J. Ackerman. Beyond PACS: the electronic triage system. Picture archiving and communication system (PACS) in medicine. NATO, 1991.

73. E. Dolev. Computerized tomography: a valuable tool in triage. Military Med 1987;152:497–499.

74. M. Burrow, M. Sinclair, and T. Gadacz. A telemedicine testbed for developing and evaluating telerobotic tools for rural health care. Paper presented at Medicine Meets Virtual Reality. San Diego, CA, 1994.

75. J. P. Brennan. Towards the delivery room of the future. Paper presented at Medicine Meets Virtual Reality. San Diego, CA, 1994.

76. M. D. Doyle, A. Noe, I. Carlbom, et al. The virtual ambryo: VR applications in human developmental anatomy. Paper presented at Medicine Meets Virtual Reality. San Diego, CA, 1994.

77. S. Hassan, M. Kahn, and T. John. A 3-dimensional medical data visualisation of temporal/spatial relationships. Paper presented at Medicine Meets Virtual Reality. San Diego, CA, 1994.

78. J. Pfeifer, M. Sinclair, R. Halebliam, et al. Virtual environment for eye surgery simulation. Paper presented at Medicine Meets Virtual Reality. San Diego, CA, 1994.

79. S. Weghorst, J. Prothero, T. Furness, et al. Virtual images in the treatment of Parkinson's disease akinesa. Paper presented at Medicine Meets Virtual Reality. San Diego, CA, 1994.

80. R. M. Satava. Surgery 2001. A technologic framework for the future. Surg Endosc 1993;7:111–113.

81. B. D. Fornage, N. Sneige, M. J. Farnoux, and E. Andry. Sonographic appearance and ultrasound guided fine-needle aspiration biopsy of brest carcinomas smaller than 1 cm^3. J Ultrasound Med 1990;9:559–568.

CHAPTER 3

Virtual Reality and Its Integration into a Twenty-First Century Telemedical Information Society

ANDY MARSH

National Technical University of Athens
Athens, Greece

Information Technologies in Medicine, Volume I: Medical Simulation and Education, Edited by
Metin Akay and Andy Marsh.
ISBN 0-471-38863-7   © 2001 John Wiley & Sons, Inc.

Virtual reality (VR) technology has long been an invaluable tool in the form of flight simulators for training military and commercial aviators. More recently, VR entertainment centers have provided many people with this same sense of total immersion in a life-like, three-dimensional (3-D) environment (1). Today the technology is making rapid strides in the medical realm as well, providing surgeons and interns with access to realistic simulations for training and surgical planning and augmenting reality by supersomposition in a growing range of operating room contexts (2–23). Virtual reality simulations include not only compute software and hardware but also the disciplines of robotics, telecommunications, head-mounted displays (HMDs), and databases. Interfaces that provide the user with a sense of touch and that offer force feedback in response to the user's motion are also entering the picture. Called haptic interfaces, they widen the applications of Virtual reality by augmenting the scenes of sight and sound provided by existing systems (24–27).

California-based Medical Data International (California) predicted that the global market for virtual reality products in medicine would exceed $6.5 billion by the year 2000. A major obstacle, however, is how to integrate this advanced technology into a health-care society that can be envisaged for the 21st century.

It is well known that health care is a major candidate for improvement in any vision of the kinds of information highways and societies that are now being visualized (28–31). In June 1994 the leaders of the Group of Seven (G7) indusrtrialized nations agreed that action should be taken to promote the development of a global information infrastructure. They identified 11 specific areas (or themes) for further development, one of which was health care. The six subprojects so far identified under the health care theme all involve the interchange of multimedia information, requiring the use of international standards for the exchange of multimedia information (i.e., telemedicine) (32). The concept of remote health care captures much of what is developing in terms of technology implementations (33), especially if it is combined with the growth of the Internet and World Wide Web (WWW) (34, 35). It is also foreseen that the WWW will become the most important communication medium of any future information society.

If the development of such a medical society is to be on a global scale it should not be allowed to develop in an ad hoc manner. For this reason the European Commission ISIS '95 supported the EUROMED project (http://euromed.iccs.ntua.gr), which identified 20 building blocks resulting in 39 steps requiring multidisciplinary collaborations (36). To date, most standardization work in health care has concentrated on single-medium objects, e.g. text, reports, biosignals, and images. There is, however, a demand for media images with an audio soundtrack and, text reports with images or biosignals. Owing to the difficulty in doing this, most work has been either on small extentions to monomedia standards (e.g., text/biosignals in DICOM) (37), or carrying separate monomedia objects for each medium. For example, an image and a text report may be sent separately: the user or the user's applications must decide the relationship between them and treat them acccordingly.

The requirement now is to find suitable multimedia standards for health-care information. In addition, new advanced imaging techniques, such as those developed in the United States, are behind new revelations about the potential of advanced medical imaging. So promising are these techniques that, for example, concerning the mechanics of human thought the U.S. Congress declared the 1990s the decade of the brain. Researchers are on the verge of accurately charting different brain functions (e.g., the U.S. project NEUROSCOPE at the University of Illinois). Modern neurology and neurosurgery make extensive use of medical images for both diagnostic and therapeutic purposes (16). Imaging modalities that are quite complementary may be used to display various anatomic structures. For example, CT is relevant for viewing the skull and ventricular system, MRI is suitable for visualize cerebral tissues, angiography is used to display blood vessels, and nuclear medicine (PET, SPECT) is used for functional imaging. Nevertheless, there are potentially many situations in which a clinician would like to inspect an area of intent using more than a single image system. Viewing different images side by side provide little detailed information of the similarities and the differences between them. Accurate alignment of such images provide anatomic and functional information a the set of superimposed data; e.g., the U.S. project ANALYZE (38) at the Mayo Clinic, made up of >60 programs that allow fully interactive display, manipulation, and measurement of multidimensional image data. Not restricted to computational neurology, this technique can be used in application fields such as radiation oncology, plastic and reconstructive surgery, medical diagnosis, and mammography and can form the basis for developing computationally intensive virtual surgery and surgery planning techniques; e.g., VRASP at the Mayo Clinic (39).

One important consideration for the 21st century is to create a telemedical information society that integrates the latest developments, ranging from telecommunications to the use of advanced imaging techniques such as VR (36, 40, 41). This chapter is divided into two areas of emphasis. First, the definition of a possible infrastructure that would allow for the integration of VR applications into a telemedical information society is presented and then the forms of VR that are envisaged to be used for future 21st century health care will be discussed (5).

It is clear from the current trends in health care that a telemedical society will exist in some form or other (32). The medical information management market is one of the largest and fastest-growing segments of the health-care device industry. In the United States alone, the revenue is expected to be $21 billion by 2000. Of this market, telemedicine currently accounts for only a small segment but it is expanding rapidly. Note that >60% of the federal telemedicine projects were initiated since 1998. In this chapter *telemedicine* refers to the (interactive) audiovisual communication between health-care providers and their patients or other health-care providers, regardless of geographic distance. The first use of telemedicine dates back to 1959 when x-ray images were transmitted across telephone lines. Nowadays, the uses vary widely, e.g., medical consultation during natural disasters, the military used telemedicine in Croatia and Somalia to help treat the wounded, and university hospitals providing second opinions and continuing medical education to community hospitals. The objective of any telemedical information society that can be imagined for the this century must be to provide a global uniform level of health care (29). To facilitate the possibilities for any international collaborations, standardized approaches must be adopted (42). There are already a number of localized nationally supported telemedical projects, examples can be found in Indonesia (43), Africa, Japan, Korea (44), throughout Europe (35, 45), the United States (46), and China. For example, as part of the Three Goldens in 1993 the Chinese government launched the Golden Bridge initiative to improve life and optimize the use of resources in China. The Golden Bridge (considered to be China's own interest) involves connecting computers among government, medical, health, educational, and financial organizations. In June 1996 Guangzhou Huamei communications unveiled a memo stating the plans to provide People's Liberation Army (PLA) hospitals with asynchronous transfer mode (ATM) interconnections that can carry 155 Mb/s.

A project titled Telehealth Africa is establishing links between European hospital centers and some African hospital centers. The goal is to transmit and receive health-related diagnostic images. In Indonesia, a communication network is being established to interconnect the 7000 medical institutions throughout the islands (43). In France, a telemedical system is providing support for AIDS suffers (47). In Nepal, a telecommunication link to institutions in the United States is supporting a telecollaborative diagnosis for unfamiliar and complex conditions and diseases. In Hungary, a weekly teleconferencing link between a Budapest institution and an American hospital is supporting telecollaborative diagnosis of pediatric movement disabilities. These applications and projects are just a few of those in existence.

A number of well-coordinated experiments have clearly shown the advantageous aspects of telemedicine. In December 1996, U.S. and Israeli physicians conducted a telemedicine exchange. The all-day event included Israel's largest medical center (Rabin Medical Centre) located near Tel Aviv, Texas Children's Hospital and Baylor College of Medicine (Houston, TX), and Duke University Medical Center (Dirham, NC). Physicians participating in the exchange presented adult and pediatric cardiology care for multisite medical consultation, including long-distance transmission of x-rays and ultrasound images. In the same month, at the Arab health exhibition held in Dubai, United Arab Emirates, two companies—VSI Enterprises (Noscross, GA) and Interclinical Ltd, (London)—demonstrated live surgical procedures from Holland to physicians in the Middle East. Live interactive demonstrations of coronary artery ballon angiography and coronary artery stent implications were transmitted from Katherina Hospital in Eindhoven. Six cases were presented via video conferencing, enabling the surgical team in Holland to demonstrate the clinical applications and techniques.

In January 1998, the Hamid Hospital in Dubai signed an agreement with both the Omnix Qatar Co. and Fore Systems to organize the installation of a health-care network based on asynchronous transfer mode (ATM) technology. The network architecture will consist of a 155 Mb/s ATM backbone. This network will enable the hospital to take up a pioneering solution throughout the whole of the region for many years to come. It is the intention of the hospital staff to serve 300 physicians and >500 users. In addition, 23 remote health-care centers will be connected to the backbone (48).

There are many alternative uses of telemedicine varying from emergency telemedicine to medical care in remote areas to home care telemedicine (e.g., cardiac monitoring). In November 1991, Dodge County Hospital situated in the rural town of Eastman, Georgia, become the pilot site for an interactive patient-examination system that was developed to eliminate distance in the provision of health care. Since then, the network has enabled hospital staff to offer definite care to about 85% of patients with complex problems without them having to leave their own familiar doctor or community hospital. Georgia's pioneering telemedicine program resides under the responsibility of the medical college of Georgia Telemedicine Center in Augusta (49).

However, the underlying foundations for the uptake of telemedicine in any future health-care society that can be envisaged is its standardized installation and interfacing. The EUROMED proposed a new standard called *Virtual Medical Worlds* that defines the foundational building blocks of a telemedical information society for the 21st century (34, 35, 50). As shown in Figures 3.1 and 3.2, a 21st-century medical environment conjures up thoughts of overwhelming technology and uniquely identified patients. How far this is from the truth is yet to be determined; however, because the concept of telemedicine captures much of what is developing in terms of technology implementation, especially if it is combined with the growth of the Internet and WWW, it may not be too unrealistic. So it can be seen that a global telemedical information society is an achievable possibility. The problem now is to develop a global standardized use of telemedicine that also encorporates the new advanced imaging techniques such as VR and subsequently the use of supercomputing support. As shown in Figures 3.3 and 3.4, realistic reconstructed 3-D models of the body can now be generated from standard imaging modalities such as CT and MRI (51–53). These models can be used not only for training purposes but also for surgery planning.

For example, 3-D, computer-generated renditions of the human body made up of thousands of digitized images of a cadaver is available from the U.S. National Library of Medicine (http://www.nlm.nih.gov). The National Library of Medicine (NLM) provides a set of digitized images of the human body for use in education and research. The project currently has both a human male and a human female (54). The process used was initial MRI and CT scanning, freezing, further MRI and CT imaging, cutting into 1-mm (male) or 0.33-mm (female) slices, and digitizing at 0.33-mm resolution. Each slice is a 2048×1216 pixel image, corresponding to 7.5 Mb of uncompressed data. These have saved as JPEG images (between 50 and 180 Kb) for ease of use.

Many projects have made use of this source data, corresponding to 1878

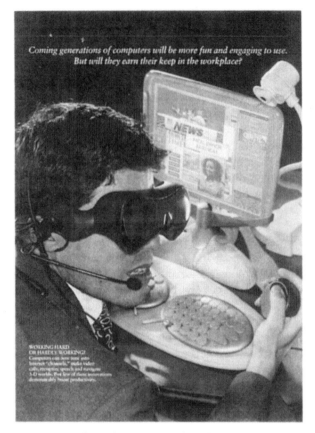

Figure 3.1. Doctor of the future?

male images and >5000 female images (38, 55, 56). Most projects reconstruct 3-D versions of the data, which can then be subjected to further image processing. The original tapes correspond to >50 Gb for the two cadavers, but many implementors work with selected and compressed subsets of the data. Projects include the following:

- The NPAC *Visible Human Viewer*, a Java applet from Syracuse University that allows interactive extraction of parts of the Visible Human Dataset over the Internet.
- CD-ROMs from Micron, Data Express, and Research Systems.
- 3-D renderings of the data via a Fujitsu 1000 supercomputer from the Australian National University.
- *The Dissectable Human*, a CD-ROM presentation from Engineering Animation.

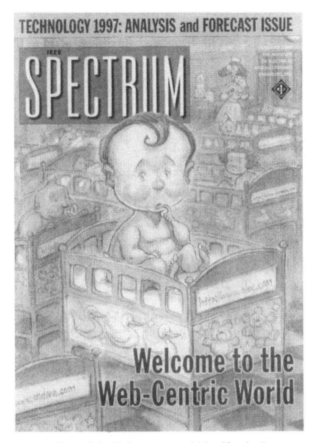

Figure 3.2. Unique personal identification?

• The Interactive Knee Program from the University of Pennsylvania.
• The Visible Human Explorer for Sun workstations from the NLM and University of Maryland.

The Visible Human Project is an outgrowth of the NLM's 1986 long-range plan to create complete, anatomically detailed, 3-D representations of the male and female human bodies. The first phase of the project was to collect transverse CT, MRI, and cryosection images of representative male and female cadavers. The long-term goal is to produce a system of knowledge structures that will transparently link visual knowledge forms to symbolic knowledge formats, such as the names of body parts. The visible human work for diagnosis treatment planning requires extensive data collection and organization coupled with the application of intelligent software to integrate the data with current medical knowledge.

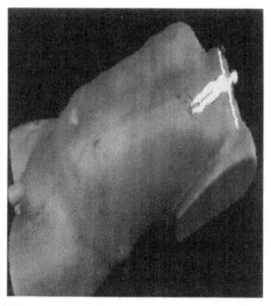

Figure 3.3. The visible human torso. (Courtesy of Richard A. Robb Biomedical Imaging Resource, Mayo Foundation, Rochester MN.)

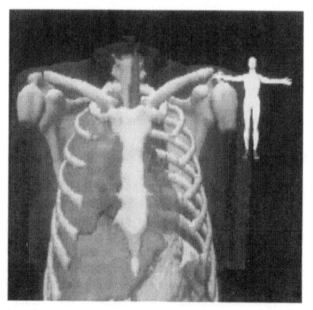

Figure 3.4. The visual human anatomy (Courtesy of Richard A. Robb Biomedical Imaging Resource, Mayo Foundation, Rochester MN.)

One result of efforts under way in many laboratories is something called a "deformable atlas," a human anatomic template that can be manipulated in software to represent the physical characteristics of any individual (57). Three-dimensional volumetric rendering of brain structures, limp nodes, and internal organs are displayed in workstations or personal computers for study and analysis. This provides a more efficient road map for surgeries and helps reduce operating time. The present and potential future uses of multimedia healthcare information are widespread:

- *Diagnosis.* The results of diagnostic tests may be delivered electronically to a clinician's workstation, including still images (e.g., x-rays of a bone failure), sequences of images (e.g., slices through a patient's brain from an MRI scanner), and moving images (e.g., video from an ultrasound examination).
- *Treatment.* Calculation of drug dosages and administration of pharmaceuticals or positioning graphics and radiation dose calculations can be stored as multimetric objects with temporal and spatial relationships.
- *Surgery.* There are many situations in which prerecorded diagnostic images may be used in conjunction with real-time scanner information (e.g., to guide the precise site of an incision). Miniature TU cameras can be passed through catheters in microsurgery.
- *Training.* Multimedia technology offers the potential for health-care procedures skills, because surgical operations can be captured in a number of media simultaneously (e.g., video, endoscope, blood pressure, ECG) for subsequent play back and analysis by students. Similarly, such records could be used as reference tools.
- *Health-care record.* Health-care practitioners have accumulated vast amounts of heterogeneous patient-related information (notes, charts, freehand sketches, images, etc.). Multimedia applications offer a way of storing and indexing such heterogeneous information within a common framework.

Concentrating on the health-care record, the medical data related to a particular patient may be in various media, from textural reports to a surgery planning video to a VR simulation. Such information may also be located in various databases and hospital information systems. One important consideration for this century is to create a telemedical information society whereby patient's medical data can be accessed globally and transparently by any retrieval and communication medium. Eventually, all patient information will be stored in a computer-accessible medium and all the computers will be connected in a global network—the essence of a 21st-century medical information system—so that multimedia systems will be accessible remotely via a homogeneous communication protocol. This protocol could be the WWW.

The building blocks of the foundational elements of a 21st-century health-care society are explained below. Associated with each building block is a tool set containing a number of generic tools and programs. As presented below, some of these are related to the use of VR techniques. Depending on its the situation, VR can be used simply as a viewer of 3-D models with the illusion of perspective added or for the interaction and manipulation of reconstructed patient-specific models. Later in this chapter, VR as a perspective image viewer of predicted tumor growth models is discussed. Its use for training and education purposes is introduced, and its diagnostic advantages are described. Clearly, VR will play an important part in maintaining a healthy community in this century, and its full potential has not even been considered.

"We are only just beginning to assess the impact of these technologies on the medical field," said Vannier (4), head of the Radiology Department at the University of Iowa Hospitals and clinics in Iowa city. "We don't know yet where the new the developments will take us." Some possible implications are introduced at the end of this chapter.

3.1 THE ELEMENTS OF A TELEMEDICAL INFORMATION SOCIETY

Whatever form of an information society related to health care we can imagine, it will be based on three basic components: raw medical data, reconstructed medical data, and derived medical data (Fig. 3.5). The raw medical data will consist of the medical data that can be ascertained directly from the patient for example x-ray, CT, and MRI. There is now a defacto standard for this data called Digital Imaging and Communications in Medicine (DICOM) (37). The ACR-NEMA DICOM standard has been developed to meet the needs of manufacturers and users of medical-imaging equipment for interconnection of devices on standard networks. Its multiple parts provide a means of expansion and updating, and the design of the standard was aimed at allowing simplified development for all types of medical imaging. DICOM also provides a means by which users of imaging equipment may assess whether two devices claiming conformance will be able to exchange meaningful information. The future additions to DICOM include support for creation of files on removable media (such as optical disks or high-capacity magnetic tape), new data structures for x-ray angiography, and extended hard copy print management. (http://www.xray.hmc.psu.edu/dicom/dicom_intro/DICOMIntro.html).

The derived medical data will be the subsequent diagnosis and in various formats, including text. The reconstructed medical data will consist of, for example, computer-generated models. All the medical data will have to be archived (Fig. 3.5). The raw medical data will be stored in DICOM picture archiving and communication system (PACS) and multimedia databases in multimedia RIS and hospital information system (HIS) databases. The reconstructed medical data will reside on some computing device. It is envisaged that this will be a WWW server. It is also envisaged that the communicating proto-

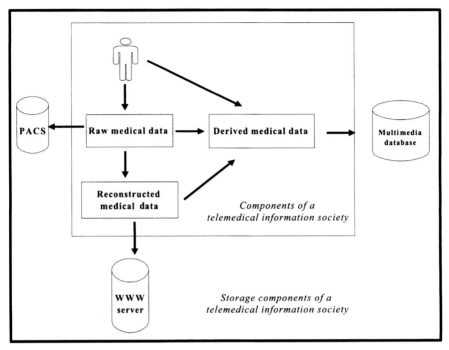

Figure 3.5. Components of a telemedical information society.

col will be the Web. The unique property of the WWW is that it provides a uniform meta-operating system, allowing computer platforms of various topologies to communicate. With the introduction of Java and Java script, it is now possible to run the same application programs (applets) on different computing platforms without any porting problems (Fig. 3.6). Based on this methodology, the accessibility of patient information is reduced to the notion of navigating or surfing the Web. There are currently a number of software providers offering WWW DICOM interfaces for archiving stores. One system, implemented at the University of Joensuu within the framework of EUROMED project (58). To use the WWW DICOM system, the user first runs a WWW browser (*Mosaic, Netscape,* or *Lynx*) and specifies a URL on one of DICOM PACS Unix workstations. This URL refers to an HTML file that contains a query form (Fig. 3.7). The query form contains a number of fields, such as patient name and medical record number. The user may specify any or all fields and can use wildcards in fields such as the name field. Once the form is completed, the user presses a button to submit the request.

The HTML form submits the query to a common gateway interface (CGI) program, which executes on the DICOM PACS server. This program accepts as input the form field values that the user specified. It then communicates with the archive via DICOM to determine patients who match the search criteria.

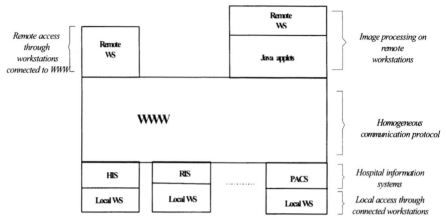

Figure 3.6. Multimodal medical information systems.

The user may then choose a patient, which in turn causes the studies for the patient to be displayed. Finally, the user may select a study that causes those images to be retrieved from the archive and be displayed via the Web browser. The result of this system is an easy-to-use interface that is accessible for any Web-supported computing platform to a DICOM PACS with the option to query and move images from the PACS.

Alternative public DICOM implementations can be found at the Pennsynvalnia State University, the University of Oldenburg, and the Mallinckrodt Institute of Radiology (the premier of publicly available DICOM implementations). There are also a number of hospitals currently using WWW browsers to access a DICOM PACS system. One such implementation is at the Medical Imaging Unit Center of Medical Informatics, Geneva University Hospital, where the conventional PACS environment was replaced by a prototype of the WWW browser that directly triggers a specific program for displaying medical images from a conventional *Netscape* or *Mosaic* browser. A specially designed interface written in HTML can be used from any conventional WWW browser or any platform.

Accessing a DICOM PACS through a Web interface is one aspect of a newly emerging telemedical information society. There are, however, many other aspects that need to be considered, for example, locating the text data and visualization data.

The development of a global telemedical information society should not be allowed to develop in an ad hoc manner. It is the objective of EUROMED (34–36, 50, 59) to standardize the foundational elements of such a society. The project identified 20 building blocks (Fig. 3.8), from which 39 steps have been defined. Each step is well defined and modular in nature. It is only when all the steps and, therefore building blocks, are put together that a telemedical information society becomes a realistic possibility. The building blocks are briefly explained below.

A   B

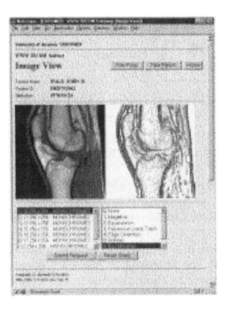
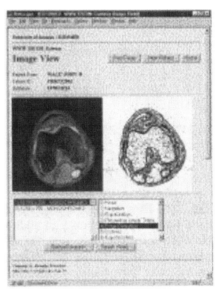

C   D

Figure 3.7. A WWW PACS system user interface. **A**, Query form to select a patient (114 Kb). **B**, Query form to select a study (109 Kb). **C**, DICOM image view (185 Kb). **D**, DICOM image view (107 Kb).

3.1.1 Communication

It is envisaged that in any image of the information society of the future, the computer will play an important part (60). It is, therefore, possible to conceive that everybody will have access to a computer, especially in a working environment. And everybody will have a unique identiifcation number or URL

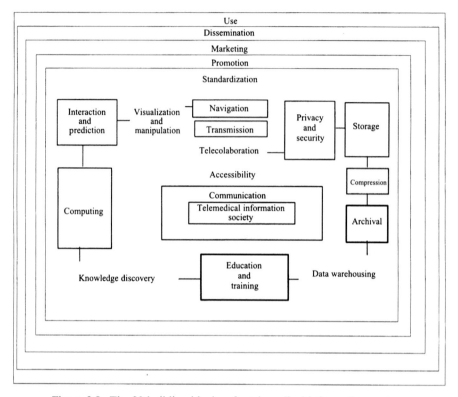

Figure 3.8. The 20 building blocks of a telemedical information society.

(Fig. 3.2). Thus, it is not unrealistic to assume that all medical practitioners will have access to a computer. In addition, with the advancement of telecommunications infrastructures, and the Internet, it is possible to imagine that all computers will be connected to Internet. The Internet is a "network of networks" that links computers around the world. These computers range from PCs to high-performance computing platforms, but they all use a set of rules called TCP/IP to exchange information.

One example of a TCP/IP networks is that used by the National Health Service (NHS) in the UK. The NHS-wide network is a strategic approach to provide a network infrastructure for all forms of health-care-related electronic communication, including computer data, voice, and mobile telemetry, throughout the country. Typical electronic communications take the form of patient-related clinical information exchanged during the referral/discharge cycle, contract-related information, items of service claims, continuing medical education, and telemedicine. The need for NHS-wide networking arose from the requirements to replace the existing network infrastructure, to introduce new applications (e.g., GP links), to support e-mail, and to encourage rapid access to the results of studies and reports providing up-to-date protocols for patient care. This supports the move toward evidence-based medicine. The project was formally conceived in mid-1992 and is undergoing pilot and acceptance testing. The WAN is exclusive to the NHS and supports e-mail, electronic data interchange (EDI), and X.400 message handling services as well as TCP/IP. Although not mandatory, the intention is that this infrastructure will become the network of choice for the NHS. Gateways to the Internet are to be installed but will be carefully controlled. The Internet gateways will be one-way, allowing NHS users to access multimedia applications on the Internet while preventing Internet users from accessing the NHS. It is expected that the NHS will set up its own Web-like servers to disseminate health-care information. (Further information can be obtained from the NHS Infoline, +44-121-625-3838.)

Another example is the Fr1 billion project awarded in 1997 by the French social security ministry to CEGETEL to setup a national Internet-based health-care computer network. Over 5 years, the project will create an open data transmission network capable of serving the country's entire health-care system. CEGETEL is a joint venture of British Telecom, the French utility Cie Generale des Eaux, Mannesmann of Germany, and SBC communications of the United States. It was formed in 1995 to capitalize on the 1997 deregulation of France's telecoms market.

In addition, with the development of modern and satellite technology, the concept of a mobile connection to the Internet is also conceivable. Mobile connections could be used to support cases of emergency, natural disasters, and temporary sites. In many remote and rural areas of the world, it has been almost impossible for sick or injured people to get to a doctor or a paramedic, let alone a specialist. With the falling cost and increased sophistication of communications and computer technologies, satellite communications—such as those provided by Inmarsat—are becoming a cost-effective means of delivering health care to remote sites, including villages, settlements, and camps, and to crew and passengers aboard ships and aircraft.

Inmarsat operates a global communications network of 10 satellites, which provides communications anywhere in the world (except for the extreme polar regions). Inmarsat was established by an intergovernmental treaty in 1979. The organization has 79 member countries but is used by >160 countries. Each member country appoints a signatory (usually, but not always, the main telecommunications operator in that country) who provides Inmarsat services to the end user. In addition to the satellites, the Inmarsat system includes land Earth stations (LESs), which provide links to the terrestrial telecom networks. There are also >55,000 mobile Earth stations (MESs) used by customers and produced by different manufacturers around the world. Inmarsat is the only global provider of mobile satellite communications for distress and safety and for commercial applications at sea, in the air, and on land.

The delivery of telemedicine services yields many social and economic benefits, including reduced travel, improved consultations, universal service, reduced waiting lists, and cost-effective training and education. Some projects for which Inmarsat has been used are the following:

- U.S. Army doctors used Inmarsat-A high-speed data systems to handle health-care emergencies in Somalia, Croatia, Bosnia, and elsewhere. Applications include telepresence, digital image delivery, triage, and obtaining second opinions.
- New Zealand Army personnel in Bosnia used Inmarsat satellite phones to provide an Internet link to Auckland. They then used the link to check health-care databases, obtain advice for specific treatments and participate in specialist discussion groups.
- Several clinics in Obninsk, Russia, used Inmarsat multimedia videoconferencing stations so that victims of the Chernobyl nuclear accident could receive regular checkups and treatment under the guidance of experts in Japan.
- WHO field workers used Inmarsat to remain in contact with international experts while dealing in situ with the e-bola epidemic in Zaire and the lahar emergency in Indonesia.
- British Airways is collaborating on development of a briefcase-size monitoring kit to be carried on long-haul flights. Heartbeat, blood pressure, oxygen levels in the blood, temperature, and other vital signs will be collected and transmitted to doctors on the ground. Cabin staff will then be helped to make a diagnosis or give treatment.
- Inmarsat is being used in the MERMAID project, funded in part by the CEU to provide delivery of 24-h multilingual telemedicine and health-care services to ships at sea.

Although networking technologies will not be covered in this chapter. A special mention should be made of ATM. Many types of multimedia information, such as voice and video, cannot be carried effectively over conventional lower-speed networks because they are not tolerant of the variable delays present in the network layers. ATM technology offers the dual benefit of allocating bandwidth on demand effectively while meeting the strict performance criteria necessary for multimedia information transfer. One project that used ATM technology is the CEU-TEN-IBC-HIM project.

The High-Performance Information Infrastructure for Medicine (HIM) project is funded by CEU DG XIII as part of the Trans-European Networks—Integrated Broadband Communications (TEN-IBC) project. Its purpose is to evaluate high-performance computer applications running over pilot ATM networks established by the European PTTs. The objectives of HIM are to evaluate the global networks available for imaging, to establish user needs and requirements for computer applications, and to develop tools for collaborative working. The HIM project comprises 18 partners over 9 countries, including health-care partners, technical partners, and evaluation partners. Currently it is investigating image conferencing using 2-D image sets (CT, MRI, etc), medical images in the management of liver disease, cardiology cine sequences, 3-D remote-image processing facility, and image mailbox (e-mailing images in support of patient referrals). Some of the tools used in the course of the project include: the display utility DisplImage, developed at University College London, which makes use of the X client-server architecture and the Berkeley Conferencing Tools vic and vat (available in the public domain). The Internet in whatever form could provide the communications infrastructure, the accessibility protocol, however, is bound to be based on World Wide Web.

3.1.2 Accessibility

The advantages of using the WWW as the accessibility protocol for a telemedical information society is that it is platform independent and thus accessibility from any platform. In addition, interpreted languages such as Java have been developed to run on the WWW. The Web can then be thought of as the generic operating system (61). The Web is a simple yet ingenious system that allows users to interact with documents stored on computers across the Internet as if they were parts of a single hypertext (62). A major reason for the accelerated growth of the Internet in the last few years is the WWW, which began in 1992 at CERN, the European Laboratory for Particle Physics, as a means of distributing and annotating specific research. Technical standards are now defined by the World Wide Web consortium, which specifies four sets of rules creating, publishing and finding documents:

- *Hypertext Mark-Up Language (HTML)*. Web documents are ordinary text files that can be created with any word-processing program. They include tags that control their appearance. Tags can also define a word or phase as a link. Selecting a link lets the user go to another document (or to another section of the same document). HTML documents (often called pages) can also include color graphics and clips of digitized audio or video. Users need a Web browser program (for example, *Netscape*) to view Web pages.
- *Virtual Reality Modeling Language (VRML)*. VRML is an open extensible, industry-standard scene description language for 3-D scenes, or worlds, on the Internet. With VRML and *Netscape's Live3D*, you can author and view distributed common interactive 3-D worlds that are rich with text, images, animation, sound, music, and even video. VRML 1.0 supports worlds with relatively simple animations, and VRML 2.0 supports complex 3-D animations, simulations, and behaviors by allowing Java scripts to act on VRML objects.
- *Hypertext Transfer Protocol (http)*. Users of the Web retrieve documents from servers (or Web sites); http allows a networked computer to listen for and respond to incoming request for files (hits).
- *Uniform Research Locator (URL)*. A URL is the Internet address for a Web document or other file. A typical URL looks like this: http://www.Euromed.iccs.ntua.gr. Web users can retrieve documents either by manually entering URLs or by selecting links that contain URLs.

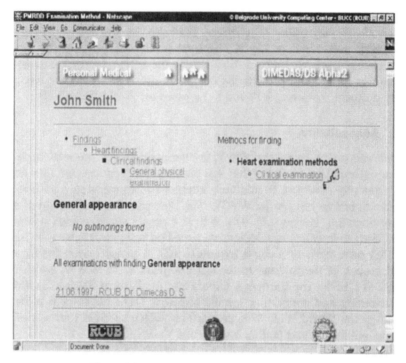

Figure 3.9. A Web-based MIS for cardiology.

3.1.3 Storage

Data storage (of medical information) is one of the most critical cornerstones of the societies building blocks. Medical imaging data should be stored in DICOM 3.0 format in PACS.

If the Web is to be adopted as the accessibility medium and the Internet as the communication medium, then there should be a WWW interface to the storage components. It is, therefore, envisaged that HIS, PACS and any other storage mediums will be Web accessible. The integration protocols between PACS/HIS and other information systems—such as the cardiology information system developed at the University of Belgrade, shown in Figure 3.9—should be based on well-defined Web protocols such as HTML, VRML, http, and shttp. Alternative databases such as the Neuronal Database in the Human Brain Project (63) and video archiving systems should also be designed with Web interfaces. Furthermore, it is envisaged that the information systems will begin to possess some processing capabilities so, the processing of an image could then be undertaken at the site of storage (64) (Fig. 3.10).

3.1.4 Privacy and Security

Making the medical information systems accessible via the Web raises problems.

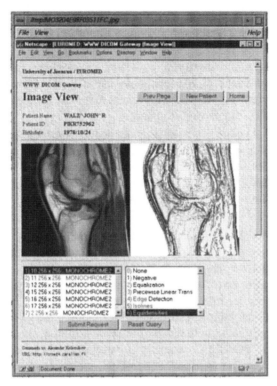

Figure 3.10. An example of WWW DICOM archiving.

- *Ownership and responsibility.* In many countries, legislation requires that all captured health-care information be preserved for a certain period of time (typically 5 to 10 years) before it can be deleted. In such cases, it should be clear who is responsible for the maintenance and integrity of the information.
- *Access rights.* Who is allowed to look at, modify, copy, or delete an item of health-care information? In some hospitals, for example, only senior doctors are allowed to delete images. Others may be allowed to look at or copy them, and yet others may not be allowed to access them at all.
- *Identification.* In clinical applications, the ability to associate patient-related information with the correct patient is vital. In such cases, linkages between diverse types of information need to be protected and must be preserved after information interchange. In other situations (e.g., research), the opposite is often the case, and anonymity is required. The situation is complicated in a distributed multimedia environment in which the relationship between some items of patient-related information, often in different formats, must be maintained and other relationships must be severed.
- *Integrity of information.* Because of the use to which it is put, the preservation of information at known and guaranteed levels of integrity is crucial

in the health-care domain. Health-care information of all types must be protected from accidental or malicious alteration during interchange and storage.

- *Confidentiality.* Confidentiality is a key requirement for patient-related health-care information. Most countries have legislation to protect the confidentiality of information. Some experts advocate the use of encryption in messages, while others would restrict it.

- *Availability.* Availability is also a key requirement for health-care information. The correct information must be available when and where it is required, otherwise patients' lives could be put at risk. Availability can be critical, especially when time is short in an emergency. Some experts argue against the use of encryption in messages for this reason.

Thus another building block in the society should control the privacy and security of the stored data. Security and confidentiality considerations are not covered in this chapter, but discussions are available (65–71). The reasons are that security requirements for health care are not well defined, they vary from country to country according to the potential and cultural beliefs, they vary from institution to institution according to local polices. The CEN/TC251/WG6 program is currently looking into these issues. In addition, there is support from the EC under the INFOSEC program to support projects related to security issues. One such project is EUROMED-ETS, which deals with the issues of security of WWW-based telemedicine (72). The recommendations of this project is to adopt trusted third-party services for the management of unique keys, such as the client certificate server developed by *Netscape* and the use of shttp for the communication protocol (see http://euromed.iccs.ntua.gr for further details).

Clearly, a lot of work needs to be undertaken regarding privacy and the issues of data protection, reliability, and integrity. However, many of these issues can be borrowed from the commercial commerce society.

3.1.5 Navigation

It is envisaged that in the telemedical information society of the future the data related to the patient will be stored in a computer-accessible medium. The data (the electronic health-care record of the patient), could, however, be distributed among many computing systems (Fig. 3.11). To avoid the pragmatics of accessing a remote computing system, EUROMED developed a Web-based interface that uses hyperlinks and the http protocol to access patient data (Fig. 3.12).

As shown in Figure 3.13, each patient will have a unique identification number. This ID number, or URL, will be similar to an e-mail address or Web home page. From the patient's home page all the medical data related to a patient can be acquired by following a combination of hyperlinks and hypergraphics. The patient's home page is in standardized HTML format, consisting

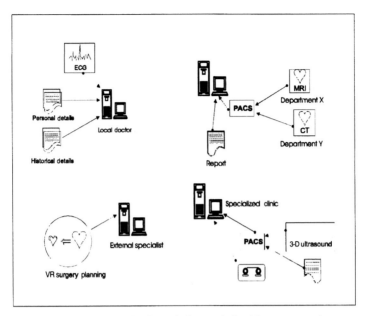

Figure 3.11. A distributed electronic health-care record.

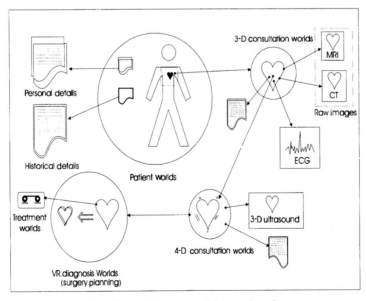

Figure 3.12. A hypergraphic user interface.

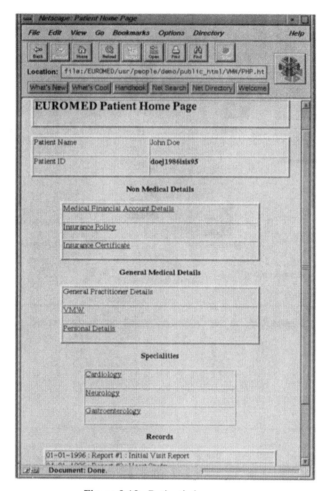

Figure 3.13. Patient's home page.

of four sections: nonmedical details, general medical details, specialities, and records. The nonmedical data will link to information such as the medical financial details (Fig. 3.14), the medical insurance policy (Fig. 3.15), and the medical insurance certificate (Fig. 3.16). From the general medical details section, an overview of the patient's health care can be seen. The specialities and records sections act as shortcuts into the patient's health-care record.

As shown in Figure 3.17, by following the virtual medical worlds (VMWs) link, a hypergraphical and hypertextual environment will present all the available data related to the patient. The hypergraphical representation of the patient's health-care record is a three-tiered hierarchy consisting of whole-body templates (patient's VMW record), atlas templates (e.g., thorax VMW),

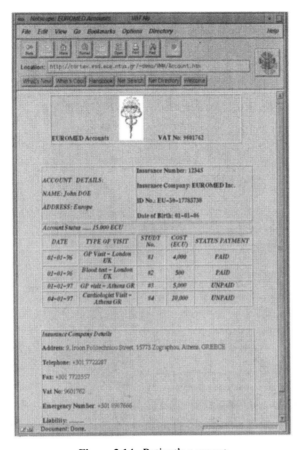

Figure 3.14. Patient's account.

and organ templates (e.g., heart VMW). At the whole-body level, annotations of the whole-body template indicate the existence of medical data related to a particular area of the body. Annotated regions of the body at the whole-body level link to atlas templates. Also visible at the whole-body level are the medical disciplines that have been used by the patient. In the foreground are disciplines that are associated with the whole body, for example, general practitioner (GP). Behind these are the speciality disciplines, for example, cardiology and neurology; and even farther behind are medical record summaries related to regions of the body. By using the zooming capabilities of the Web browser, a practitioner can examine which specialities have been applied to the patient and even the extent of the examinations. All the named disciplines are hyperlinks to the related medical information systems. For example, the patient VMW record shown in Figure 3.13, the practitioner could follow the cardiology hyperlink to the cardiology information system without having to pass through the atlas

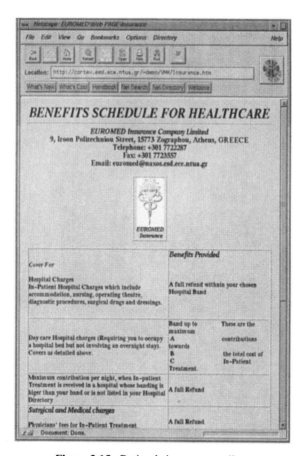

Figure 3.15. Patient's insurance policy.

and organ templates. Similarly, the cardiology information system could be accessed directly from the patient's home page by following the cardiology link in the specialities section. By following the hypergraphical link in Figure 3.17, from the whole-body template, the practitioner could access the thorax VMW. At the atlas and organ levels, general and specialized disciplines related to the region of the body can also be seen. For example, in Figure 3.17, the specialized discipline related to the thorax and heart VMW is cardiology. Each of the body templates is in VRML format and is constructed from the Visible Human Dataset. At the organ level, related examinations are also visible. Therefore, by following either hypergraphical or hypertextual links to the medical informa- tion system, the data of the patient can be accessed as shown in Figure 3.18.

To make the virtual medical worlds as general as possible, the following types of general procedures, actions, entities, and data were identified: exami- nation, examination method, specific finding, parameter, diagnosis, and ther- apy. Each of these is added as a hyperlink in each of the virtual medical world,

Figure 3.16. Patient's certificate.

if applicable, dynamically. *Examination* was defined as a collection of actions by some examination methods selected by a physician. *Examination method* is a collection of actions performed to collect some medical parameters. An examination method can include examination submethods and/or specific findings. *Specific finding* is a collection of medical parameters that have something in common. *Medical parameters* represent information about the medical condition of some part of the human body. A parameter can be a numerical value; text; image(s); audio signal; video; a 3-D, 4-D, or VR model; or some other form of information.

Each instance of examination, examination method, specific finding, parameter, diagnosi, or therapy is defined as a personal medical resource (PMR). A physician should have an opportunity to reach data related to any PMR of any patient existing in any medical database throughout the world. Thus each PMR has a corresponding personal medical resource locator (PMRL) to make that task possible (73). This locator makes it possible to reach the PMR from any

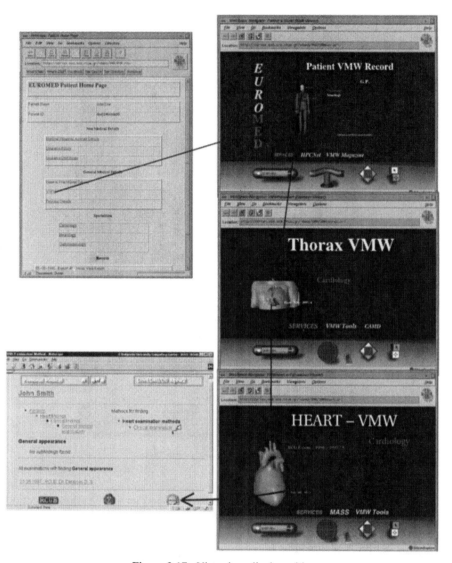

Figure 3.17. Virtual medical worlds.

Web page on any Internet-connected computer. Obviously, the PMRL must be unique.

PMR are stored in personal medical resource databases, and the basic rule is that the PMR is stored in the database of the hospital where it was generated. That is how a distributed database of medical data is generated. With a PMRL, there is the potential to reach a PMR throughout the medical world on the Internet. The basic question is where to find the PMRL of a patient. The per-

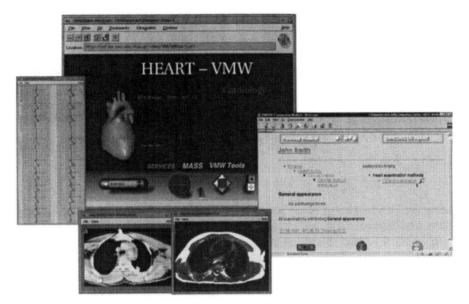

Figure 3.18. Patient cardiology data.

sonal home page site as the place to find the collection of all of the PMRLs related to the patient. This collection is actually a personal medical resource locator database that (conceptually) exists only on the personal home page site. The PMRLs are available on the patient's home page, this is transparent to the user. To easily reach the home page, there could be some mapping between it and the patient's ID number. However, mapping is not needed because the patient's ID number could be the same as the URL to the home page.

The crucial point is how to generate Web pages with mutually related PMR(s), what descriptions to put on those pages, and how to make surfing through Web pages a process in which the physician could easily reach all logically related PMR(s). This is the point where the expert knowledge of medical doctors is necessary. This information should be incorporated in a personal medical resource description database. It should exist as identical copies at each node in the medical worlds. As the representation of expert knowledge through the database is improved, the Web pages and surfing options will change; but these modification need not to be done simultaneously throughout the network. Obviously, new versions of the databases could be easily distributed through the Internet.

3.1.6 Transmission

Identifying the location of medical information is the first step toward its use. The transmission of these data over the network becomes critical when consid-

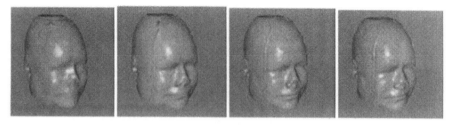

Figure 3.19. Progressive transmission.

ering the bandwidths of today's networks. The issues of transmission of medical data and compression are closely linked. For the purposes of this chapter, compression relates to storing the medical data and minimizing the required space, whereas transmission relates to minimizing the time the practitioner has to wait to view the medical data. Of course, if the data to be transmitted are compressed, the amount of information transmitted is reduced, which saves time. Medical images may be transmitted in a progressive or even a selective manner. This approach allows the users to decode images from the lowest to the highest resolution and is ideally suited for image transmission across the Internet. This method allows the user to download a small portion of the compressed file and view the image at lower resolution to determine if the entire image is needed. This feature also ensures that the viewer does not lose interest while the image is downloaded because the decompressed image will appear quickly, first with low resolution and then progressively building up in detail as it is downloaded (Fig. 3.19). One example of this approach is the *Lightning Strike Wavelet* compression software (www.infinop.com/fhtml/encrypt.html).

If the practitioner wishes to wait, all the data as presented in the original format will be acquired. However, at any instance the practitioner may have enough information to make diagnosis. In addition, the practitioner could indicate at the general level a specific area of interest that could be transmitted first, with the remaining data following progressively. Progressive transmission is an ongoing area of research, but it is hoped that it will be enclosed in the definition of virtual medical worlds for both 2-D and 3-D medical images. Its implications for VR also need to be investigated.

3.1.7 Telecollaboration

Conferencing is defined as the interactive exchange of information in real time between two or more participants. Real-time conferencing is often used for remote consultation between clinicians. There are several distinct types of conferencing, the most familiar being the simple telephone call. Other types include

- Voice conferencing, which allows multiple parties to connect to each other and participate in a discussion, using audio technology such as a telephone or radio.
- Video conferencing, which allows the presentation of many types of visual and audio information via videocameras, microphones, and display stations.
- Pictorial information can be sent as an image, for example, a digital x-ray is displayed on a screen and imaged by the camera rather than being transmitted in its native format. There are refinements, including digitizing whiteboards whose contents may be transmitted at the touch of a button. High-quality videoconferencing requires dedicated high bandwidth links, whereas slow-scan video can work satisfactorily over two 64 Kb/s ISDN B-channel links.
- Data conferencing allows participants to manipulate shared data in real time, typically in conjunction with voice conferencing. An area of the computers' memory or disk storage is synchronized between two users by means of the conferencing software. Each has control of a cursor, which moves simultaneously on both the local and remote displays. A bearer technology such as ISDN is well suited to this type of application.

Document conferencing assumes that all participants are supplied with a copy of the conference documents (e.g., an x-ray image and report) in advance of the conferencing session. Operations can then be performed on the remote copy of the document.

Telecollaboration could be thought of as conferencing using basic Web-based tools such as e-mail, newsgroups, and links to educational databases (Fig. 3.20). However, the real benefit of telemedicine is that more that one practitioner can telecollaborate (e.g., view the same medical data simultaneously). With Web-based tools this becomes easy by using plug-ins such as *Cooltalk*. *Cooltalk* has a shared whiteboard, has talk facilities, and can even be combined with videoconferencing facilities. The shared whiteboard can be used to view and annotate the same image simultaneously on two Web-connected workstations, facilitating the tele-aspect of telemedicine (Fig. 3.21). Together sophisticated plug-ins and video make up the first easy solution.

3.1.8 Visualization and Manipulation

For visualization purposes, a VRML browser can be used to view virtual medical worlds and reconstructed images generated from raw medical data (74). For example CT slices to VRML could be done on the fly by a Java applet. Java could also be used to manipulate the VRML models, performing tasks such as intersection and measurement analysis, as shown in Figure 3.22. Java is platform independent; therefore, the developed applets could run on any

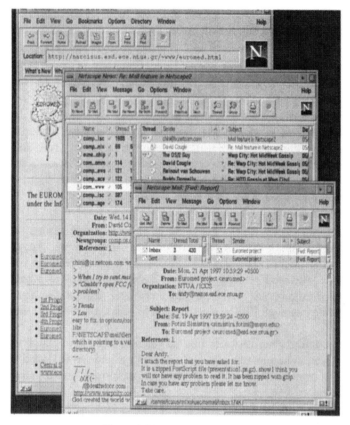

Figure 3.20. Web-based tools.

Web browser. An example of the same applet, a region-growing algorithm, running on two different platforms is shown in Figures 3.23 and 3.24. A Java applet could be used to reconstruct the VRML representation from MRI images, as shown in Figure 3.25. These models could be fused to produce a new model whereby the movement of the endocardium is denoted by color (Fig. 3.26).

3.1.9 Interaction, Prediction, and Computing

The ultimate objective for imaging is interaction and prediction with medical models. The 3-D and 4-D models generated by the Java programs should be augmented so they can be viewed by VR techniques. The interaction could be in the form of surgery planning and surgery assistance, making use of VR techniques, such as VRASP developed at the Mayo Clinic. Virtual endoscopic techniques could then be developed to examine the body, e.g., virtual endos-

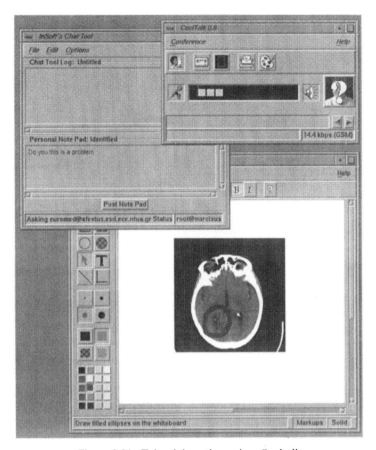

Figure 3.21. Telecolaboration using *Cooltalk*.

copy performed on a 3-D reconstructed model of the colon (10, 12, 75) (Fig. 3.27).

The prediction aspect includes medical physics for determining blood flow analysis and tumor growth. Clearly, both interaction and prediction require a vast amount of computing. This should be provided either by a connection from a hospital to a computing site or by using the hospital computers in a collaborative network. It is envisaged that a meta-computing environment will be made available for a variety of medical applications. The locations of the computational resources need not be known (76). Interaction and prediction will be discussed later in this chapter.

3.1.10   Archival and Compression

Returning to the cornerstone of storage, a general hospital over a 1-year period will require on average 6,000,000 Mb of disk storage (Table 3.1). The idea of

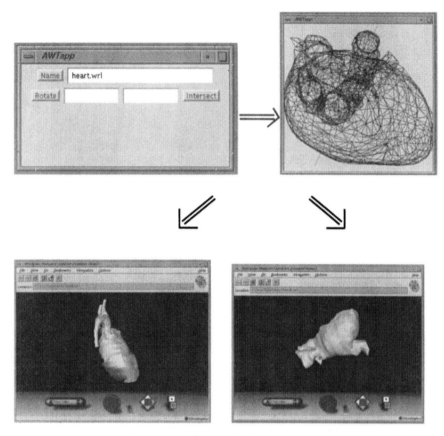

Figure 3.22. An example of a VMW 3-D intersection tool.

an archive is to store images for as long as they might be needed which must include legal requirements. Generally, this is much longer than can be cost-effectively supported by the technologies used in the on-line storage system. If a PACS should provide digital archival it must be decided how many images should be made accessible. Since any archive system will in principle overflow in time most systems provide for an on-line and an off-line archive.

In terms of an optical disk jukebox, on-line pallets are those located on a shelf in a storeroom, ready to be manually inserted in the jukebox on request. The on-line storage capacity is best thought of in terms of time depth. Studies have shown that <10% of images are accessed ever again after the first year. The results of an example study are shown in Table 3.2. In terms of disk space, this represents approximately 10% of 6,000,000 Mb. The example study showed the storage requirements in a general hospital over a 1-year period. Taking into consideration time depth and storage capacity, the requirements of an archival system might read as follows:

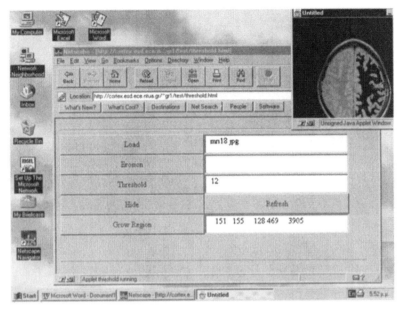

Figure 3.23. A Java applet running on a PC platform.

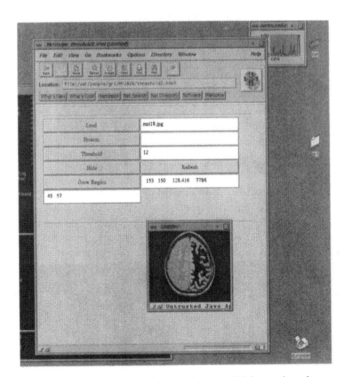

Figure 3.24. A Java applet running on a Unix workstation.

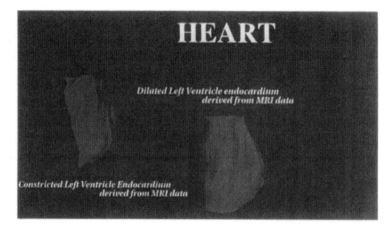

Figure 3.25. 3-D reconstructed models of the endocardium.

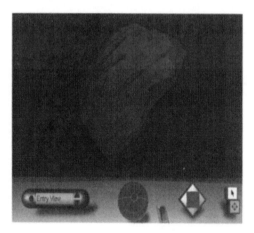

Figure 3.26. A 4-D model of the endocardium.

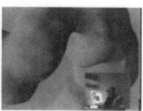

Figure 3.27. Virtual colonoscopy.

TABLE 3.1. Average annual Storage Requirements

Modality	Procedure	Annual Volume	Images/ Study	KB/ Image	MB/ Study	MB/year without Compression
Radiography	Chest 1 view	37,500	1	7,500	7.5	281,250
	Chest 2 view	32,000	2	7,500	15.0	480,000
	Portable Chest	6,250	1	7,500	7.5	46,875
	Other Portables	4,100	2	7,500	15.0	61,500
	Upper Extremity	6,900	3	7,500	22.5	155,250
	Lower Extremity- Pelvis	11,000	2.5	7,500	18.8	206,250
	Spine—Cervica	4,000	8	7,500	60.0	240,000
	Spine—Toraco- lumbar	4,000	2	7,500	15.0	60,000
	Head	1,250	5	7,500	37.5	46,875
	Mammography	6,500	5	7,500	37.5	243,750
	Tomography	50	13	7,500	97.5	4,875
	Miscellaneous	2,300	6	7,500	45.0	103,500
Fluoro	Upper GI/Small Bowel		25	2,000	50.0	50,000
	Burium Enema/ Colon		25	2,000	50.0	250,000
	Abdomen/KUB		1	7,500	7.5	29,250
	3-way Abdomen		3	7,500	22.5	76,500
	IVP		15	2,000	30.0	18,900
	Other GU		8	2,000	16.0	9,600
	Oral Cholecysto- gram		10	2,000	20.0	400
	Gall Bladder. All other		10	2,000	20.0	600
	Myelography		20	2,000	40.0	4,000
	Arthrograms		15	2,000	30.0	3,600
DSA	Special/Neuro	325	1200	500	600.0	195,000
	Arteriography Vascular	3,250	800	500	400.0	1,300,000
	Cardic	3,300	800	500	400.0	1,320,000
CT	Head + Body	19,000	75	500	37.5	712,500
MR	Head	4,900	128	140	17.9	87,808
	Body	2,100	150	140	21.0	44,100
Nuclear Medicine	Body	7,850	90	3	0.3	2,120
	Heart	7,650	90	3	0.3	2,066
Ultrasound	Cardiac	9,200	36	60	2.2	19,872
	Body	14,000	36	60	2.2	30,240
Total		202,225				6,086,680
Total without DSA						3,271,680

TABLE 3.2. Diagnostic Requests per Image for Seriously Ill Patients

Timing	
First 3 days of hospital stay	10
Next 6 days of hospital stay	4
Rest of first year	3
Outpatient studies	2
PACS operational load	
Initial acquisition	1
QC/examination verification	1
Initial archival	1
Dearchivals	5
Total number of request per image	27

1. The system shall include sufficient on-line archive storage to provide access to at least 2 years of image production without manual intervention by a human operator.
2. Images older than 2 years shall be accessible. Accessibility can be satisfied by requiring a human operator to inset storage media into the system.
3. If a human operator is requested to upload an archival system, it shall automatically provide instructions identifying the location of the media involved and the action to be performed.

With current technology and the evolution of data warehousing, there appears to be a thin line between where on-line archives in a PACS system ends and a data warehousing environment begins. It is envisaged that archiving sites will be set up so that a hospital can download the requirements of vast amount of storage to an external site. In conjunction with archives is the compression of data. Compression is a current topic with a large amount of interest, owing to its legal implications. However, techniques such as a wavelet compression could provide the answer.

3.1.11 Data Warehousing

New technology in the form of data warehousing provides the potential to store the required amount of medical data. It is envisaged, however, that a hierarchical approach will be adopted for data storage. This also has implications for the networking infrastructure. The hierarchical infrastructure will consist of hospital PACS, regional PACS, national PACS, and a european PACS (Fig. 3.28). Each PACS system outside of the hospital PACS can be regarded as a

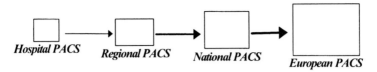

Figure 3.28. Hierarchical data management.

data warehouse, consisting only of the archiving component of a complete hospital PACS environment.

It is envisaged that the medical imaging data related to a particular patient will reside on the hospital PACS up to a set date, before this expiring date is reached, the medical imaging data will be copied to the regional PACS. The medical imaging data will then reside on the regional PACS up to a set date. Again before of the expiring date is reached, data will be copied to the national PACS, and so on. After a period of maybe up to 1 year, the data will finally reside on the national PACS with a copy on the European PACS. At any time after the initial period, the patient's medical imaging data will reside on two PACS systems, facilitating backing up the data. It is also envisaged that the VRLs given to each PACS system on the EUROMED network will reflect the hierarchical native of the data warehouse as shown in Figure 3.28. Further more, the expiring times will be uniform for each level of data warehouse. Therefore, from the date that the medical data were created it is possible to determine which PACS systems the data reside:

Week 0–12	Hospital PACS
Week 4–36	Regional PACS
Week 12–48	National PACS
Week 36+	European PACS

If the medical data were required at week 8, they would be found on the hospital PACS where it they were created and on the associated regional PACS.

3.1.12 Knowledge Discovery and Educational Training

When vast amounts of medical data become available as a result of the data warehousing, then knowledge discovery techniques can be applied to identify pathologies and disease trends. The data can also be used for educational and training purposes, because unique cases can be identified and used in VR and expert system applications to advise practitioners.

3.1.13 Standardization

So that the core building blocks cooperate in a collaborative manner, their interfaces and individual components must be standardized (42). It will be the role of European Commission–funded programs (e.g., Information Society Industrial Standardization) and the standardized bodies (e.g., CEN TC 251) to coordinate such interactions.

3.1.14 Promotion, Marketing, Dissemination, and Use

The remaining four building blocks relate to how this new society will be used. The society must be promoted through various marketing channels so that medical vendors take an integral part in the development of the society. Does the general practitioner really want to look like the one portrayed in Figure 3.1. By varying initiatives the implications on the health-care community should be presented so the results can be disseminated to the end users. One example for promoting the update of Web-based technology within the medical discipline is the on-line magazine *Virtual Medical Worlds* (http://www.hoise.com/vmw). All aspects relating to the update of a telemedical information society are being addressed by the e-zine (Fig. 3.29).

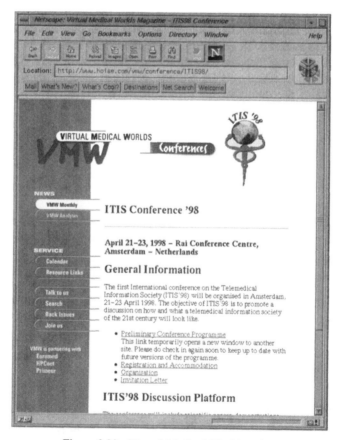

Figure 3.29. *Virtual Medical Worlds* e-zine.

3.2 INTEGRATION OF VR INTO A TELEMEDICAL INFORMATION SOCIETY

The most important aspect of a 21st-century information society is the personalized visualization of stored data. As presented above, the use of the WWW with a hypergraphical and hypertextual manipulation and interface can allow a transparent homogeneous access to a patient's data (61, 62, 77). The next step is the visualization and manipulation of these data, as shown in Figure 3.17.

At each virtual medical world, the practitioner has the possibility to initiate a service, which may be local or remote. For example, it may be to initiate a publicly available Web plug-in such as a *Cooltalk* session. A service may also be used to construct 3-D models from 2-D slices, manipulate the generated 3-D models, and create a 4-D model (78). For example, by using VRML 2.0, a model of a pulsing heart could be constructed from a series of 3-D models. Another service may take these 3-D or 4-D VRML reconstructed models and use a VR interface to perform, for example, a virtual colonoscopy (39). The advantages of the services approach is analogous to that of Web-based plug-ins; they are used when and where required and where they are supported. It is envisaged that a hospital information system of the future will consist of a local application server and access to remote services (Fig. 3.30). These remote

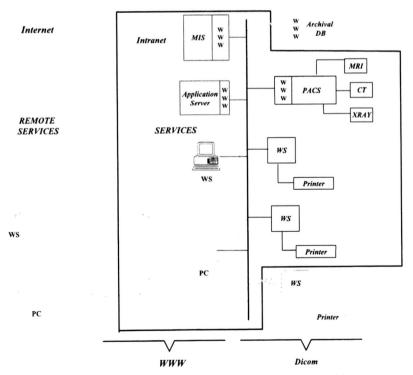

Figure 3.30. The services approach to the virtual medical world.

services may be data management services and computational services, as introduced above. The services could also be advanced visualization services, such as using VR techniques to provide a true 3-D model (79). A VR service, however, needs to use a number of other services.

For example, to sustain the illusion of reality, a surgical planning interface needs to generate smoothly animated images (80). To do this, the system must be able to sustain a display update rate of at least 30 frames per second. In addition to a high display rate, the interface must respond to the user's commands in near real time; that is, the delay between user input and system response must be <100 ms and would, ideally, approach 10 ms. Research has shown that delays above 300 ms can cause the user to overcompensate for system delay, and delays above 300 ms can cause user discomfort, including motion sickness (7, 81, 82). Owing to the currently available computer hardware, these requirements limit the complexity of the generated images and/or of the immersive simulation of real-world tasks. Remote services may be required to supply supportive computation facilities.

To further the illusion of reality and to increase the degree of immersion in VR systems, the display should be coupled to the user's head position. Work done by Arthur and Booth (83) and by Sollenburger and Milgram (84) shows that error rates for such tasks as tracing, movement, and localization improve when users are given a head-coupled stereo display over a noncoupled (static) display, with head coupling being the dominate factor (83). The use of biomedical data as the basis for models within a virtual environment poses some unique problems. Although currently available rendering algorithms can generate photorealistic images from rather dense volumetric data (78, 85, 86), ray tracing algorithms cannot sustain the visual updated rate required for real-time display. In addition, most surface-display algorithms generate images from polygon representations of the surface(s), using extremely high numbers of polygons. To be successful, a medical VR system requires a means of transforming volumetric image data into reasonable geometric (polygonal) models. This requires the ability to accurately segment the desired object from the scan data, detect its surface, and generate the best possible polygonal representation of the surface from a fixed polygonal "budget" (defined as the constraint on the number of polygons for effective display rates). Currently available hardware is able to render and manipulate in real time approximately 20,000 complex polygons (including shading, texture mapping, and anti-aliasing). Current polygonization algorithms—such as marching cubes (87, 88), spiderweb (84), and the wrapper (89)—produce high-resolution surfaces with polygonal counts ranging from 40,000 to several million polygons.

The VR system must also be able to simulate some, if not all, of the physical properties of the objects being modeled to generate an illusion of reality (6, 90). At a minimum, the biomedical model should properly deform when exposed to external forces and give the appearance of weight. Ideally, for surgery, a VR system would react properly to directed manipulations, i.e., the specific motions and functions employed by a surgeon. Combined with the pragmatic problems

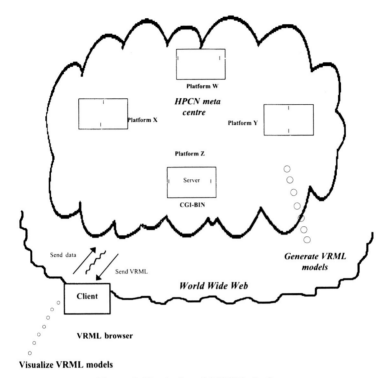

Figure 3.31. A virtual HPCN platform.

of VR is the coupling with computing resources. The resources must also be homogeneous and transparent to the user, who will be able to request the generation of a reconstructed model. The computation of the reconstructed model may be executed on a number of computing platforms. However, this is abstracted from the user who is presented with a virtual computing platform (Fig. 3.31). The concept of using a remote computing resource can be extended to include other computationally intensive tasks, such as creating a stereoscopic VR model from a 3-D VRML model.

There are two main ways to display data gathered by modem 3-D methods such as CT: surface and volume rendering. Each places limits on what can become a virtual object. With surface rendering, a 3-D grid of density above a chosen threshold τ from densities with values less than τ. The marching cubes algorithm of Lorensen and Chine (87, 91). Currently, most favored for this task produces Σ with hundreds of thousands of triangles. Building a sum of square faces across voxels, as do Udupa and Hung (92), or between them, like Chen et al. (93), places a similar burden on the graphics hardware. Users may have to choose between a crude surface and one too slow to use as a real-time virtual object. Mesh optimization techniques reduce the triangle count with less sacrifice of quality (94, 95), but they take tens of minutes. Clearly, this time is not acceptable to a surgeon who wants to explore what a tumor or artery looks like with different choices of threshold τ. Alternatively, volume rendering treats the 3-D dataset as a set of absorbency values and computes the effect of passing light through it under various rules, such as accumulating absorption or recording the highest absorbency or ray meets. The task of preserving distinct objects such as tissues or tissue boundaries found by segmentation or surface extraction is left to the user.

Until recently, volume rendering objects were unavailable for real-time interaction. A single view takes tens of seconds to render, and there can be no changing relation between the data and the viewpoint. However, the technique of 3-D texture mapping allows presentation of volume data at remarkable speeds (62, 96–98). This approach is used in the hardware implementations of the reality engine. It displays the data via a scheme of interpolated texture mapping in polygonal slices, making it much easier than with classical volume techniques to introduce a surface-rendered object. Displayed in stereo, a volume image becomes for clearer because humans can ignore noise that appears at a different length than the image features of interest. Stereo, of course, requires that each image be drawn twice. With an SGI Onyx, using one 4400 Mi/s CPU with RE2 graphics and two raster managers, a stereo frame of a pulsating heart can be rendered 7 times per second. The resulting delay makes it hard to use a 3-D cursor to locate a particular point in the image without oversboling. If the image were smaller in volume, a stereo frame could be rendered 14 times per second which makes manipulation, rotation, and dissection possible.

Clearly, there is a need to support a virtual computing platform that can be made available to the medical staff when required. In addition, one of the most important criteria in developing a modular infrastructure to support advanced imaging techniques, with a homogeneous approach, is the intermediate file formats. To satisfy this objective, it is envisaged that the format for the 3-D, 4-D and, VR image processing be VRML 2.0 (and its successors). As seen in the previous example, VRML allows 3-D models to be constructed from raw data 2-D slices. In turn, a 3-D model represents a state (a snapshot of the 3-D image); if a number of states are put together whereby each state represents a time instant, a 4-D model can be constructed. The benefits of 4-D visualization allow the user to get an impression of how the 3-D model is changing over time (e.g., the heart beating). Reprsenting the 4-D model in VRML 2.0 and using a standard VRML 2.0 browser, the model can be examined from various non-predefined viewpoints. The next logical step is to allow some form of interaction with the models (3-D or 4-D).

VR techniques could be integrated into the telemedical information society building blocks into both the visualization and manipulation toolset and the interaction and prediction toolset. They must also use a number of other toolsets, e.g., the computing toolset. First, within the visualization and manipulation toolset there must be a tool to reformat a VRML models into a stereographic models. The stereographic models could then be visualized using VR headsets. The rationale of using the headsets as simple viewers is to provide the

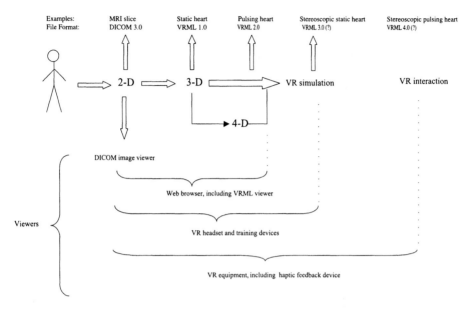

Figure 3.32. From true life to true life-like images.

user with an image perspective that gives a true feel for the model's shape. The model can even be manipulated in a similar manner as 3-D and 4-D models. Second, the interaction and prediction aspect of VR is when head movement–tracking devices and hand movement (DataGloves) begin to interact with the model being visualized (25). The overall interconnection from 2-D to 3-D to VR is shown in Figure 3.32. It seems logical that future versions of VRML will include stereoscopic images to facilitate VR viewing and to include haptic feedback devices (98, 99). Of course, these versions of VRML do not yet exist and are simply hypothetical. All versions of VRML would then be accessed through a standardized browser that would be platform integrated.

3.3 VR AS A PERSPECTIVE IMAGE VIEWER

One example of how virtual reality techniques could be used as an extra visualization technique is for predicted tumor growth (100). A program developed at the ICCS-NTUA, in Greece, uses the World Wide Web as the communication medium, allowing a practitioner via a Web interface to enter the initial parameters of a tumor growth prediction program that has been parallelized to execute on an Onyx infinite Reality^2 with four processors located at the ICCS (Fig. 3.33). The program is executed under the control of a cgi-bin Perl script, and the results are placed on an ftp server. The user is informed of the program's completion by e-mail and via an html script that has hyperlinks to access an ftp

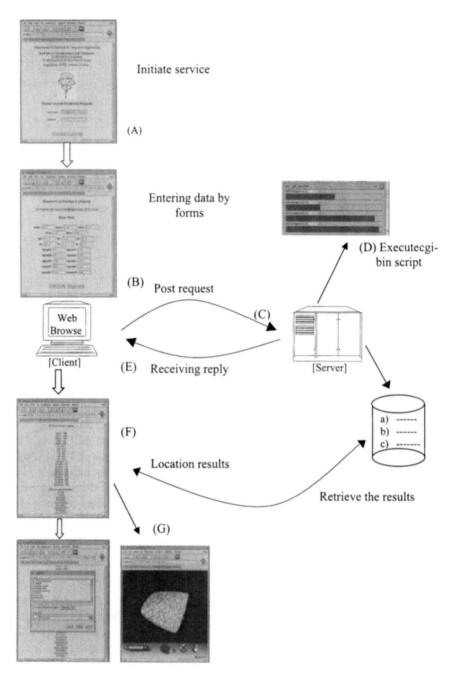

Figure 3.33. A Web-based interface growth-prediction program. A, User enters password and e-mail address. B, User enters data. C, Data sent to sewer. D, Program estimates tumor growth and creates data files. E, User receives notification. F, User downloads files. G, User visualizes tumor.

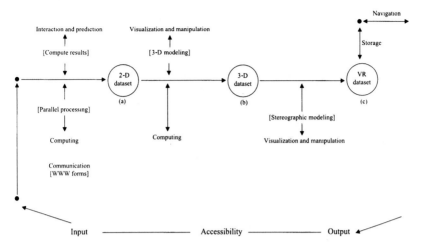

Figure 3.34. A collaboration of toolsets.

protocol and retrieve the stored results. The results can then be viewed by the user's Web browser and downloaded to a local machine. At present, the results are in two formats: asci-numeric and 3-D/4-D VRML. The envisaged third format is a stereographic image that can be viewed by a VR headset. The VR version would allow the practitioner to see the predicted tumor growth from a perspective view. The ICCS/NTUA tumor growth–prediction program uses elements of a number of the foundational building blocks: accessibility, communication, storage, navigation, transmission, visualization and manipulation, interaction and predicition, and computing (Fig. 3.34). This program will probably use VR techniques as a perspective viewer. Examples of the tumor growth program in 3-D VRML format are shown in Figure 3.35. It is thought that with the addition of a VR headset and the conversion to stereographic models, that data will be visualized perspectively.

Similar work is being done at the Helene Fuid Medical Center in Trenton, NJ, where 3-D reconstruction and computer graphics techniques are being used to assess the progress of a disease in virtual space. According to Siderits, head of experimental pathology, researchers used a digital camera to image thin stained slices of normal breast tissue obtained from a premenopausal woman during a biopsy. The stain highlighted lobules, ducts, and epithetical tissue. The supercomputer at David Sarnoft Reseach Center was used to recompile the images, producing a 3-D rendering. By applying rotation and sectioning, physicians can get a more realistic perspective of breast structure. Clearly, the next stage of this work is to include a VR interface. With these type of approches, it is possible to create a virtual cancer within a digital biodomain. By assigning attributes and behaviors to specific portions of the model, pathologists will be able to watch the progress of a virtual disease without leaving a computer workstation. The virtual approach can enhance several areas of cancer

A

B

Figure 3.35. Tumor growth.

research. Physicians may digitally test different combinations of chemotherapy drugs before ever trying them on a patient. They may grow tumors in virtual space and model invasive and metastatic carcinogmas. They could easily add features to the model, such as immune cells, and then to assess a patient's response.

Researchers at the National Cancer Centre in Tokyo are also using VR systems combined with audiovisual technology. A team led by Oyama, head of medical virtual reality projects in the centre's department of neurosurgery, is evaluating the use of VR tools to increase the information provided to cancer patients (101). A cancer-information VR theater allows a patient wearing a HMD to point to an organ image on a projection screen, observe a cancer image specific to that organ, and hear information about the cancer from an audio system inside the display (100). A patient should thus be able to gain a more realistic perspective during doctor–patient consultations. This VR system could also be an instructional tool for medical students and nurses (102, 103).

3.4 VR FOR EDUCATION AND TRAINING

Virtual reality techniques can play a vital role in educating and training young practitioners (102–106). Practicing doctors can get an insight into parts of the body that would otherwise be inaccessible without surgery and, with the full complementary use of all related virtual technology, get a realistic idea of what should be done (17, 107–111). One specialization being examined is using virtual reality to aid the trainee othorinolaryngologist (ear, nose and throat). The ear is made up of three major parts (outer, inner and middle). The outer ear is visible by the human eye, and part of the inner ear can be seen via endoscopic investigation from the nose (Fig. 3.36). However, the rost of the ear can be seen only by cutting the ear drum. Clearly, for a trainee this is not possible. VR allows the trainee doctors to see this part of the ear (Fig. 3.37).

Making a virtual model of the ear is a complex issue because of the size and level of detail that can be extracted from CT and MRI examination. Typically, MRI provides 0.8-mm slices and CT provides 1.0-mm slices. The accuracy required is for these slices to be 20 to 50 μ. This can be acquired only by taking a temporal bone, freezing it, shaving slices off, and taking an image of the exposed surface with the images in a different format. This was the approcah was adopted by the EUROMED laboratory at ICCS/NTUA. A 3-D model in VRML format is now being produced. This model can be viewed by any Web browser. A converting program could then create a stereoscopic image from the VRML model. This model could then be visualised using VR headsets to obtain a model with perspective. By using navigation and tracking hardware the trainee practitioner could then perform virtual endoscopic examinations of the model of the ear. This approach has lead to a generic static model that can be used for anantomy training.

The same approach of creating a 3-D model was taken by the virtual tem-

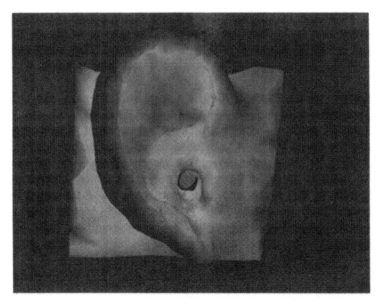

Figure 3.36. External view of the human ear. The tympanicmemberance (eardrum) is visible at the end of the ear canal. (Courtesy of the Virtual Reality in Medicine Laboratory, University of Illinois at Chicago.)

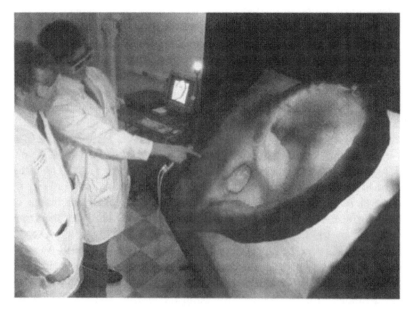

Figure 3.37. Physician using a wand to begin a tour of the virtual temporal bone on the ImmersaDesk. (Courtesy of the Virtual Reality in Medicine Laboratory, University of Illinois at Chicago.)

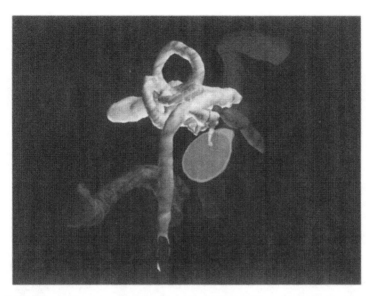

Figure 3.38. The human temporal bone in its entirety. Here the bone has been made transparent to reveal the delicate anatomic structures imbedded within bone: the organs of hearing and balance, nerves, blood vessels, muscles, the eardrum and ossicles. (Courtesy of the Virtual Reality in medicine Laboratory, University of Illinois at Chicago.)

poral bone project of the University of Illinois at Chicago. The project uses an interactive environment (ImmersaDesk, a projection-based system that includes audio capabilities) to give viewers an inside perspective on the human temporal bone. Examples of the temporal bone from this project are shown in Figures 3.38 and 3.39. The user wears special goggles to see the images in virtual space (Fig. 3.37). By speaking into a microphone the user can see the middle ear bones vibrate to the sound of the human voice.

If this type of model could be constructed on patient-specific data, it would allow the practitioner to investigate defects in the patients ear without any invasive surgery. One approach could be that of the deformable atlas, a human anatomical template that could be manipulated in software to represent the physical characteristics of any individual (57). This work is still ongoing. However, despite the inroads that VR technology has made into many areas of the medical field, some physicians argue that there is no substitute for the experience gained by performing hands-on surgery. Mason of the University of Illinois, who helped develop the virtual temporal bone model, believes that although virtual environments and sensory augmentation devices may provide useful training aids, they do not replace the years that physicians must spend in the operating room. He (4) noted,

Figure 3.39. With the bony superstructure of the model removed, a clearer view of the complex 3-D interrelationships of the structures within the temporal bone are revealed. (Courtesy of the Virtual Reality in Medicine Laboratory, University of Illinois at Chicago.)

> In my mind, there are two distinct aspects of surgery that the surgeon in training needs to learn—the purely technical or procedural aspect and the artistic aspect. Virtual training tools may be good for learning how to proceed stepwise through an operation, but there is no substitute for actually handling the tissues of a real patient when learning how to perform surgery.

An alternative view is expressed by HT Medical Systems (Rockville, MD), a 10-year-old U.S. developer of simulation technology that signed a $3.5 million partnership and funding agreement with the U.S. Commerce Department's National Institute of Standards and Technology. The research will focus on the company's interactive 3-D *PreOp* technology, which allows realistic rehearsal of surgical procedures without risk to patients. The extremely important aspects of this rehearsal capability is to help close the experience gap among surgeons. A recent American Heart Association study, for example, found that complication rates are 69% higher for doctors who perform <70 angioplastics than for doctors who perform >270. Moreover, this gap is widening as the technology involved in the procedure becomes more complex. Clearly, an approach as adopted by HT Medical Systems may be able to reduce the errors, improve the outcomes, and even reduce the costs. One approach that is achieving these goals is virtual colonoscopy, which is discussed below.

3.5 VR FOR DIAGNOSTIC PURPOSES

One application in medicine for which VR can make immediate impact is to perform virtual endoscopic evaluations (e.g., virtual colonoscopy). Colonoscopy is a medical term that has two parts: *colon*, which refers to the colon or large intestine, and *scope*, which means "looking into." Therefore, colonoscopy is a test that enables doctors to look inside the colon.

Colon/rectal cancer is the second most common cause of death, yet among the most preventable when detected in its early stages. The traditional diagnostic procedures cause tremendous discomfort and are deeply invasive. Because 9 out of 10 people prove healthy, those who should be getting the annual screening often decide they would rather run the risk of disease than go through the harsh examination.

The instrument used to perform this test is the colonoscope, a long flexible tube about the width of the index finger. Within the end of the tube is a miniaturized color TV camera with a wide-angle lens. After passing the scope through the rectum and into the colon, the doctor then directly examines the lining of the lower digestive tract on a television monitor. In this manner, it is possible to evaluate intestinal inflammation. Ulceration, bleeding, diverticulities, colitis, colon polyps, tumors, etc. Colonoscopy is associated with a small risk of preforation. In addition, it also requires intravenous sedation and takes 40 to 60 min. Frequently, owing to either technical difficulties or patient discomfort, the proximal colon cannot be fully evaluated. Furthermore, the cost of colonoscopy is approximately $1600.

Another technique used to examine the colon is Barium enema, which is an x-ray examination of the large intestives, pictures are taken after rectal installation of barium sulfate (a radiopaque contast medium). A small tube is inserted into the rectum and the large intestive is filled with barium, allowing the radiologist to accurately diagnose many conditions that affect the large intestive. Although less expensive (approximately $350), the test requires a good deal of patient positioning and thus physical cooperation from the patient. Results vary according to the technical quality of the procedure and the expense of the interpreter.

The motivation for this work is, therefore, to develop an alternative technique for visualizing the inner mucosal surface of the colonic wall and help the physicians detect the tumors and their possible extensibility outside of the colonic walls. Currently, there are two different techniques for 3-D visualization. The first is using CT images of the patient to reconstruct a 3-D volume of the area of interest and the second is using CT images of the patient to reconstruct the models of organs of interest. The second technique was used by the joint ICCS/NTUA–Mayo Clinic project (Fig. 3.40).

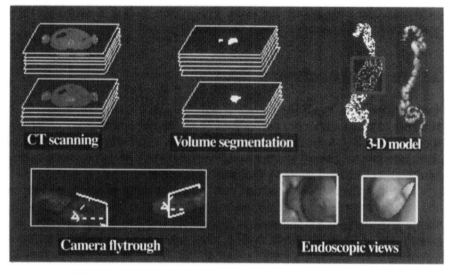

Figure 3.40. From CT scanning to virtual endoscopic views.

For the implementation of the technique, the software called *Vega* was used in conjunction with a graphical user interface called *LynX* and two input devices (a spaceball and a fastrak). *Vega* is a high-performance software environment and toolkit for real-time simulations and VR applications. It consists of a graphical user interface called *LynX Iris Performer*, *Vega* libraries, and header files of *C*-callable functions. *LynX* is the graphical user interface for defining and previewing *Vega* applications.

The Spaceball 2003 is a compact desktop input device for controlling 3-D graphic images or eyepoint/viewpoint for flythrough applications. The default operation setting for the Spaceball 2003 is full simultaneous 6 degrees-of-freedom control, which means the users can move the graphical image smoothly in all directions simultaneously, as if they were reaching out and holding onto it. Diverse common modes of operation are provided through a set of eight programmable function buttons on the back of the Spaceball 2003 and pick button on the back of the PowerSensor ball. Trackers are fundamentally sensors whose task is to detect position and/or orientation of an object and make the information available to the rest of the virtual environment. The most common function is to report the position and orientation of the head. In this application we the Polhemus Fastrak. It is a magnetic tracking system that computes the position and orientation of a tiny receiver as it moves through space. It provides in real time 6 degrees-of-freedom measurement of position (x, y, and z Cartesian coordinates) and orientation (azimuth, elevation, and roll). It includes a system electronics unit (SEU), a power supply, one receiver, and one transmitter. The transmitter is a triad of electromagnetic coils enclosed in a plastic shell that emits

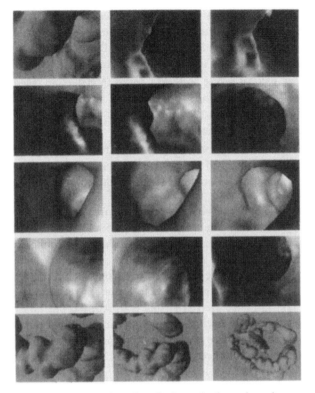

Figure 3.41. An interface flythrough along the colon.

the magnetic fields. The transmitter is the system's reference frame for receiver measurements. The Fastrak system uses a single transmitter and can accept data from up to four receivers. It can also be attached to a head mounted display.

HMDs are typically headsets incorporating two small LCD or CRT screens with optics to bring their images to the user's eye. Head motion is usually monitored with a tracker so that the image can be updated to reflect the current head position and orientation, which gives an illusion of presence in the virtual environment. In this application, a CyberEye CE-200S was used, which accepts separate left and right eye inputs and supports a resolution of 230 × 789 pixels/ eye and a field of view (FOV) equal to 27.5 diagonal. This application is currently running on a SGI Onyx2 Infinite Reality machine (Fig. 3.41).

In this application the spaceball is used to walk (navigate inside or outside of the colon) and the HMD is used for viewing the colon. The 3-D model of the colon is currently in an Inventor file format and has been reconstructed from CT images of the Visible Human Male Dataset. The reconstruction was made with the *Analyze* software package developed at the Mayo Biomedical Imaging Resource Laboratory (24, 92). Currently, the application supports the following modes and features:

Mode 1. Free flythrough using the input devices that give the user the ability to examine the inner and the outer surface of the colonic wall. This is helpful when the user detects a tumor on the inner surface and wants to see if the tumor extends to the other surface.

Mode 2. The second mode supports collision detection, meaning that the user's motion is contained by collisions with the walls of the object (colon). The mode gives the impression of relating to the user and keeps him or her inside the colon.

Mode 3. This mode supports a flythrough to a predicted or dynamically defined path. It is helpful for quick examination of the colon and does not warn the user when he or she is stuck on the colonic wall.

The three features allow the viewing position to be reset to an initial position and increase and decrease the scale. All the modes are accessible through the first six buttons of the spaceball. Figure 3.41 shows 12 frames of an interface flythrough along the colon.

The main advantages of the virtual colonoscopy include comfort and speed. Much less patient discomfort results because there is no need to reposition the patient. The radiation dose used in virtual endoscopy is one half of one quarter of the average exposure in barium enema and an unlimited number of viewing angles can be exploited. There is also no need for sedation, and the patient can resume normal activities immediately after the CT scanning procedure.

3.6 THE FUTURE FOR VR AND ITS ROLE IN A TELEMEDICAL INFORMATION SOCIETY

It can be seen that by adopting the foundational building blocks approach, in creating a telemedical information society advanced imaging techniques such as Virtual Reality can easily be integrated. In addition, by adopting a virtual medical worlds interface, the pragmatics of defining and creating virtual environments are abstracted from the practitioner. VR techniques can, therefore, be provided as an additional visualization service. A practitioner then has a choice, depending on the availability of supportive hardware, on how to visualize patient data. This chapter was not concentrated with the specifics of virtual reality techniques and did not provide detailed explanations of its use. It outlined a possible framework for how these advanced imaging techniques could be integrated into a general telemedical information society. Presently, the cost of VR hardware and software has restricted its usage to only a few medical institutions. However, it is envisaged that as these costs are reduced, the technology will become more widespread. It is thus important to promote an integrated framework so that today's futuristic techniques can be used tomorrow. Surgery planning programs such as VRASP are already available to allow a surgeon to practice an operation on a virtual model of the patient and then use this virtual operation to assist during the real operation. It seems quite possible that this approach could be taken even further so that a surgeon could be in one location and either a robot or another, less specialized, surgeon could perform the operation at another location (112–118). This approach could be used in specialized cases, natural disasters, isolated regions, and even military situations. It is also possible that VR techniques could be used for telepresence to create a virtual practitioner to guide a less qualified practitioner—a VR form of teleconferencing. An example is a ship's doctor performing an emergency operation at sea. However, with the introduction of any new technology the factors of its safe and healthy use need to be considered along with its ethics (119).

Clearly, there are many diverse potential uses of VR techniques; and even through VR is in its development stages, it is providing another tool to aid practitioners not only in training but also in diagnosis and treatment planning (120, 121). It is my opinion that only if such techniques can be truly integrated into a uniform framework—including telecommunications, computing, and data management—with all other forms of medical imaging techniques and developing technologies (e.g., GPS tacking systems and robotics with haptic feedback) that a telemedical information society can be created for the 21st century.

REFERENCES

1. C. Esposito. Introduction to virtual reality and user interface issues for virtual systems. Paper presented at IEEE VRAIS. Los Alamitos, CA, 1997.

2. S. M. Blumenfeld. A glimpse at the surgery of the next century. In H. Sieburg, S. Weghorst, and K. Morgan, eds. Health care in the information age. IOS Press, 1996:319.

3. N. Durlach. VR technology and basic research on humans [Keynote Address]. Paper presented at IEEE VRAIS. Los Alamitos, CA, 1997.

4. B. Grant. Virtual reality gives medicine a powerful new tool. Biophoto Int 1997.

5. J. Rosen. From computer-aided design to computer-aided surgery. Paper presented at Medicine Meets Virtual Reality. San Diego, CA, June 1–2, 1992.

6. R. Satava. Virtual Reality and Surgery. Minim Invasive Surg 1994;3(suppl 1):2.

7. K. F. Kaltenborn and O. Rienhoff. Virtual reality in medicine. Meth Inform Med 1993;32:407–417.

8. R. A. Robb and D. P. Hanson. A software system for interactive and quantitative analysis of biomedical images. In Hohne et al., eds. 3D imaging in medicine. Vol. F60. NATO, 1990:333–361.

9. J. W. Peifer, W. D. Certis, and M. J. Sinclair. Applied virtual reality for simulation of endoscopic retrograde cholangio-pancreatoraphy (ERCP). In H. Sibery, S. Weghorst, and K. Morgan, eds. Healthcare in the information age. IOS Press, 1996:36.

10. B. Geiger and R. Kikinis. Simulation of endoscopy. Paper presented at the AAAI Spring Symposium Series. Stanford, CA, 1994.

11. M. Kobayashi, T. Fujino, and T. Kaneko, et al. Virtual surgery for fracture of the mandible. In K. Morgan, R. M. Satava, H. B. Sieberg, et al., eds. IOS Press, 1995:175–179.

12. S. B. Jones and R. M. Satava. Virtual endoscopy of the head and neck: diagnosis using three-dimensional visualisation and virtual representation. In H. Sieburg, S. Weghorst, and K. Morgan, eds. Health care in the information age. IOS Press, 1996:152.

13. M. Dinsmore, N. Langrana, G. Burdea, and J. Ladeji. Virtual reality training simulation for palpation of subsurface tumors. Paper presented at IEEE VRAIS. Los Alamitos, CA, 1997.

14. H. Fuchs, A. State, E. D. Pisano, et al. Towards performing ultrasound-guided needle biopsies from within a head-mounted display. Paper presented at VBC 4th International Conference. Berlin, 1996.

15. K. Glantz, N. I. Durlach, R. C. Barnett, and W. A. Aviles. Virtual reality (VR) and psychotherapy: opportunities and challenges. Presence Teleoper Virtual Environ 1997;6:87–105.

16. J. Leigh, C. A. Vasilakis, T. A. DeFanti, et al. Virtual reality in computational neuroscience. In R. A. Earnshaw, J. A. Vince, and H. Jones, eds. London: Academic Press, 1995:293–306.

17. M. D. Snow, J. A. Graham, W. J. A. Yates, and C. Phillips. The dimensionally integrated dental patient record: digital dentistry virtual reality in orthodontics. Paper presented at the 12th International Symposium on the Creation of Electronic Health Record System and Global Conference on Patient Cards. San Diego, CA, 1996.

18. J. P. Wann. Virtual reality environments for rehabilitation of movement disorders. Paper presented at ECDVRAT. Reading, UK, 1996.

19. K. J. Zuiderveld. VR in radiology: first experiences at university hospital. Utrecht. Comput Graph 1996;30:47–48.

20. M. Bajura, H. Fuchs, and R. Ohbuchi. Merging virtual objects with the real world: seeing ultrasound imagery within the patient. Comput Graph 1992;26:203–210.

21. R. A. Robb and B. M. Cameron. Virtual reality assisted surgery program. Paper presented at Medicine Meets Virtual Reality III. San Diego, CA, Jan 1995.

22. K. Kaplan, I. Hunter, N. I. Durlach, et al. A virtual environment for a surgical room of the future. In K. Morgan, R. Satava, H. B. Sieburg, et al., eds. Interactive technology and the new paradigm for healthcare. IOS Press, 1995:161–167.

23. S. Grosskopf, A. Hildebrand, R. Malkewitz, et al. Computer aided surgery-vision and feasibility of an advanced operation theatre. Comput Graph 1996;20:825–838.

24. B. Marcus. Hands on: haptic feedback in surgical simulation. Paper presented at Medicine Meets Virtual Reality. San Diego, CA, 1994.

25. W. J. Greenleaf. The DataGlove and DataSuit technology for medical applications. Paper presented at Medicine Meets Virtual Reality II. San Diego, CA, 1994.

26. P. Astheimer. What you see is what you hear. Acoustics applied in virtual worlds. Paper presented at IEEE VRAIS. 1993.

27. D. R. Begault. 3-D sound for virtual reality and multimedia. Boston: Academic Press, 1994.

28. R. Earnshaw. 3D and multimedia on the information superhighway. IEEE Comput Graph Appl 1997;17:31.

29. R. Mattheus. Global information society. In K. Morgan, R. M. Satava, H. B. Sieburg, et al., eds. Interactive technology and the new paradigm for healthcare. IOS Press, 1995:423–432.

30. Williams and M. Moore. Telemedicine: its place on the information highway. In W. W. Cooper, F. Phillips, D. V. Gibson, et al. eds. Impact: how IC2 research affects public policy and business markets.

31. Kuhn. Frontiers of medical information sciences. New York, 1988.

32. D. C. Balch and J. M. Tichenor. Telemedicine expanding the scope of health care information. J Am Med Inform Assoc 1997;4:1–5.

33. M. Burrow, M. Sinclair, and T. Gadacz. A telemedicine testbed for developing and evaluating telerobotic tools for rural health care. Paper presented at Medicine Meets Virtual Reality. San Diego, CA, 1994.

34. A. Marsh. EUROMED—the creation of a telemedical information society. Paper presented at the 10th IEEE Symposium on Computer-Based Medical Systems. Maribor, Slovenia, June 11–13, 1996.

35. A. Marsh. EUROMED—A WWW based multi-media medical information system. Paper presented at the 19th Annual International Conference of the IEEE Engineering in Medicine and Biology Society. Chicago, IL, Oct 30–Nov 2, 1997.

36. A. Marsh. The creation of a 21st century telemedical information society. Future Gen Comput Sys In press.

37. S. Horil, F. Prior, W. Bidgood, et al. DICOM: an introduction to the standard. http://www.xray.hcm.psu.edu/dicom/dicom-intro/DICOMIntro.html.

38. R. A. Robb and D. P. Hanson. The ANALYSE software system for visualization and analysis in surgery simulation. In Lavalle, et al., eds. Computer integrated surgery. Cambridge, MA: MIT Press, 1996.

39. A. Marsh, F. Simistira, and R. Robb. VR in medicine: virtual colonoscopy. J Future Gen Comput Sys. In press.

40. F. Simistira, A. Marsh, R. A. Robb. Coupling HPCN and virtual reality in a telemedical information society. Paper presented at the International Conference and Exhibition on High Performance Computing and Networking (HPCN 1997). Vienna, Austria, Apr 28–30, 1997.

41. R. A. Robb, J. J. Camp, and D. P. Hanson. Computer-aided surgery and treatment planning at the Mayo clinic. Comput Graph Appl.

42. R. Mattheus. European standardisation efforts: an important framework of medical imaging. Eur J Radiol 1993;17:28–37.

43. Y. Irawan and S. Soegijoko. Development of appropriate telemedicine to improve the management information system for community healthcare in indonesia. Paper presented at the 19th Annual International Conference of the IEEE Engineering in Medicine and Biology Society. Chicago, IL, Oct 30–Nov 2, 1997.

44. H. Lee, S. Park, and E. Woo. Remote patient monitoring service through World Wide Web. Paper presented at the 19th Annual International Conference of the IEEE Engineering in Medicine and Biology Society. Chicago, IL, Oct 30–Nov 2, 1997.

45. S. Krishnan, P. Goh, and Y. Datian. A multimedia based medical database networking system for special clinical procedures in health care delivery. Paper presented at the 19th Annual International Conference of the IEEE Engineering in Medicine and Biology Society. Chicago, IL, Oct 30–Nov 2, 1997.

46. M. Moore. Elements of success in telemedicine projects. Austin, TX: Graduate School Library of Information Science, 1993.

47. R. Beauscart, J. Kulik, M. Valette, et al. Telemedicine for home care: applications for AIDS patients. Paper presented at the 19th Annual International Conference of the IEEE Engineering in Medicine and Biology Society. Chicago, IL, Oct 30–Nov 2, 1997.

48. L. Versweyveld. Health care ATM network introduces telemedicine to the Middle East. Virtual Med Worlds 1998.

49. L. Versweyreld. Dodge County Hospital: chronicle of a telemedicine pilot site. Virtual Med Worlds 1998.

50. A. Marsh. EUROMED—visualisation suites for medical imaging. Paper presented at the 3rd International Workshop on Community Networking. Antwerpen, Belgium, May 23–24, 1996.

51. R. A. Robb. Three-dimensional biomedical imaging. Principles and practice. New York: VCH, 1995.

52. T. K. Capin, D. Thalmann, I. S. Pandzic, and N. M. Thalmann. A dead-reckoning algoritm for virtual human figures. Paper presented at IEEE VRAIS, Los Alamitos, CA, 1997.

53. N. M. Thalmann and D. Thalmann. Towards virtual humans in medicine: a prospective view. Comput Med Imaging Graph 1994;18:97–106.

54. V. Spritze, M. J. Ackerman, A. L. Scherzinger, and D. Whitlock. The visible human male: a technical report. J Am Med Info Assoc 1996;3:118–130.

55. K. H. Hohne, M. Bomans, A. Pommert, et al. A 3D anatomical atlas based on a volume model. IEEE Comput Graph Appl 1992;12:72–78.

56. A. Pommert, R. Schubert, M. Riemer, et al. Symbolic modeling of human anatomy for visualization and simulation. In R. A. Robb, ed. Visualisation in biomedical computing 1994. Rochester, MN, 1994:412–423.

57. T. W. Sederberg and S. R. Parry. Free-form deformation of solid geometric models. Comput Graph 1986;20:151–160.

58. A. Kolesnikov, O. Kelle, and T. Kauranne. Remote medical analysis with Web technology. Paper presented at the Finish Symposium on Signal Processing, FINSIG '97. Pori, Finland, May 22, 1997.

59. A. Marsh. EUROMED—combining WWW and HPCN to support advanced medical imaging. Paper presented at the International Conference and Exhibition on High Performance Computing and Networking (HPCN 1997). Vienna, Austria, Apr 28–30, 1997.

60. R. Rockwell. Infrastructure and architecture for cyberspace communities. Comput Graph 1996;30:19–24.

61. R. Barrett, P. P. Maglio, and D. C. Kellem. How to personalize the Web. Paper presented at CHI '97: Human Factors in Computing Systems. New York, 1997.

62. K. Perlin and E. M. Hoffert. Hypertexture. Comput Graph 1989;23:253–262.

63. D. Beeman, J. M. Bower, E. De Schutter, et al. The GENESIS simulator-based neuronal database. In S. H. Koslow and M. F. Huerta, eds. Neuroinformatics: an overview of the human brain project. Mahwah, NJ: Erlbaum, 1997:57–80.

64. Logan. Whole frog technical report [Pub. No. LBL-35331]. Berkley, CA: Imaging and Distributed Computing Group.

65. V. Ahuja. Network & Internet Security. New York: Academic, 1996.

66. B. Barber. Towards an information technology security policy for the NHS. In B. Richards et al., eds. Current perspectives in health care computing 1991. British Computer Society, 1991.

67. B. Barber, A. R. Bakker, and S. Bengtsson, eds. Caring for health information: safety, security and secrecy. Amsterdam: Elsevier Science, 1994.

68. B. Blobel. Open information systems and data security in medicine. In B. Barber, A. Treacher, and K. Louwerse, eds. Towards security in medical telematics: legal and technical aspects. Amsterdam: IOS, 1996:168–182.

69. D. Hamilton. Application layer security requirements of a medical information system. Paper presented at the 15th National Computer Security Conference. 1992.

70. S. L. Pfleeger. A framework for security requirements. Comput Security 1991;10:515–523.

71. Architecture and general specifications of the public key infrastructure, COST. Telematics Engineering/ICE-TEL, Sept 1996.

72. D. Polemi and A. Marsh. Secure telemedicine applications. Paper presented at the Conference on High Performance Computing and Networking Europe. Amsterdam, Apr 21–23, 1998.

73. I. Milojevic and N. Djukanovic. Distributed personal medical data storage and access. Paper presented at Information Technologies. Zabljak, Yugoslavia, Mar 15, 1997.

74. K. H. Hohne, M. Bomans, A. Pommert, et al. Rendering tomographic volume data: adequacy of methods for different modalities and organs. In Hohne et al., eds. 3D imaging in medicine. Vol. F60. NATO, 1990:197–215.

75. W. Lorensen, F. A. Jolesz, and R. Kikinis. The exploration of cross-sectional data with a virtual endoscope. In K. Morgan, R. M. Satava, H. B. Sieburg, et al., eds. Interactive technology and the new paradigm for healthcare. IOS Press, 1995:221–230.

76. B. Chinoy and K. Fall. TCP/IP performance in the CASA gigabit network. Paper presented at the Usenix Symposium on High-Speed Networking. Aug. 1994.

77. C. Hand. Some user interface issues for hypermedia virtual environments. Paper presented at the 5th International World-Wide Web Conference. 1996.

78. P. B. Heffernan and R. A. Robb. Display and analysis of 4-D medical images. Paper presented at CAR'85. 1985.

79. T. Berlage, T. Fox, G. Grunst, and K. J. Quast. Supporting ultrasound diagnosis using an animated 3D model of the heart. Paper presented at the International Conference on Multimedia Computing and Systems. Los Alamitos, CA, 1996.

80. T. Poston, L. Serra, M. Solalyappan, and P. A. Heng. The graphics demands of virtual medicine. Comput Graph 1996;20:61–68.

81. C. Artur. Did reality move for you? New Sci 1991;134:22–27.

82. R. Holloway, H. Fuchs, and W. Robinette, Virtual worlds research at the University of North Carolina at Chapel Hiils as of February 1992. In T. L. Kunii, ed. Computer graphics—international visual computing. Springer, 1992:109–128.

83. K. W. Arthur and K. S. Booth. Evaluating 3D task performance for fish tank virtual worlds. ACM Trans Info Sys 1993;11:239–265.

84. D. B. Karron, J. Cox, and B. Mishra. New findings from the Spiderweb algorithm: toward a digital morse theory. Paper presented at Visualization in Biomedical Computing. 1994.

85. L. L. Fellingham, J. H. Vogel, C. Lau, and P. Dev. Interactive graphics and 3-D modeling for surgery planning and prothesis and implant design. Paper presented at NCGA. 1986.

86. R. Drebin, L. Carpenter, and P. Harrahan. Volume rendering. Paper presented at SIGGRAPH. 1988.

87. W. E. Lorensen and H. E. Cline. Marching cubes: a high resolution 3D surface construction algorithm. Comput Graph 1987;21:163–169.

88. C. Zhou, R. Shu, and M. S. Kankanhalli. Handing small features in isosurface generation using marching cubes. Comput Graph 1994;18:845–848.

89. A. Gueziec and D. Dean. The wrapper: a surface optimization algorithm that preserves highly curved areas. Paper presented at Visualization in Biomedical Computing. 1994.

90. I. B. Simon. Surgery 2001: concepts of telepresence surgery. Surg Endosc 1993;7:462–463.

91. W. E. Lorensen and H. E. Cline. System and method for the display of surface structures contained within the interior region of a solid body. U.S. Pat. 4,710,876 (1987).

92. J. K. Udupa and H.-M. Hung. Surface versus volume rendering: a comparative assessment. Paper presented at the 1st Conference in Visualisation in Biomedical Computing. 1990.

93. L.-S. Chen, G. T. Herman, R. A. Reynolds, and J. K. Udupa. Surface shading in the Cuberille environment. IEEE Comput Graph Appl 1985;5:33–43.

94. A. Guezzec and R. Hummel. The wrapper algorithm: surface extraction and simplication. Paper presented at IEEE Workshop on Biomedical Image Analysis. 1994.

95. H. Hoppe, T. DeRose, T. Duchamp, et al. Mesh optimisation. Comput Graph 1993.

96. B. Cabral, N. Cam, and J. Foran. Accelerated volume rendering and tomographic reconstruction using texture mapping hardware. Paper presented at ACM/IEEE. 1994.

97. U. Cullip and U. Neumann. Accelerating volume reconstruction with 3D texture hardware [UNC Tech. Report TR93-0027]. 1993.

98. O. Wilson, A. Van Gelder, and J. Williams. Direct Volume rendering via 3D textures [U.C. Santa Cruz Technical Report, UCSC-CRL-94-19]. 1994.

98. W. Broll. Extending VRML to support collaborative virtual environments. Paper presented at the CVE Collaborative Virtual Environments. Nottingham, UK, 1996.

99. W. Broll and T. Koop. VRML: today and tomorrow. Comput Graph 1996;20:427–434.

100. H. Oyama, T. Miyazawa, M. Aono, et al. VR medical support for cancer patients. In K. Morgan, R. M. Satava, H. B. Sieburg, et al., eds. Interactive technology and the new paradigm for healthcare. IOS Press, 1995:433–438.

101. R. Kijima and M. Hirose. Virtual sand box: a development of an application of virtual environment for the clinical medicine. Paper presented at the 3rd International Conference on Artificial Reality and Tele-Existence, ICAR. Tokyo, Japan, 1993.

102. H. Hoffman. Virtual reality meets medical education. In K. Morgan, R. M. Satava, H. B. Sieburg, et al., eds. Interactive technology and the new paradigm for healthcare. IOS Press, 1995:130–136.

103. H. Hoffman. Virtual reality and medical curriculum: integrating extant and emerging technologies. Paper presented at Medicine Meets Virtual Reality. San Diego, CA, Jan 27–30, 1994.

104. J. J. Cromby, P. J. Standen, J. Newman, and H. Tasker. Successful transfer to the real world of skills practised in a virtual environment by students with severe learning difficulties. Paper presented at ECDVRAT: 1st European Conference on Disability, Virtual Reality and Associated Technologies. Reading, UK, 1996.

105. J. J. Cromby, P. J. Standen, and D. J. Brown. The potentials of virtual environments in the education and training of people with learning disabilities. J Intellect Disabil Res 1996;40:489–501.

106. K. Vosburgh, W. E. Lorensen, and G. Burdea. Virtual reality in medicine practice and training. Paper presented at IEEE VRAIS. Los Alamitos, CA, 1997.

107. J. R. Merrill. Surgery on the cutting edge: virtual reality applications in medical education. Virtual Reality World 1993.

108. C. Shaw, M. Green, J. Liang, and Y. Sun. Decoupled simulation in virtual reality with MR Toolkit. ACM Trans Info Sys 1993;11:287–317.

109. A. State, M. A. Livingston, W. F. Garrett, et al. Paper presented at SIGGRAPH '96. New York, 1996.

110. A. Wagner, O. Ploder, G. Enislidis, et al. Image guided surgery. Int J Oral Maxillofacial Surg 1996;25:147–151.

111. A. Wagner, O. Ploder, J. Zuniga, et al. Augmented reality environment for temporomandibular joint motion analysis. Int J Orthodont Orthognath Surg 1996;11:127–136.

112. W. Broll. Distributed virtual reality for everyone—a framework for networked VR on the internet. Paper presented at IEEE VRAIS. Los Alamitos, CA, 1997.

113. D. J. Brown, S. V. Cobb, R. M. Eastgate, and J. R. Wilson. Desktop VR as a practical tool in industry and education. Paper presented at Virtual Reality Universe. San Diego, CA, 1997.

114. T. K. Capin, H. Noser, D. Thalmann, et al. Virtual human representation and communication in VLNet. IEEE Comput Graph Appl 1997;17:42–53.

115. W. Lamotte, E. Flerackers, F. Van Reeth, et al. Visinet: collaborative 3D visualization and VR over ATM networks. IEEE Comput Graph Appl 1997;17:66–75.

116. M. R. Macedonia and M. J. Zyda. A Taxonomy for networked virtual environments. IEEE Multimedia 1997;4:48–56.

117. B. S. Mahal, D. E. R. Clark, and J. E. L. Simmons. Software advances in virtual environments: a survey. Paper presented at FIVE '96: Framework for Immersive Working Environments. London, UK, 1996.

118. K. Osberg. A teacher's guide to developing virtual environments: VRRV project support [HITL Technical Publication No. R-97-17]. Seattle: University of Washington, Human Interface Technology Laboratory, 1997.

119. K. Osberg. But what's behind door number 4? Ethics and virtual reality: a discussion [HITL Report No. R-97-16]. Seattle: University of Washington, Human Interface Technology Laboratory, 1997.

120. D. J. Brown, S. J. Kerr, and A. Eynon. New advances in virtual environments for people with special needs. Ability, in press.

121. E. A. Attree, B. M. Brooks, F. D. Rose, et al. Memory processes and virtual environments: i can't remember what was there, but I can remember how I got there: implications for people with disabilities. Paper presented at ECDVRAT: 1st European Conference on Disability, Virtual Reality and Associated Technologies. Reading, UK, 1996.

CHAPTER 4

Virtual Reality and Medicine— Challenges for the Twenty-First Century

JOSEPH M. ROSEN

Dartmouth-Hitchcock Medical Center
Lebanon, New Hampshire
Thayer School of Engineering
Hanover, New Hampshire

Robert Mann (1) first proposed a virtual reality (VR) system for medical applications in 1965. His initial ideas were for a rehabilitation application for virtual reality. Later, his vision was to develop a system that would allow surgeons to test out multiple operations for a given orthopedic problem (Fig. 4.1). Then in a virtual environment (VE), the clock could be speeded up to predict the future outcome of different surgical approaches. In effect, the patient could leave the operativng table, go through rehabilitation, and then return for evaluation. The surgeon could then pick the best choice for the real operation. This approach would need a model that was not only patient specific but also accurate in terms of the deformity and its response to treatment over time. This is the ultimate goal for the twenty-first century for a VR system in surgery.

Information Technologies in Medicine, Volume I: Medical Simulation and Education, Edited by Metin Akay and Andy Marsh.
ISBN 0-471-38863-7 © 2001 John Wiley & Sons, Inc.

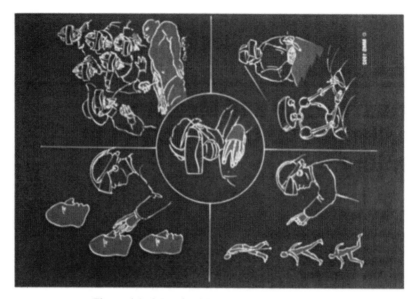

Figure 4.1. Mann's vision of VR applications.

Althought the first reported VR system was by Sutherland (2) in 1970, my first introduction was through the space program in the 1980s. VIEWS was developed at NASA to create an environment for simulating space operations. One of the first major efforts was to simulate a space station. This provided two specific application scenarios. One simulated a control room with multiple control panels. The other simulated teleoperations or telepresence (Fig. 4.2). Both of these applications are important in surgery, and key lessons can be learned from the NASA experience.

The NASA system had specific goals, and the models they were based on were well known and predictable. Although the power of the computing available was limited, the model that was a simple wire frame mock-up of the space station and space shuttle. The interface included vision, sound, and manipulation. This system provided a method to simulate the space station and have astronauts and engineers interact with a proposed design before implementation. There are many lessons from this system that are still applicable to present medical systems.

It is difficult to create a model of the human body that is realistic enough to accurately portray the surgical mission that is planned. The interface tools that are presently available are much more advanced than the ones available to NASA in the 1980s; however, without a true model to interact with they are unable to provide the realism for surgical education and training that is needed. Present cadaver laboratories and training through hands-on experience provide the majority of medical education today in surgery. It is unlikely that present VR simulators will change this without a significant improvements in the models.

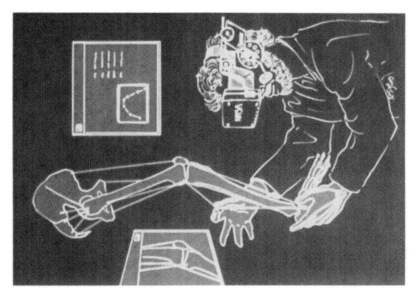

Figure 4.2. NASA's VIEW system.

During my experience at NASA, I used the scenarios of teleoperations and a command cockpit for applications. These scenarios provided the tools to create a medical simulator and to develop tools for performing surgery at a distance. The performance of surgery could either be at a distance (telesurgery) or by superimposing the virtual image on the real patient (datafusion). Virtual reality provided the tools for taking a digital model and placing it into a virtual interactive world. Most of my work has been directed at creating digital models of humans. I will review some of this work and will emphasize what needs to be done, rather than focus on what has already been accomplished.

To reach the goal of a truly realistic virtual human it is good to provide a test as a milestone for achievement. In 1950, Turing (3) provided a test, (the Turing test) to determine if a computer could be created to respond the way a human would respond to a number of questions asked to both the computer and a human. If the human interrogator could not distinguish between the answers of the computer and the human then the Turing test parameters would be met. A VR Turing test would do the same except with respect to a human interacting in a multidimensional way with both a virtual human and a real human (Fig. 4.3). If the interrogating interactive human could not tell the virtual human from the real human by sight, hearing, touch, or feel—even through dissection—then the parameters of the test would be met. I hypothesize that we still have a long way to go before we can approach meeting those goals with our present-day virtual humans, interactive tools, and surgical simulation systems.

Such models were rigid at first but are now more lifelike, giving mathematical properties to the tissue to mimic the response of normal tissues to surgery.

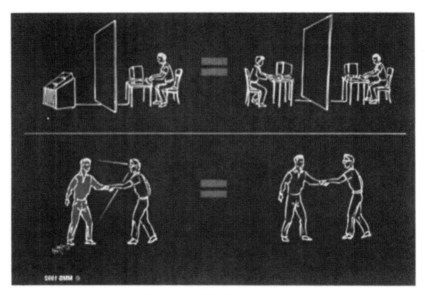

Figure 4.3. VR Turing test.

The interface equipment that comprises the eyes, ears, and hands of these systems have evolved rapidly since 1990, driven by commercial and military applications. The VR trainers have just recently begun to develop educational environments to enhance the teaching of care providers. The initial systems have not yet fully succeeded in providing an improved educational environment over conventional methods of teaching anatomy and basic surgical skills.

Systems are presently available for many medical training applications, including microsurgery, urology, general surgery, heart surgery, vascular surgery, eye surgery, otolaryngology, military wound débridement, and obstetrics. Ultimately these systems will be able to provide teaching at a distance for telemedicine and telesurgery. The goal of this chapter is to better define where we need to make improvements in the human body models for all of these systems. Most of these systems assume normal tissue properties and do not address the response over time of the tissues to the disease state, to the surgical intervention, or to the healing process. The pathologic state of tissues and the tissue's response to interventions over time should be the next grand challenge in virtual reality and medicine.

4.1   VIRTUAL HUMAN

A realistic human alone will not solve all of the problems faced by VR in improving the methods of medical education; but without first improving the models of humans, we will probably be unable to move beyond our present state of the art. Just like the work done by Muybridge (4) at Stanford 100 years

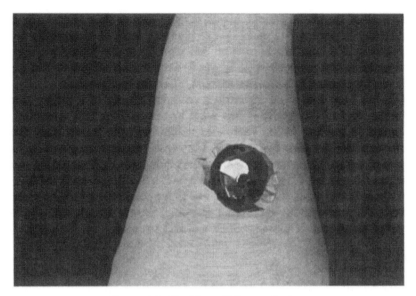

Figure 4.4. The Virtual Human Project.

ago, we must study human motion in great detail before we can understand it. We must also study the human body in great detail to be able to convert all of the physical properties of humans to engineering software models that can be manipulated and viewed in virtual reality systems.

The recent National Library of Medicine's (NLM) Virtual Human Project provided a three-dimensional (3-D) digital model of the human (Fig. 4.4). This can also be seen as a starting point toward creating a realistic human that could be used for VR. However, the model must behave like a human with disease. It must animate the ways that tissues are altered by various disease processes and the healing process that interacts with the disease and its curative interventions, such as surgery.

The human body provides a grand challenge that must be overcome before one can build successful surgical simulators and performance machines. As a plastic surgeon, I have spent my career manipulating and viewing all of the tissues in the human body from early infancy to the very aged. I have seen pathologic states from cancer, trauma, congenital anomalies, infection, inflammation, burns, and myriad other common and rare disorders. Each provides a unique challenge to the modeler of the human body. Time itself and the healing process provide a daunting challenge. The human body responds to injury by a complex set of actions, called healing, that must be understood and converted into mathematical models. This will allow a realistic representation of the healing process so that a repair done on a virtual face can show how the response to improper surgery can cause contractures and distortions to the stuctures of the nose, lips, and eyelids. And the response of each of these structures is unique and different in each individual.

Because of the above factors, plastic surgery—more than almost any other subspecialty in surgery—requires unique planning tools to successfully predict the outcome of a nasal reconstruction or a cleft lip repair. Therefore, many of the operations that are performed by plastic surgeons are unique to that patient and must be planned in a creative manner, often for the first time.

This has been true since the earliest recorded history of a plastic surgical operation, that of the forehead flap nasal reconstruction. This operation was performed in ancient India. Templates made from the leaves from specific plants were used for planning surgery. The use of physical templates continues to be used today. These templates are often made from rigid materials, such as paper, and do not have the plasticity that skin has and thus are not realistic. VR environments and mathematical models of tissue properties provide a means to improve the predictability of surgery planning. Plastic models will also allow improved datafusion of virtual models and real patients.

4.2   COMPUTER VIRTUAL MODELS

The computer is a tool that can handle the complexity of real tissues. Dynamic mathematical models of the mechanical behavior of materials have been used in engineering for many years. Work in computer animation has yielded simulations that behave like human skin, muscle, and bone. An interactive graphic interface to this computer model would allow a surgeon to plan and simulate the outcome of surgical procedures of these tissues.

The computer has been used for surgical planning by using expert systems, two-dimensional (2-D) and 3-D graphics, and mechanical analysis. An expert system is an algorithm or flow chart summarizing that expert's approach to a certain problem. The computer functions as an interactive textbook for training or decision making. It presents predetermined case histories and images as well as a menu of possible actions for the user to choose from. The system then displays a prediction of outcome based on the procedures chosen. All possible outcomes are stored in the simulation system. The rhinoplasty simulator developed by Constantian et al. (5) is an elegant example of the use of an expert system.

Computer paint programs and image processors are currently used to design rhinoplasties, midface advancements, and mandibular osteotomies (6). The computer is used to display 2-D images that have been digitally retouched by the operator. Because graphic representations have no information about the physical properties of tissue, they rely solely on the surgeon to predict the outcome of the surgical plan and then on his or her ability at photo-retouching to create the final image. The patient-specific data obtained from radiology studies such as CT and MRI scans can be formatted by computer graphic rendering techniques into visual 3-D objects. Surgical-simulation systems have been based on segmentation (cutting) and rearrangement of the volume data. This technique is useful in bone surgery, such as craniofacial surgery (7, 8) because the modeled tissue is rearranged in blocks, and elasticity is not as significant as in surgery of the soft tissues.

For a computer to predict the outcome of surgery, it must have a model of the physical properties of the tissue to analyze relevant mechanical consequences of a proposed surgical procedure. The ultimate goal of the patient model is that it accurately accounts for the patient's tissue at each location of the body for computer simulation. Three-dimensional patient data currently obtained in medicine (e.g., CT, MRI, and PET scans) are encoded volumetrically, i.e., each point in space is defined by an absolute reference frame independent of the patient, and the material is encoded at each of these points. These data are not immediately amenable to modeling, because there is no information about how each piece of material connects to other pieces of the material. A finite element mesh (FEM) divides a material with complex geometry into regions (elements) that, taken together, approximate the behavior of the entire material. Each region (element) is defined by the boundaries it shares with other elements. A matrix with the material properties of the elements will predict each element's distortion, given the restriction that it must still share the same borders with the other elements. There are several mathematic algorithms for the construction of FEMs based on data in volume datasets (9).

One of the first areas of the body to be the subject of computer mechanical models is the leg. Delp and co-workers (10) constructed a computer simulation of the lower extremity musculotendonous system that can walk in a computer-simulated environment and be used to analyze tendon transfer operations. Using a computer-generated model of the hip joint with muscle and tendon actuators, Delp and Maloney (11) were able to predict the outcome of hip arthroplasties (total hip joint replacements). By simulating 41 muscle–tendon complexes, they determined the maximum force generated by leg abduction, adduction, flexion and extension in relation to the position of the hip joint itself (Fig. 4.5). Using this model, one can predict the effect of hip prosthesis position on individual muscle groups. Displacing the hip prosthesis off-center alters the moment-generating capacity of the muscles. Expanding the model to include major muscles of the entire lower extremity, Delp and Zajac (12) made several interesting observations concerning the affect of tendon lengthening and transfers on muscle strength. These procedures are often performed on patients with gait or posture abnormalities caused by stroke or cerebral palsy. The significance of accurately predicting outcomes of reconstructive surgery is great.

Chen and Zeltzer (13) presented a method that combines realistic computer animation and valid biomechanical simulation of muscle. Taking human animation beyond simulating surface geometry of skin, they detailed the modeling of individual muscles. Using reconstructed 3-D images from CT and MRI data and the *Swivel 3-D Professional Modeling Program*, Chen and Zeltzer constructed a polyhedral model of the human calf muscle (gastrocnemius). The biomechanical model was synthesized using the finite element method. By developing a model with the capacity to simulate actual muscle force and to

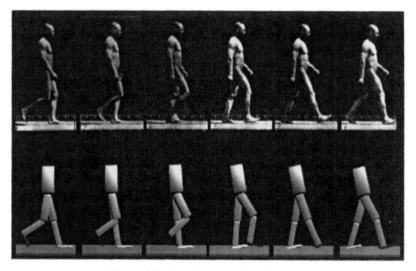

Figure 4.5. Gunshot wound to the leg.

visualize the dynamics of muscle contraction, they created an animated character that changes shape accurately and realistically.

McKenna (14) developed a system to simulate complex human kinematics. His model of the human figure contains 90 degrees of freedom (dof) with 28 dof in each foot, incorporates anatomic diagrams, a 3-D digitized skeleton, and clinical and cadaver studies of the biomechanics of limbs and joints. Simulated actions include rising to standing from knees, reaching, rising on toes, and walking and falling under gravity.

Satava (15) created a virtual abdomen to teach medical students specific anatomic details of abdominal organs and to instruct surgical residents in techniques and operative procedures. This computer model allows the viewer to see the anatomy from outside of the organs, as in a traditional open laparotomy, but also from the inside in the fly-through mode, as in an endoscopic procedure. There are also laparoscopic tools in the model to perform simulated minimally invasive surgery.

Larabee and Galt (16) compared a 2-D FEM simulation of human skin to pigskin to analyze flap advancements. Kawabata et al. (17) used a 2-D FEM to analyze the effect of various Z-plasty parameters. Motoyoshi et al. (18) used an FEM model of facial soft tissue to predict the outcome of orthognathic surgery. Lee et al. (19) used an FEM with overlying detail similar to CAPS to generate computer-synthesized facial expression.

One of the most difficult areas of the human body to simulate is the face. Through it, we communicate verbally and nonverbally, express emotions and thoughts, and feed our bodies. The fluidity, individuality, and complexity of the musculature of the face complicate attempts to accurately model the subtlety of facial expression. Although early efforts at key frame animation of the face proved satisfactory for 2-D modeling, the time required to specify the large number of key frames required for 3-D simulation is impractical (20). In the early 1980s, Platt and Badler (21) simulated the human face using a three-layered model of skin, muscle, and bone. Skin is represented by a set of points with 3-D coordinates. Bone is a represented as a rigid surface below the skin. The muscle is a group of muscle-fiber points that are connected by elastic arcs to the overlying skin and underlying bone. Points on the skin are also connected to neighboring points through arcs. By integrating the network of points, one can demonstrate how the application of force or tension on one section of the model will effect more distant areas of the same surface (16).

Pieper (22) created a detailed model of the face using reconstructed images from CT and MRI scans of a patient. His program, *Computer-Aided Plastic Surgery* (CAPS), allows the planning, analysis, and visualization of plastic surgery on the soft tissues of the face. It is a prototype computer program that a surgeon could use as a sketch pad to predict and compare the outcome of facial plastic procedures on a patient-specific physical model. One can select incision placement, can move tissue, and can suture. The CAPS program uses a FEM to simulate plastic surgery by removing certain elements and then redefining the remaining elements as sharing their (formerly separate) borders, just as a surgeon excises tissue and defines new shared edges with sutures. When the computer calculates the distorting forces and applies this to the patient-specific model, it is possible to visualize the consequences of the surgery. This has been used for excisions of tumors, for cleft lip repairs, and for rhinoplaties.

Although the above projects have begun to put together a virtual human, to a large extent these models are based on normal anatomy and physiology. They generally use a patient data, like the Virtual Human Data from NLM, to create a generic person. To provide a realistic human, many other factors need to be addressed. I will now elaborate on some of the factor that need to be addressed by future mathematical models and software programs.

4.3 INTERFACE TOOLS

Interface tools include systems for seeing, hearing, and touching with or without force feedback. These systems made great advances during the 1990s. They are important for not only medical applications but for many commercial and military applications. Although they are critical for medical applications, they have advanced beyond the capabilities of the human body models. The virtual human body models will need to be improved before the present sight, sound, and touch systems can be fully be taken advantage of for VR applications in medicine.

4.3.1 Complete Systems

In the early twentieth century, flight simulators were introduced and soon became a proven means of training pilots in complex tasks (23, 24). Flight simulators provided an environment for training and instruction, a tool for prediction, and an aid for experimentation. Their advantages include decreased costs and increased safety compared to real flight experience.

For the most part, these advantages hold equally true for surgical simulation. In addition, surgical simulators provide a concentrated environment that lends itself to learning complex tactile maneuvers in a relatively quick and proficient manner. Moreover, simulation of infrequent but highly hazardous events provides experience in handling scenarios that may not be available during a period of routine procedures.

Similar to flight simulation, surgical simulators allow the user to practice complex tasks using an interactive computer environment. Over the last century, this interactive environment progressed from a 2-D screen (i.e., photographs and radiographs) to a 3-D VR. Two-dimensional sources of data were initially modified by hand using drafting tools. Later, the 2-D data were introduced into a computer to facilitate manipulation and allow the surgeon to better plan and demonstrate the possible outcomes of the proposed procedure. More recently, volumetric data obtained from computer-aided scans provided 3-D information for surgeons to help plan complex operations. Using a computer simulator for planning, a surgeon may try out many different possible reconstructions on a patient-specific model before operating.

Surgical simulators consists of three basic components, similar to a flight simulator: the computer, the interface, and the physical model. The physical model for the surgical simulator is a realistic computational representation of the patient, the operating room, and the surgical instruments (25, 26). The interface uses either a force-feedback mouse or a glove to allow the user to manipulate surgical instruments three-dimensionally and uses internal motors to give the user force-feedback. In other words, the user can move a scalpel into virtual tissue and can actually feel the resistance.

4.3.2 Battlefield Simulator

To look at the present state of the art, I would like to look at great detail at one system with which I have been inovlved. Delp's group (27) at Musculo-Graphics, Inc. has developed a model of the leg that predicts the result of a gunshot wound (GSW) to the thigh. As the bullet passes through the thigh, it lacerates, crushes, and burns the tissue in its path. The injuries caused in this way define the permanent wound cavity. Delp et al. built a polygonal surface with the appropriate size and shape for the thigh model and for the bullet parameters. The beginning of the wound tract is cylindrical (about 1 cm in diameter). When the bullet hits the lateral edge of the femur, it is assumed to break the bone and then deflect about 15° laterally. The wound tract behind the femur is roughly cone shaped, with several large spikes representing the tissue destroyed by bone fragment projectiles.

The four bone fragments in the model were created by determining the intersection of the permanent cavity and the femur. The resulting piece of bone was divided into four smaller pieces of roughly equal size. One was assumed to have been expelled from the thigh; the other three were embedded in the thigh model, at the ends of the spikes in the permanent cavity. For future injury simulations, the software developed by Mission Research Corporation will more accurately calculate the sizes and positions of the bone fragments given the parameters of the projectile.

Further damage is caused by the transfer of kinetic energy from the bullet to the surrounding tissue (27–29). This energy transfer stretches and devitalizes some tissue outside of the permanent cavity. This region of devitalized tissue is known as the temporary cavity. To approximate the geometry of the temporary cavity, they performed nonlinear scaling operations on the permanent cavity and increased its average diameter. After determining the shape of the cavity, it was checked for intersection with each structure in the thigh model. If the two objects intersected, the intersecting portion of the thigh structure was labeled as nonviable by marking the vertices and polygons within that region with a special label. The portion of the structure outside of the temporary cavity was labeled as viable. The nonviable portion of the structure is then rendered using a darker color and texture map to indicate that it is devitalized.

Delp's group (27) has evaluated the functional consequences of the injury by computing how it affects muscle strength. Strength is quantified as the maximum moment-generating capacity of each muscle group based on the muscle's physiologic cross-sectional area. muscle fiber length, pennation angle, and moment arm. Muscle strength after injury and repair were compared to the strength required for walking to evaluate the functional consequences of the injury.

They have also analyzed the functional consequences of the injury to the circulatory system. In fact, the circulatory effects of the injury are more important for an accurate simulation of the treatment process, because they affect the patient's vital signs and the bleeding of the tissues as the wound is débrided. As a result, the researchers have produced a system to evaluate the effects of trauma to the musculoskeletal and circulatory systems.

To evaluate the functional consequences of the injury to the musculoskeletal system, Delp et al. (27) adapted a generic musculoskeletal model of the lower limb to the injured thigh model. This model consists of seven rigid-body segments (pelvis, femur, tibia/fibula, patella, talus, foot, toes) and 43 muscle–tendon actuators. The circulatory model developed for this training system calculates the time-dependent changes of several key hemodynamic properties, such as blood loss, heart rate, and cardiac output. As the user interacts with the wound using the virtual surgical tools (e.g., scalpel, hemostat), the patient's tissues should bleed or stop bleeding as appropriate. These changes in blood loss will then affect the vital signs, which will be updated and displayed when needed.

The circulatory model has two components. The first component is a mathematical model governing the flow of fluid through a network of closed conduits (16, 20). These equations calculate the steady-state flow of blood (modeled as a viscous fluid) through the arteries, veins, and capillaries. The flow must satisfy the basic principles of the conservation of mass and energy.

The second component is a set of equations describing the transient response of several hemodynamic properties as blood is lost from the system. The key properties in which Delp et al. are interested are cardiac output, heart rate, and arterial pressure. Other properties that affect the calculations are peripheral resistance and stroke volume. They used the results of experimental studies on animals to generate the relations between these properties and the total amount of blood loss (18).

Delp's group (27) is also developing tools to create virtual surgical instruments to assess and treat the injury. The user will select the instruments from a virtual surgical tray and use them to perform activities such as moving soft tissue and bone; realigning fractured bones; viewing the color and assessing the contractility of muscle; débriding the wound; and repairing nerves, blood vessels, and skin. Simulating the mechanical response of the soft tissues during these activities is a key element of the training scenario. When tissues are prodded, they should deform as would real tissue, whether healthy or devitalized. When tissues are cut with a scalpel or scissors, they should cut or tear realistically and should bleed as appropriate. Delp et al. will implement physiologically based algorithms to simulate these responses and will make the tools interactive so that the user can observe the effects in real time. They have thus far implemented two surgical instruments: a hemostat and a scalpel. The hemostat can be used to grab and pull tissue or to push it to check the tissue's consistency. In either case, the tissue deforms according to a second-order deformation function centered on the contact point. The specific form of this function depends on the tissue type and its healthy or devitalized status.

4.4   CONCLUSION

This chapter focused on the challenge of the human body and the need for an improved model for virtual surgery. Although further work needs to be done on the interface tools to interact with this model, this is a seconday challenge to be met after the virtual human model is better developed. The other key factor is that many fields are developing the interface tools in parallel to medical applications. However, the human body is unique to the medical field, although overall human body models still have practical applications in transportation for crash testing, in the military for ballistics research on tissue injury, and in commerce for ergonometric design. The present human body models are only a beginning to what is needed to move the field of virtual reality and medicine to a new state of the art in medical education and training.

Telemedicine and telesurgery will also benefit greatly from better human body models. However, strictly speaking, both telemedicine and telesurgery can be done without virtual human body models; it is only in projecting surgical simulators and performance machines at a distance does the human body model become critical. Progress will also be made in parallel with many other fields that are improving the interface tools for teleoperations and teleconferencing for a number of other commercial and military applications.

In summary, plastic surgery provides a unique view of the human body. More than any other single field it requires a robust model of the human body. This model is needed to aid in the planning of surgery. From the leaf template for forehead flap nasal reconstruction employed by Indian surgeons to plastic templates milled from CT scan reconstructions, all may be regarded as an attempt to simulate the operation in a medium other than the patient. More work is needed to refine the particular model discussed here and to validate its results. In the future computers will be involved not only in the planning of surgery but also in the training of surgeons and in the aiding of the performance of surgery. Help will extend to telemedicine and telesurgery, but ultimately the acceptance of these simulators and trainers will depend heavily on the realism of the underlying virtual human body models. These models will need to be multidimensional, accurately predicting the outcomes of surgery and the healing process over time, as first suggested by Mann in the 1970s.

REFERENCES

1. R. Mann. 1965.
2. Sutherland. 1970.
3. Turing. 1950.
4. Muybridge. 1900.
5. M. B. Constantian, C. Ehrrenpries, and J. H. Sheen. The expert teaching system: a new method for learning rhinoplasty using interactive computer graphics. Plast Reconstr Surg 1987;79:278.
6. R. C. Mattison. Facial video image processing: standard facial image capturing, software modification, development of a surgical plan, and comparison of pre-surgical and post-surgical results. Ann Plast Surg 1992;29:385.
7. M. D. Cutting, F. L. Bookstein, B. Grayson, et al. Three-dimensional computer-assisted craniofacial surgical procedures: optimization and interaction with cephalometric and CT-based models. Plast Reconstr Surg 1986;77:877.
8. D. E. Altobelli, R. Kikinis, J. B. Mullikin, et al. Computer-assisted three-dimensional planning in craniofacial surgery. Plast Reconst Surg 1993;92:576.
9. H. E. Cline, W. E. Lorensen, S. Ludke, et al. Two algorithms for reconstruction of surfaces from tomographs. Med Phys 1988;15:320.
10. S. L. Delp, P. Loan, M. G. Hoy, et al. An interactive graphics-based model of the lower extremity to study orthopaedic surgical procedures. IEEE Trans Biomed Eng 1990;37:757.
11. S. L. Delp and W. Maloney. Effects of hip center location on the movement-generating capacity of the muscles.
12. S. L. Delp and F. E. Zajac. Force- and moment-generating capacity of the lower extremity muscles before and after tendon lengthening.

13. D. T. Chen and D. Zeltzer. Pump it up: computer animation of a biomechanically based model of muscle using the finite element method. Comput Graph 1992;26:89–98.

14. M. A. McKenna. A physically based human figure model with a complex foot and low level behavior control. Doctoral dissertation, Massachusetts Institute of Technology, Boston, June 1994.

15. R. Satava. Virtual reality surgical simulator: the first steps. Paper presented at the Virtual Reality and Medicine Conference. San Diego, CA, June 1992.

16. W. F. Larabee and J. A. Galt. A finite element model of skin deformation. III The finite element model. Laryngoscope 1986;96:413.

17. H. Kawabata, H. Kawai, K. Masada, and K. Ono. Computer-aided analysis of Z-plasties. Plast Reconstr Surg 1989;83:319.

18. M. Motoyoshi, A. Yoshizumi, A. Nakajima, et al. Finite element model of facial soft tissue. J Nihon Univ School Dent 1993;35:118.

19. Y. Lee, D. Terzopoulos, and K. Waters. Realistic modeling for facial animation. Paper presented at SIGGRAPH. Los Angeles, CA, Aug 6–11, 1995.

20. F. I. Parke. Parameterized models for facial animation. Paper presented at IEEE CG&A. Nov 1982.

21. S. M. Platt and N. I. Badler. Animating facial expressions. Comput Graph 1981.

22. D. S. Pieper. CAPS: computer-aided plastic surgery. Doctoral thesis, Massachusettts Institute of Technology, Boston, Feb 1992.

23. R. N. Haber. Flight simulation. Sci Am 1986.

24. J. M. Rolfe and K. J. Staples. Flight simulation. Cambridge, UK: Cambridge University Press, 1986.

25. J. D. Foley. Interfaces for advanced computing. Sci Am 1987.

26. D. Sturmin, D. Zeltzer, and S. Pieper. Hands-on interaction with virtual environments. Paper presented at UIST '89: ACM SIGGRAPH/SIGGHI Symposium on User Interface Software and Technology. Williamsburg, VA, Nov 13–15, 1989.

27. S. L. Delp, J. P. Loan, C. Basdogan, et al. Surgical simulation: an emerging technology for military medical training, military telemedicine on-line today. IEEE Press, in press.

28. M. L. Fackler. Wound ballistics: a review of common misconceptions. JAMA 1990;155:685–690.

29. J. J. Hollerman, M. Fackler, D. Coldwell, and Y. Ben-Menachem. Gunshot wounds: 1. Bullets, ballistics, and mechanism of injury. AJR 1990;155:685–690.

Virtual Reality Laboratory for Medical Applications

GABRIELE FAULKNER

University Hospital Benjamin Franklin
12200 Berlin Germany

5.1   Definition

5.2   Aim

5.3   Human Senses

5.4   Human Factors

5.5   User and Task Analyses

5.6   Technical Components of a VR System
      5.6.1   Restrictions
      5.6.2   Hardware
      5.6.3   Software

5.7   VR Input Devices
      5.7.1   3-D Sensor
      5.7.2   Glove Based
      5.7.3   Stationary Desktop
      5.7.4   Hand Held
      5.7.5   Haptic
      5.7.6   Stereoscopic Video Capturing
      5.7.7   Two-Dimensional

5.8   VR Output Devices
      5.8.1   Glasses
      5.8.2   Head-Mounted Display
      5.8.3   Head-Coupled Display
      5.8.4   Virtual Model Display
      5.8.5   Spatially Immersive Display
      5.8.6   3-D Audio

Information Technologies in Medicine, Volume I: Medical Simulation and Education, Edited by
Metin Akay and Andy Marsh.
ISBN 0-471-38863-7   © 2001 John Wiley & Sons, Inc.

5.1 DEFINITION

Virtual reality (VR) is the term given to a new human computer interface, and illusion is the key component. The aim is to give the user the illusion of an alternative reality. Immersive environments are often named in this context and describe VR systems that are intended to block out the real world and help the user become part of the virtual scene. VR has been described as being

> about the computer graphics in the theatre of the mind. It's about the use of high technology to convince yourself that you're in another reality, experiencing some event that doesn't physically exist in the world in front of you. Virtual Reality is also a new medium for getting your hands on information, getting inside information, and representing ideas in ways not previously possible (1).

In addition, building virtual environments (VEs) requires the understanding not only of the existing technical components but also of the pattern and behavior of human perception.

5.2 AIM

The aim of this chapter is to give a description of a VR laboratory in the context of medical applications. In 1990, I started to set up a test bed for three-dimensional (3-D) input and output devices at the Technical University of Berlin. This led to the installation of a VR laboratory, which, was moved into the medical environment at the University Hospital Benjamin Franklin (UKBF), as part of the Free University of Berlin.

To set up the VR laboratory, user and task analyses must be performed. A VR system is composed of different components, which are explained and described by example. The individual components must be carefully selected, depending on their functionality and their use within the medical environment. The devices need to be regarded from the point of view of their technical description and their limitations. The advantages of the individual components, however, are not the only criteria for choosing them, because the interrelation with the system must also be taken into account. The costs are often an important limiting factor for influencing the choice of a particular device.

5.3 HUMAN SENSES

Each of the organs responsible for one of the senses reacts to a specific physical energy—the stimulus. The activity of the sense organs has to be organized so that perception, learning, and decision making can take place (2, 3). Human beings receive stimuli from their environment by means of the five major senses, which are processed in parallel using different percentages of the available bandwidth (as noted in parentheses below) (4).

Vision (70%) is fulfilled by the visual system and is our primary sense. In the development of a VR system, special attention should be given to focusing action (accommodation), the color vision of humans, and the foveal vision in combination with visual perception phenomena (e.g., the perception of visual cues regarding an object's size, position, or occlusion). The fovea is a small area in the retina that contains only cone receptors. If a human looks directly at an object, its image falls on the fovea, because the fovea is located directly in the line of sight.

Audition (20%) is the perception channel for which the auditory system is responsible. With respect to VR systems, the physical specification of sound waves and their behavior in space should be taken into account. Olfaction (5%), the sense of smell, is carried out by the olfactory system and allows humans to distinguish between various scents.

Cutaneous (4%) senses refer to the sensory receptors of the skin. Human beings have the ability to sense haptic information (sense of touch), such as the temperature or texture of an object's surface, and an applied force, such as the resistance, weight, or pressure caused by an object. Gustation (1%), which tells us how something tastes, is carried out by the gustatory system. It plays a minor role in VR in medicine today.

The sense of balance, which gives information about the position and movement of the head and limbs, does not belong to the classical five senses but should be taken into account when using 3-D output devices that suffer from a response lag (discussed later). The ratings of each perception channel represent the available bandwidth for the perceived information but do not necessarily correspond to the importance of the stimulus. For example, a simulation of cutting tissue would require more tactile feedback than audible feedback.

5.4 HUMAN FACTORS

In selecting a component for the desired VR system, the effect of that component on the user regarding all human factors has to be carefully considered. Research has taken place concerning the effect on the health of the operator (5).

The use of VR systems can also have an effect on the user in the form of the so-called simulator sickness, which includes drowsiness, nausea, headache, disorientation, and oculomotor disfunction. Currently, there are no definitive results indicating any long-term health problems that could be attributed to the regular usage of VR systems.

5.5   USER AND TASK ANALYSES

Thoroughly performed user and task analyses help produce a good system, which will be more suitable to the needs of the user and his or her expectations. Thus, in the concept phase, the designer of medical VR systems should thoroughly examine topics before starting to implement a medical application system within the scope of VR. User and task analyses help define user groups and the tasks to be performed by the system. The analyses could follow the guidelines of the user centered design Allison et al. (6), which aims at answering such questions as:

- Who are the medical users of the system and in what circumstances will they use it?
- What is the purpose of using the system and what are the tasks to be performed?

Accordingly, information must be gathered on the participating user groups pertaining to the following factors: age, sex, education, job, job experience, computer experience, intelligence, handicaps, physical ability, motor skills, and language. To describe the task to be performed, the following factors must be analyzed: performance speed, frequency of use, duration of sitting, ability to change tasks, security factors, and problems. In addition, the work environment should be examined in regard to temperature, light, noise, and the danger of theft or vandalism.

Work conditions must also be noted. Important questions are

- Will the system be operated by a single user or by a group?
- Are there likely to be any interruptions of the work at any time?
- In what kind of environment will the work take place (open or private)?
- Are there any special work conditions?

5.6   TECHNICAL COMPONENTS OF A VR SYSTEM

A VR system consists of various components that dependent on three factors: the costs of the whole VR system, the purpose of the application, and the working environment. The individual parts are described below, but first it is necessary to discuss the technical restrictions.

5.6.1 Restrictions

The objectives and key tasks of the VR system have to be specified before a serious system can be developed. Adequate prototyping is necessary for recognizing potential task-oriented problems. Besides the technical restrictions, the price of an input/output (I/O) device is often the main limitation to purchasing VR components. Most I/O devices are expensive because they are sold in small quantities and are usually assembled by hand, the expenses of prototype development can be enormous, and success in sales is risky.

One more technically limiting factor of VR components is the environment in which the VR system has to be tailored. For example, a VR system for an operating theater should meet the special requirements of sterility, which are not easy to accomplish, and take into account the limited amount of space available during the operating procedure. The freedom of movement and field of view of the surgeon must not be restricted during the operation. For teaching and simulation purposes, a special room is required with appropriate low lighting and enough space for the VR system and the audience.

Technical variables of the VR components can have a dramatic effect on the quality of the whole VR system (7, 8). The main ones are as follows:

- *Accuracy.* With respect to the precision of a simulated image and the corresponding image in the real world or the amount of error in the transformation of the real movements into the actions within the computer system, such as the accuracy of the sensor values (coordinates in space) delivered when changing the sensor's position or orientation.
- *Resolution.* The number of pixels on the screen or the granularity of measurement values of an analogue sensor after an analogue to digital (A/D) conversion.
- *Lag time.* Corresponds to the time difference between sending a signal and receiving that particular signal, e.g., the time between sending data by an interaction device and receiving those data by the VR application.
- *Response time.* Refers to the time between an action and the delivered feedback caused by this action, e.g., between a change in the head position tracker and the corresponding movement on the display.
- *Weight.* The weight of a head-mounted display (HMD).
- *Ergonomics.* The lack of comfort of a HMD or a glove-based interaction device (direct cabling to the computer).

The VR computing hardware must generate and render the images before displaying them. The images have to be computed with minimal delay, taking into account the position and orientation of the head of the user. If the components are not correctly connected by adequate technology, perceivable visual lags will be revealed. These lags can cause some health problems (explained later).

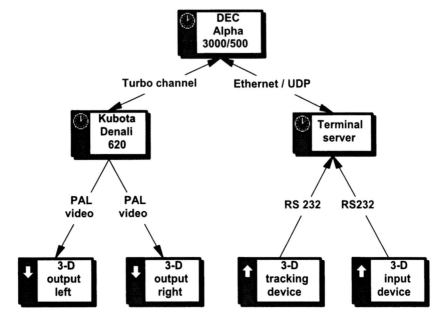

Figure 5.1. The VR system used in the laboratory at the Technical University Berlin and UKBF.

To connect the different components, special interfaces and/or specialized computers for serving the interaction devices are required. These specialized computers must achieve the synchronization and the minimization of the computing load of the imaging computer. Network solutions using a high-speed network can help spread the computing load and improve the throughput of the system (Fig. 5.1). In both configurations it must be ensured that stereoscopic output and 3-D input can be created in real time.

5.6.2 Hardware

The graphical system provides the computing power necessary for the specific needs of an application. The classes described are PC based, workstation based, and high-end system (9). Table 5.1 compares typical representatives of these three classes.

5.6.3 Software

To build a VR environment, software is, of course, needed. Figure 5.2 shows the individual components required for handling data. The import filter provides the necessary data transformation from the data source and the data format required for the modeling process. In a medical application, where the goal is to visualize real anatomic data, the data sources are usually CT or MRI

TABLE 5.1. Computing Hardware Applicable for VR

Type	Components	Ability	Price (approximate)
PC	P90, 64 MB RAM, 1 GB disk, high-resolution graphics and audio board	Low-level VR through-the-window system with limited quality in regard to the detail of the rendered scene, update frame rate, and real-time interaction	$7000
Workstation	Digital AlphaStation 600 5/266, 128 MB RAM, 2 GB disk, ZLX-L2 graphics	Medium range VR through the window system with restricted quality in regard to the detail of the rendered scene, update frame rate, and real-time interaction	$53,000
High end	SGI Onyx, 512 MB RAM, 6 GB disk, 4 processor R4400, 2 reality engine graphics, 8 raster manager 5, sirius video board	High-range immersive VR system with tolerable quality in regard to the detail of the rendered scene, update frame rate, and real-time interaction	$930,000

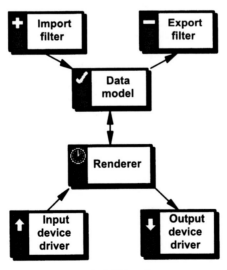

Figure 5.2. Graphics pipeline of a typical VR software system with its major components.

scanners that deliver 3-D information in a consecutive sequence of 2-D image slices.

The choice of representation of the transformed source data on the computer has to be made depending on the intended application and its interactions. The result is the data model as part of the database. The database itself can also contain artificially created objects describing, for instance, the objects involved in an operation scenario. Volume (voxel-based) and surface modeling in the form of polygonal representations are commonly used to build the data model. Volume modeling is most suitable for medical purposes, because it is possible, by using cutting planes or transparencies, to show the interior of an object, which surface modeling is not able to perform.

Rendering is defined as the "process of going from a database representation of a three-dimensional object to a shaded two-dimensional projection on a view surface" (10). The process of visualizing the volume data set is called volume rendering. The process either directly projects the volume primitives or reduces the volume data into a 2-D pixel space, which is then stored as a raster (a pattern of horizontal scanning lines) image in the frame buffer. Volume rendering comprises the viewing and the shading of the volume image. Surface rendering is the process that renders the geometric primitives to the screen by conventional geometric rendering techniques and involves viewing and shading. To transform the voxel-based source data into a polygonal representation, the technique called isosurfacing can be applied. To be sufficiently accurate however, this technique generates an extremely large number of polygons.

Export filters serve the purpose of transforming the rendered model, or parts of the model, into the format required for postprocessing by specialized hardware such as numerically controlled (NC) machines, by stereo lithography, or by specialized software (e.g., finite element calculations or radiation therapy planning).

Driver software must be installed for the I/O devices used. In most cases, the driver software must be developed first for the particular combination of equipment. To achieve a user-friendly interaction, an appropriate task-dependent interaction method has to be designed and special attention has to be given to the suitable feedback. Table 5.2 shows examples of VR development systems for the above-mentioned classes of VR hardware computer systems.

5.7   VR INPUT DEVICES

To set up a VR environment for medical applications, the facilities offered by the following classes of 3-D input devices should be considered:

- A sensor for measuring state changes in 3-D, such as force, position, and orientation.
- A glove-based input device for all interactions that require the high dexterity of the hand. The hand inherits more than 20 degrees of freedom (dof).

TABLE 5.2. VR Development Software Systems

Name	Components	Ability	Price
PC: WorldToolKit V 2.0 (Sense8)	Intended for single users running on a single workstation with low-level support for networking; runs on IBM PC compatibles, SUN, and Silicon Graphics workstations; support for many I/O devices; C library; multiple viewport and light sources, 3-D paths, portals, 2-D texts and shapes, and object animations; support for graphics hardware	Low-level VR through-the-window system with limited quality in regard to the detail of the rendered scene, update frame rate, and real-time interaction	$800 (developer's licence)
Workstation: OpenGL (Silicon Graphics)	Software interface for applications to generate interactive 2-D and 3-D computer graphics; designed to be independent of operating system, window system, and hardware operations; supported by many vendors; provides a wide range of graphics functions from rendering a simple geometric point, line, or filled polygon to texture mapping; nonuniform rational B-spline curved surfaces, geometric primitives, α blending, anti-aliasing and atmospheric effects	Medium-range VR through-the-window system with restricted quality in regard to the detail of the rendered scene, update frame rate, and real-time interaction	Bundled with OS licence (Digital)
High-end: IRIS Performer (Silicon Graphics)	Software development environment providing high-level support for visual simulation, VR, graphics-intensive applications, and advanced image-generation functions; implements functions such as culling, controlling many different display channels, and performing fast intersection tests; Designed for maximum performance	High-range immersive VR system with tolerable quality in regard to the detail of the rendered scene, update frame rate, and real-time interaction	$600

141

- A stationary desktop input device, which is suitable for through-the-window VR systems, with a stationary output device such as a computer monitor.
- A hand-held input device, which is most suitable in an immersive environment where the user can freely interact in all directions.
- A haptic interface, which allows the user to interact with the computer by applying and receiving an appropriate and variable resisting force.
- A 2-D input device, which has been used for 3-D interaction.

In the following sections, representatives of each class—with their technical descriptions and medical application purposes—are discussed. The specific device are used in my laboratory and do not represent an exhaustive list.

5.7.1 3-D Sensor

The 3-D sensors must have 6 dof and the ability to detect the position and orientation of the object at any instant. There are currently five basic position- and orientation-sensing methods (11): mechanical, ultrasonic, magnetic, optical, and image extraction. As examples of sensors, two devices that use the magnetic and optical principles are described because they are widely used for medical applications.

The underlying concept of the magnetic sensing method is that a magnetic field oriented along a single axis is generated by an electrical current that is sent through a coil of wire (transmitter coil). On the other hand, if a coil of wire (receiver coil) is exposed to a magnetic field, an electrical current proportional to the strength of the magnetic field is generated. The generated electrical charge is greater if the receiver coil is closer to the axis of the magnetic field. If three coils of wire are mounted at right angles to each other and are fed with electrical current, the coils create three magnetic fields along three axes. Then if another three-coil set is moved through those magnetic fields, the second set produces three distinct electrical charges, depending on its position and orientation. This yields a total of nine measurements, which are processed by the control box to determine six values for position and orientation.

There are two main problems with this technology: lag time and accuracy. Lag time (the delay time between the movement of the magnetic tracker and the time when the computer receives and processes the information) is too long for current developments. The lengthy lag time is caused by the signal processing and filtering of each set of nine measurements (1). Accuracy of the measurements is influenced by the side effect that the magnetic field generated by the transmitter is also picked up by other large highly conductive objects in the working area because those magnetic objects give off their own fields.

5.7.1.1 *Fastrak.* Owing to its wide use in the VR field, the Fastrak tracking system (Polhemus) is described as a representative of magnetic sensors. The

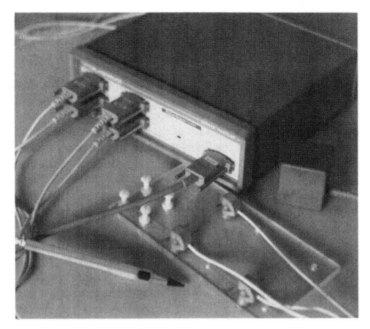

Figure 5.3. The Fasttrack (Polhemus Navigation Science, Colchester, VT) controller box (background). In the foreground from left to right: stylus, three receivers mounted on a plate, and the transmitter.

transmitter, made of an assembly of three collocated stationary antennas, generates near-field, low-frequency magnetic field vectors (Fig. 5.3). They are detected by the receiver, which is made up of an assembly of three collocated remote-sensing antennas. The sensed signals are mathematically transformed into the position and orientation of the receiver relative to the transmitter (6 dof). The position coverage is within 30 in. (0.76 m) of the receiver from the transmitter and with reduced accuracy within 120 in. (3.05 m). The static accuracy is 0.03 in. (0.08 cm) RMS for the x, y, and z receiver position and 0.15° RMS for the receiver orientation. The resolution is 0.0002 in./in. (0.0005 cm/cm) and 0.025°. The latency is 4.0 ms from the center of the receiver measurement period to the beginning of the transfer from the output port. It delivers 120 updates/s for one receiver. If the system uses four receivers, it can deliver only a fourth of the updates. It has an RS-232 interface, ranging from 300 to 115000 baud as well as an IEEE-488 parallel port at a maximum of 100 Kb/s.

The Fastrack has some limitations. The tracker should not be put into action in the presence of strong magnetic fields or ferrous material. Large metallic objects (e.g., an operating table) that are near the transmitter or receiver may affect the performance of the tracking system. It works only within 3.05 m^3 and offers good accuracy in the working range. Tests showed that it is sensitive to interference.

In my laboratory, the Fastrack has been used for the definition of the point of view of the operator and for intraoperative determination of the position and orientation of parts of the patients and surgical instruments.

5.7.1.2 Optical Tracking. The idea of optical tracking is that several light-emitting diodes (LEDs), which are normally infrared, are placed on top of a HMD and a video camera (often black and white) plus the required image-processing software, tracks the position of the LEDs. The camera can be placed on the head of the person and the lights mounted in stationary positions.

At the University of North Carolina, a configuration of three cameras and about 1000 LEDs, spread uniformly across the ceiling, are used. The computer sequentially pulses the LEDs and simultaneously processes the images of the camera to detect a flash and uses this information to determine position and orientation (1).

In another set up, there are several cameras that point to a target on the human who wears a special headset. Using image-processing functions, the computer correlates the different camera views into a single position and orientation. The camera is equipped with an image sensor, called a lateral effect photo diode, which is extremely efficient at tracking and locating the ceiling-mounted LEDs.

Problems occur if the person stands too close to a wall or leans over too far, causing the camera to point to a place where there are no LEDs. Optical tracking requires the sensor and source to be in line of sight, and this is a major limitation. It is also fairly exhausting for the user to carry the camera on his or her head. However, the accuracy of this technology is good, with fast update rates being achieved.

5.7.1.3 FlashPoint. At the UKBF, the FlashPoint 5000 (Image Guided Technologies) was installed and is presented as a typical system with an optical working principle. It is based on a three-camera sensor assembly that detects special LEDs. It has 6 dof.

Unfortunately, if too many LEDs are hidden by an object or the user's body, the optical method cannot work. Therefore, in a small operation field, the usability of FlashPoint might be too restricted.

At the UKBF, FlashPoint has been used for the intraoperative determination of the position and orientation of neurosurgical instruments. The medical staff involved in this procedure were satisfied with the results, and the advantages of the online visualization of the current position of the surgical tip were obvious.

5.7.2 Glove Based

At present, there are various types of gloves available, which differ in accuracy, robustness, price, and application suitability. The glove converts hand gestures and positions into computer-readable form. It uses a tracking device, such as

A

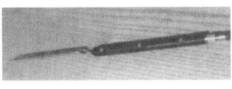

B   C

Figure 5.4. FlashPoint 5000 (Image Guided Technologies) **A**, The camera. **B**, The reference object probe. **C**, The reference object head ring.

the Polhemus tracker. This tracker is mounted on the back of the glove and senses the hand's position (x, y, z) and orientation (yaw, pitch, roll). There are also sensors mounted on the glove that detect the finger flexion. Only a limited number of gloves offer force and tactile feedback.

The disadvantages of gloves depend on their technical realization. The following is a list of common drawbacks:

- No force or tactile feedback.
- Problems when put to use in the presence of strong magnetic fields or ferrous materials, owing to the working principle of the tracker.
- Direct cabling to the computer.
- Fragile construction.
- Glove must fit exactly.
- Long calibration time.
- Unpleasant to wear after the recent use of another user.
- Wearer not accustomed to fulfilling interaction tasks with static gestures.
- Interaction can tire the involved muscles.
- The position and rotation sensor mounted on top of the glove; thus if the user rotates the hand, a translation is automatically performed as well.
- The human hand can rotate only to a certain degree owing to physiologic constraints.
- High price.

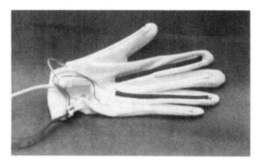

Figure 5.5. The UKBF glove.

- Not suitable for daily routine work in a clinical environment owing to acceptance problems with medical people.
- Restrictions in application in the sterile area of the operating theater.

Owing to all the problems with gloves, especially when used in the medical field, it was decided to perform tests in my laboratory with a self-made model (Fig. 5.5) (8). It should be pointed out however that the technique employed for measuring the finger movements are not as accurate as when performed by a state-of-the-art commercially available model. The prototype is a cotton glove with the Flock of Birds tracking system, which is a magnetic field 3-D sensor and hence inherits a full 6 dof for position and orientation. The flexion of the fingers is measured with 5 dof. The resolution of the bending angle is 8 bit; 150 updates/s are delivered.

The cotton glove does not fit properly because of the softness of the material. There are no measurements for single finger joints. At my hospital, however, it has been used for the translation of gestures into interaction commands and thus for navigation in a VR scene.

5.7.3 Stationary Desktop

The Geoball is a stationary desktop device offering 6 dof: 3 for the three rotations (pitch, yaw, roll) in x, y, and z and 3 for the three translations in x, y, and z. The user pushes, pulls, and twists the ball in any direction. Performing translations and rotations with the Geoball involves the application of force pressure to the ball along a specific axis or torque pressure around a specific axis. The values for translation and rotation are derived from the forces that the user applies. Inside the ball are six LEDs in the center, six diaphragm apertures around the LEDs, and six position-sensitive detectors (PSDs). The sensing procedure is based on the measurement of the deflection of the light's position and is converted into voltage, which supplies the data for position and orientation (12).

The Geoball contains optical PSDs, which are mounted in a rigid sphere.

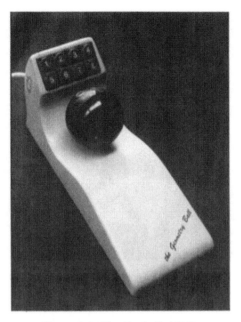

Figure 5.6. The Geoball, (CIS).

The position and orientation are specified by pushing or rotating the sphere. It has full 6 dof. It offers a maximum of 80 data packages/s at 9600 baud. It inherits a RS-232 interface with 300 to 19200 baud.

Because the Geoball is a stationary desk-based input device, it is difficult to put into action in an immersive VR environment, because it cannot be carried around. The Geoball delivers relative positioning values in relation to a 3-D scene but not absolute values.

For my group, it has been useful for the positioning of an arbitrary cutting plane in 3-D CT or MRI datasets. The medical operator performed well when using the ball for rotation and translation interaction tasks, even though the reset to the original position had to be activated often to get back to a well-defined position.

5.7.4 Hand Held

The Logitech 3-D mouse is a typical example of a hand held-device (Fig. 5.7) (13). It consists of three major components: First, the position reference array, which is a triangle of the ultrasonic speakers that send signals to the mouse. Second, the mouse itself contains a triangular set of three microphones that sample signals from the position reference array. The mouse and the triangle communicate along a line of sight. Third, the control unit with a CPU connects the mouse, the speaker triangle, the power supply, and the computer.

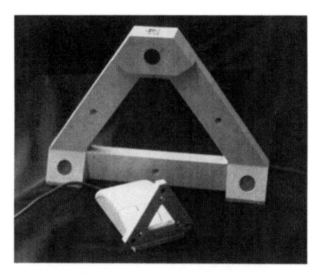

Figure 5.7. The Logitech 3-D mouse (Logitech).

The Logitech 3-D mouse is based on ultrasonic waves. The device can be used as a 2-D and 3-D input device. It can operate in the ordinary 2-D mode as a conventional three-button mouse moving on the desktop. The resolution is 400 dpi. In the 6-D mode it has 6 dof. The device operates using a 3-D Cartesian coordinate system reading x, y, and z axes and pitch, yaw, and roll movements in fine (0.1°) increments within 2 ft.^{3} along each axis. The resolution is 200 dpi along the x, y, and z axis and 0.1° in the pitch, yaw, and roll rotations. The Logitech 3-D mouse delivers absolute values of position and orientation. It has a sample rate of up to 50 updates/s and a RS-232 interface.

The Logitech 3-D mouse has some limitations. It offers high resolution only within 0.6 m^3. The tracking speed is up to 0.76 m/s. The mouse has to face the transmitter triangle and all microphones must be free of obstructions. Tests showed that when, for instance, the operator performs the rotation of an object with the 3-D mouse, the mouse moves out of the working range. This results in picking the object again and then rotating it to the required position. The same occurs for translations. This is a distinct disadvantage. The tests also showed that the mouse is not ergonomically designed for use in free space, as holding it in the hand leads to cramp.

The mouse has been useful for the planning of the treatment of hyperthermia and could also be of help in the planning of radiation treatment. It is interesting to note that this mouse can be used in both 2-D and 3-D modes, making it a device with which the user is already familiar.

5.7.5 Haptic

The most commonly used haptic input device, called PHANToM, was developed by Massie and is now marketed by SensAble Devices (14). It is a 3-D input device with force feedback based on a thimble interface connected to a linkage mechanism. A trio of direct current (dc) brushed motors are responsible for the x, y, and z forces applied to the user's fingertip, which is inserted into a thimble. My project team did not test the PHANToM device and so the following descriptions were taken from the company's information (http://www.sensable.com/products.htm).

The PHANToM is a 3-D input device with force feedback based on linkage mechanism and a thimble interface. The 3 dof and, thus the fingertip's position in space, are measured by optical encoders that are mounted on each motor. It has 400 dpi resolution, offers an exertable force of 8.5 N by the motors, and 1000 updates/s.

The PHANToM works in a limited working space ($0.13 \times 0.18 \times 0.25$ m). It also needs a specialized interface (PC ISA bus board). In medical applications, the PHANToM was used for the cutting of human tissue in a simulated surgical procedure and for performing the simulation of minimal invasive surgical tasks.

5.7.6 Stereoscopic Video Capturing

At UKBF, I began a project to capture stereoscopic video. The Headcam was designed, implemented, and modified as part of a student project by Weingartner (15). The principal idea is that two cameras capture two videos from different viewpoints, producing a stereoscopic video that delivers a 3-D impression.

The implementation of the Headcam resulted in three prototypes. The first prototype was mounted on a headlight for surgical operations (Fig. 5.8). The fixed part of the camera contained a metal stick, mounted at a 90° angle on a metal moveable arm and another metal stick containing two threads. The threads were used to mount the cameras. The prototype had the following disadvantages:

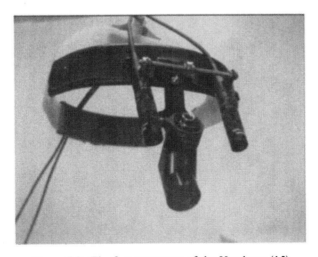

Figure 5.8. The first prototype of the Headcam (15).

- The distance of the two cameras could be changed only with tools.
- The distance of the two cameras was not adjustable with respect to the middle point.
- The convergence of the cameras was not adjustable.
- The vertical parallelism had to be manually adjusted and controlled by looking at the monitor image, which was time-consuming.
- The freedom of movement of the surgeon was reduced.
- The construction was too elastic and not sufficiently rigid.
- The fixation of the cameras was not stable enough; they changed position too easily.

This prototype was evaluated twice in the area of maxillofacial surgery, but improvements were required. This led to the design of the second prototype.

The second prototype had advantages over the first prototype (Fig. 5.9). The distance of the two cameras was easily changeable by a gear wheel around the middle point of the camera installation. The convergence of the cameras was adjustable. The vertical parallelism of the cameras was achieved by fixing them on a common horizontal metal plane.

Nevertheless, some disadvantages should also be mentioned regarding the second prototype:

- The mechanism for adjusting the convergence of the cameras was inexact.
- The convergence angle of the cameras could be changed only individually and could not be done synchronously.

Figure 5.9. The second prototype of the Headcam (15).

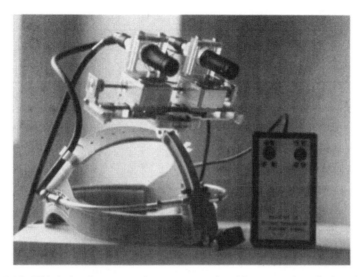

Figure 5.10. Third development of a stereoscopic video-capturing device, including remote control.

- The minimal camera interdistance should be 25 mm, but the prototype provided only 40 mm.
- The pointing directions of the headlight and cameras were not combined.
- The whole mechanics for adjustment were too heavy, too big, and too clumsy and could not be remotely controlled.

Because the results of the second prototype were not fully acceptable, it was decided to have the third prototype built professionally to ensure precise fabrication (Fig. 5.10). This fabrication is more precise than the other two prototypes and ensures a better adjustment of the position and angle of the two cameras. Two motors drive the distance between the cameras and their viewing angle. The remote control for both motors was developed at my laboratory. Tests in the operating theater have yet to be carried out.

5.7.7 Two-Dimensional

Two-dimensional input devices are useful for delivering numerical value and text data that are generally necessary for all types of interactive systems. In my laboratory, we use these devices for 3-D interaction as well, which requires the software to question the user about the individual rotation and orientation values. The main disadvantage of this type of interaction is that it is intuitive for the user to understand the individual transformation but not the 3-D combination. Owing to its widespread usage, the 2-D mouse has often been used for inputting rotation and translation values. Devices have been developed for stationary desktops and hand-held devices (Table 5.3).

TABLE 5.3. Self-Made 2-D Input Devices

Class of Device	Example of 2-D Input Device	Description	Limitations	Medical Application
Stationary desktop	Dialbox (Krauss, TU Berlin)	Dialbox with potentiometers; 8 dof; resolution of 8 bit/axis; 150 updates/s; RS-232 interface at 9600 baud	Nonintuitive knob layout	Could be used for positioning an arbitrary cutting plane in a 3-D CT or MRI dataset
Hand-held	ZAP (Krauss, TU Berlin)	Input device based on an infrared remote control; 17 buttons; 4 updates/s. RS-232 interface at 9600 baud	Nonintuitive button layout of infrared control; poor update rate for real-time interaction	Could be used for navigation in 3-D CT or MRI datasets

5.8   VR OUTPUT DEVICES

Human beings normally perceive the real world as it is, which means in 3-D. Therefore, 3-D output is one of the key features determining the quality of VR applications. The following classes of 3-D output devices will be discussed:

- Special glasses can be worn to create the 3-D impression of the 2-D view of the VR scene. The multiplexing of the two stereoscopic images on a single display must be achieved so that the glasses can de-multiplex the images for the correct eye.
- Head-coupled displays (HCDs) are usually CRT-based stereoscopic viewing devices with a wide-angle optic. They present the two stereoscopic images on its two displays (one for the right eye and one for the left). The device is placed on a moveable stand. Tactile feedback can also be given.
- HMDs are typically made of image display elements, optics, and electronics and provide wide-angle stereoscopic imaging. They also usually present the two stereoscopic images on two screens (one for the left eye and one for the right), which are fused by the user's brain. The special optics are required not only to bring the user's vision of the displayed images into focus but also to widen the field of view.
- Projection areas consist of a certain number of screens in combination with the same number of video projectors to create a VR room; the aim is

Figure 5.11. SGS 610 (Tektronix).

to fill the visual field. Special glasses have to be worn to get the stereo-scopic impression.

• 3-D audio displays provide spatial audio cues.

5.8.1 Glasses

One technique for providing stereoscopic display is the multiplexing of the two stereoscopic images onto a single display (usually an ordinary video monitor). The realization of this technique requires the wearing of special glasses to de-multiplex the images for the correct eye.

One type of stereo glasses is based on polarization, e.g., the glasses from Tektronix with their shutter or liquid crystal modulator (Fig. 5.11). When used with stereo glasses, the shutter acts as a fast optical switch and transmits the left image of the stereogram only to the left eye, blocking it from the right eye. The glasses then switch and do the same to the right eye. The stereoscopic modula-tor encodes each of the two images differently: left circularly polarized light for the left eye and right circularly polarized light for the right eye.

The SGS 610 system contains a 19-in. active liquid crystal shutter, which has to be mounted in front of the monitor, and passive polarization glasses. The active shutter works so that, for the right eye, it provides the turn on time of 0.35 ms maximum; for the left eye, it is 3.25 ms maximum. Therefore, each picture for each eye has the required specific polarization. The average light transmission is 12%. It works with 60 or 120 fields/s.

A   B

Figure 5.12. CrystalEyes (Stereo Graphics). **A**, Glasses with sync box. **B**, Glasses with the PC controller box.

The SGS 610 has limitations. The vertical resolution of the frame buffer is only half of the normal nonstereo mode (V sync is doubled). There is no total immersion into the 3-D graphic scene.

The device could be employed for molecular structure visualization. At UKBF, we found it useful for the visualization of 3-D CT and MRI datasets. The lightweight passive glasses are comfortable to wear. It is also satisfying that, owing to the passivity of the glasses, the user can look in another direction from the monitor and can see the environment in the normal way.

Some systems time multiplex stereo images on the display, showing each image alternately. The user has to wear see-through shutter glasses and to look at the monitor (Fig. 5.12). This technique involves the multiplexing of the two images on a display that is stereo ready. The glasses de-multiplex the image for the correct eye.

The active shutter glasses consist of cells mounted in front of each eye (liquid crystal lenses) that turn opaque when a voltage is applied. These are synchronized with the display, so that each eye sees the correct image when it appears, by detecting the infrared signals broadcast by the emitter to switch the liquid crystal lenses in exact synchronization with the image fields as they are displayed by the monitor. CrystalEyes is a field-sequential, electrostereoscopic system in which the views are alternated at 120 fields/s.

The CrystalEyes are active liquid crystal shutter glasses (LCD) with a transmittance of 32%. The field rate is 90 to 150 fields/s. The synchronization with the computer monitor is performed by a sync box via wireless infrared signals.

The limitations of CrystalEyes include the following. The vertical resolution of the frame buffer is only half of the normal nonstereo mode (V sync is doubled). There is no total immersion into the 3-D graphic scene. If the user looks in another direction from the monitor, the glasses are still active and thus the shutter opens and closes all the time. Consequently, the view of the real environment is disturbed.

The glasses are used at the UKBF with the Silicon Graphics and the PC for the visualization of rendered 3-D CT and MRI datasets.

5.8.2 Head-Mounted Display

HMDs are often seen within the VR context and are the most commonly associated output devices for this purpose (16). There are a variety of models on the market, which differ in price, resolution, color, viewing angle, and weight. A HMD is typically made up of image display elements, the optics, and the electronics and provides wide-angle stereoscopic imaging.

Head-mounted displays generally have a binocular optical system that is worn on the head of the user, presenting an image of the stereo pair directly to each eye. Therefore, stereoscopy is used to give the illusion of depth in the overlapping display area between the two eyes. Most HMDs also have a 3-D tracking subsystem that allows the absolute location and orientation of the helmet in space. Hence the viewing direction of the user can be determined, which updates the presented image. The precise location of the head of the user has to be accomplished in real time. HMDs are often equipped with a 3-D sound system.

The disadvantages for medical usage are the relatively low resolution, considering some of the fine structures in medical visualization; the uncomfortable helmet construction; and its direct cabling to the computer.

For the surgical teaching, the project team at the UKBF is examining the suitability of the VISTA HMD (Fig. 5.13).

The VISTA is a head-mounted stereoscopic viewing device. The displays are LCD type with full color and a resolution of 640 × 480 pixels per eye. The field of view is 30° diagonal with 18° (V) by 24 in. (H). They are not see through, but the optics can be easily folded up so that the view onto the real operation field is free. The optics consist of plastic aspheric lenses that have an independent optical path for each eye and provide 100% overlap for stereoscopic viewing. The headset is adjustable for the size of the head of the wearer and the user's interpupillary distance (IPD). The possible IPD range is aimed at being suitable

A   B

Figure 5.13. Prototype of the VISTA HMD. **A**, Side view. **B**, Inside view showing the two displays.

for 95% of adults. The VISTA weighs 907.2 g. It contains Sennheiser digitally compatible headphones and a built-in microphone. The head tracker can be a Polhemus or an Ascension sensor. The control unit provides a horizontal scan rate of 31.5 Hz and a vertical scan rate of 60 Hz. It provides genlocked inputs (genlocking supplies a common sync signal), so that there is the possibility of independent phased locked loops for the left and the right eye. It has connectors for VGA, BNC, RGB, H&V, and RCA connectors.

Unfortunately, HMDs are relatively heavy and uncomfortable to wear. The direct cabling to the computer restricts action. If the user turns more than once in the same direction, there is a possibility of being trapped in the wires. It is not usable for intraoperative procedures by the main surgeon, as the view of the real scene is possible only when the optics are folded up. HMDs could, however, be used for treatment planning, for surgical simulation, and for surgical teaching purposes.

5.8.3   Head-Coupled Display

An HCD provides a full 3-D impression by transmitting stereoscopic images to two output devices and being equipped with an appropriate viewing optics. It seems that the HCD is a more suitable 3-D output device for certain medical applications, such as in research or teaching, than the HMD. The Binocular Omni-Orientation Monitor (BOOM) is a development in the area of head-coupled CRT-based stereoscopic viewing devices with wide-angle optics. One BOOM was developed at Fake Space Laboratories in the United States (17). It consists of a box that contains two small displays for stereoscopic visualization, thus one for each eye. The user views the scene through this optic and sees the 3-D computer-generated world. Using two handles, the user moves the display in any direction. The resolution of the BOOM depends naturally on the resolution of the used CRT, and it could be also monochrome.

In my laboratory at UKBF Krauss developed an HCD named SimStim (Fig. 5.14).

The SimStim is a head-coupled, monochrome, CRT-based stereoscopic viewing device with optics and tactile feedback. It has PAL resolution (768 × 576 pixels per eye). The Logitech US head tracker for sensing position and orientation has been integrated. There are two buttons for user input. Among its limitations is a disturbing image distortion caused by optics is perceivable. It was used in my laboratory for the visualization of 3-D CT and MRI datasets.

5.8.4   Virtual Model Display

Virtual model displays (VMDs) allow the user to see and interactively work with the 3-D objects that are projected onto a flat surface. The Responsive Work-bench (German National Research Centre for Computer Science) belongs to this class (18). The Responsive Workbench consists of a rear projected table with a

Figure 5.14. SimStim (Krauss, TU Berlin).

horizontal screen and allows one to work with virtual objects. It is aimed at showing the possibilities for future cooperative work within a VR environment.

5.8.5 Spatially Immersive Display

Spatially Immersive Displays (SIDs) rely on wraparound video from multiple sources projected onto either a dome or panoramic rectangular screens. The viewer walks into the SID environment and has the "you are there" experience in the virtual world.

The CAVE (CAVE Virtual Reality Theater) is a projection-based VR system (http://evlweb.eecs.uic.edu/EVL/VR). Created by scientists at the Electronic Visualization Laboratory in 1992, the CAVE is a 10 ft.^{3} structure that sits in a 35- × 25- × 13-ft. darkened room. It is a room with an open side and no ceiling in which the user can walk around wearing a pair of CrystalEyes glasses.

5.8.6 3-D Audio

In a VR environment, there is the need to have interactive 3-D sound in real time. It should inherit the full spectrum of acoustics, including Doppler effects (the phenomenon characterized by a change in the apparent frequency of a sound wave as a result of relative motion between the observer and the sound), the spatial relation of the object to the environment, and the acoustics influencing parameters of the environment's objects in accordance with the original environment. The reproduction of a stationary or freely moveable sound source in space has to be exactly positioned. The acoustics parameters of the environment should be changeable so that rooms of different sizes or outside environments with all the involved reflections and transmissions can be modeled. In my laboratory, we did not purchase any kind of 3-D audio system. Therefore, the following descriptions were taken from the sales information.

The Acoustetron II of Crystal River Engineering is an interactive 3-D audio sound server that provides the full spectrum of 3-D sound to high-end graphics workstations, such as Silicon Graphics computers (http://www.cre.com/ acoust.html). It is a stand-alone, spatial sound-processing system (the audio server). It is controlled from a central simulation computer (the audio client) over a communication line (RS 232 by default). The client sends information, such as audio source and listener positions, to the server via RS232. The server continually computes source, listener, surface relations, and velocities and renders up to 16 separate spatialized sound sources accordingly. The audio output can be presented over headphones, nearphones, or speakers. Sounds can originate from digitized sound samples (wave files) or external live inputs, such as CD tracks or microphones. The sounds are processed at the rate of 44,100 16-bit samples/s (CD quality) from 8 simultaneous sources, or 22,050 16-bit samples/s from 16 sources. An ANSI C function interface allows the development of 3-D sound spaces and the integration of real-time 3-D audio into existing VEs. At an update rate of 44 Hz, sounds are rendered at their exact position and orientation in space, as perceived by the listener and appear to move seamlessly in the VE. Medical application areas are rehabilitation, training, and simulation for which additional cues for nontransferable information can be delivered.

5.9   PARTICULARITY OF A MEDICAL VR SYSTEM

A major application area for VR lies in medicine, because all patients are 3-D and even 4-D, if time is taken as another dimension. The fourth dimension could, for example, describe physiology. A 3-D system with complete 3-D interaction is convenient and user-friendly. However, the multidimensionality increases the complexity of the system and, consequently, the interaction process. The hope is that a VE system will include a "natural user interface" providing a self-explanatory, intuitive, user-friendly but powerful interaction.

VR offers the ability to look inside a patient without making any incisions. Three-dimensionally reconstructed data from CT or MRI provide a good database for this purpose. After building a simulator based on 3-D data, training can be undertaken easily and without harm to a patient. This can enhance the quality of an operation performed on a real patient. VR is advantageous for the simulation of different surgical techniques. A medical student or inexperienced surgeon can train in the techniques he or she needs to perfect. The whole operative process, including the result of the operation, can be simulated without the direct involvement of a patient. Training with a VR system can also be helpful when the available patient data are derived from a video signal; such as with endoscopy (a minimally invasive medical technique).

To create a VR system that receives full user acceptance, an additional functionality (such as assistance for the navigation of the surgical instruments during surgery) should be given to the doctor to fulfil the routine working task. The pure imitation of a real working situation gains no real benefit for the user because, first, the realization is often technically difficult or even impossible, and, second, it is an effort for the user to learn to handle a new system when fully content with the current working situation. Systems for the daily clinical routine are not yet possible, owing to the lack of appropriate solutions because the currently existing systems are still being researched.

A VR system in surgery, when it is used in an operating theater, technically differentiates from a nonsurgical VR system by the sterility and security requirements. It should be stressed that the quality and accuracy of the data calculation and visualization have to be high enough to satisfy the demands of the surgeon for a VR system that assists a real surgical incision.

5.9.1 Application Areas

In medical applications, the three senses of sight, sound, and touch should be thoroughly considered and an appropriate feedback provided to these senses. The given feedback has to be in accordance with the stimuli within the real world, so that the user receives, for instance, when sound is expected, audio and not visual feedback.

To build a VR system, user and task analyses should help define the users, their tasks, and thus the purpose of the system. Six main areas exist for medical applications and, which are discussed below; an example is given for each category:

> *Diagnosis.* At the University of North Carolina, Chapel Hill, a system has been developed that provides an augmented view of an unborn child. (Augmented reality is a special type of VR that aims at enhancing the reality by adding computer-generated information.) The intention is to show live ultrasound data for the pregnant woman (19). The visualization is accomplished by a small video camera on the front of a HMD worn by the observer. The images of the video camera are composed with computer-generated images, which comprise one or more 2-D ultrasound images that have been transformed to the current viewing position of the observer. These echographic images are obtained by an ultrasound scanner, and then the position and orientation in 3-D are tracked with 6 dof. Simultaneously, the position and orientation of the HMD are tracked. Based on this geometry, an imaging system is able to generate 3-D renderings of the 2-D ultrasound images.

Planning. Lorensen et al. (20) developed a system that claims to "enhance reality in the operating room." The acquisition of CT or MRI data is followed by image processing to improve signal-to-noise ratios by applying the edge-preserving diffusion algorithm as a noise-reduction and edge-sharpening filter. The subsequent segmentation process classifies tissues within the 3-D volume, identifying brain surface, cerebral spinal fluid, edema (fluid), tumor, and skin. The model can then be constructed for the surfaces of each tissue by applying the marching cubes and dividing cubes algorithms (21). The surgical plan is generated the night before the operation. Before preparing the patient for the operation, the video and computer-generated surfaces of the patient are aligned and combined. During the operation, this fused video signal gives the surgeon additional help for the localization of the tumor.

Simulation. At Georgia Institute of Technology, researchers are trying to simulate surgery on the human eye, where they also include force feedback for the interaction (22). This is of interest not only to the performing surgeon but also to medical students, because they can get the feeling of the surgical procedure.

Tele (remote) medicine. The Artma Virtual Patient (ARTMA Inc.) belongs to the stereoendoscopic systems and uses augmented reality to merge a video image with 3-D data (23). Data fusion is a complicated task, because the system has to find the correct location where the data are to be superimposed. The calibration has been achieved by fiducial markers and surface fitting. Therefore, 3-D sensors actively track the position of the stereotactical instruments. The 3-D graphics are extracted from CT data or x-ray images. During the operation, the surgeon sees the endoscopic image in combination with predefined reference points that specify important anatomic structures, thereby helping him or her to avoid critical regions. This image fusion also helps find the best trajectory for the surgical incision.

Rehabilitation. At the Loma Linda University Medical Center a 17-year-old patient was suffering from a car accident and VR was applied for rehabilitation purposes. The patient "was motivated to rehabilitate his impaired psycho motor skills through an 'air guitar' interactive system, which converted the weak bioelectric signals from his impaired muscles into 'rock and roll' music" (24).

Teaching. Dumay (25) elaborated on VEs for surgical training at the TNO Physics and Electronics Laboratory. He stated that it is not surprising that surgical simulation systems are accepted because people like to train with hands-on systems in which they are actively committed to the learning task. The aim is to give the human an experience with a VR surgical simulation system that is near to reality.

After the user and task analyses, the data of the scene with all its objects have to be specified. The major subject of medical activities is the patient.

Medical imaging equipment, such as CT and MRI, delivers the source data of the patient. Depending on the purpose of the imaging system and the diagnosis or treatment-planning technique, a different amount and type of patient data are available. After acquisition, these data have to be transferred into the VR system, assuming the data format can be handled. Under certain circumstances, the data are preprocessed, for example, to eliminate artifacts. By interacting with the computer, the user determines the parts of the scene that are to be either visible or obscured. Like in the real world, it should be possible to manipulate objects including their position, orientation, and physical properties.

5.9.2 Applications at the University Hospital Benjamin Franklin

Co-operation with the Clinic for Oral Surgery and Plastic Surgery at the UKBF was the precondition to the proposal of a joint project in the field of VR applications. The project is now funded by the German Research Council.

The aim of the whole project is the visual 3-D control of planning and conducting the surgical operation. Therefore, the surgeon needs a tool to preoperatively perform a computer-based planning in 3-D based on CT or MRT scans. The lack of a variable and inexpensive model on which a surgical planning procedure can be performed as often as desired led to the concept of the Interactive Articulator, which is a computer-simulated interactive planning tool for maxillofacial surgery. Another aim of the project is the intraoperative visualization of the 3-D planning results.

5.9.2.1 Current Planning. The current planning of the operation is carried out using different sources of information and conventional tools, such as ortho-pan-tomogram (OPTG), WINCEPH (a PC-based program), an articulator, and in special cases a stereo lithographie. The OPTG is a panoramic slice image procedure that offers the possibility of obtaining the whole of both dental arches on one film (Fig. 5.15). It mainly serves diagnostic purposes. The PC-based program WINCEPH offers a 2-D analysis of the patient's profile (Fig. 5.16). It compares these values with standard values and is used mainly for documentation purposes. A gypsum model is used for performing the proposed

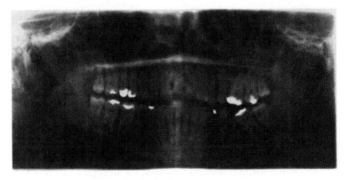

Figure 5.15. Ortho-pan-tomogram.

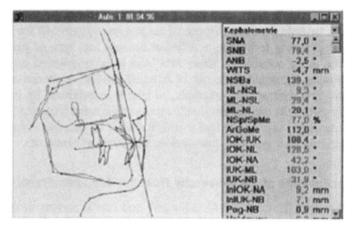

Figure 5.16. Screen shot of the kephalometric planning tool WINCEPH.

surgical procedure. The model is placed in the articulator, which allows the possibility of measuring the jaw in three dimensions and simulating the joints of the jaw (Fig. 5.17). It is used, for example, to show where exactly an abnormal occlusion occurs. The stereo lithography creates a synthetic resin model based on the CT scan. The skull is selected by a segmentation process. The model is very costly and, as a result, is only produced in special cases (Fig. 5.18).

The surgeon uses the two models to gain a 3-D impression of the patient's anatomy and the planned surgical operation. Inherent in these planning tools are the following problems: They are expensive, owing to the production costs of the plastic model, and they are invariable, because if a part has been cut out of the gypsum model, it is difficult to put it back.

Figure 5.17. Articulator with the patient model of the upper and lower jaw made out of gypsum.

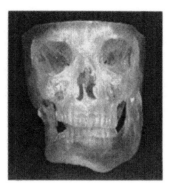

Figure 5.18. Plastic model of the patient's skull.

5.9.2.2 Real-Time Rendering. The crucial question of VR systems is the real-time visualization of complex structures with sufficient detailed information. Virtual sphere rendering (VSR) was developed by Neumann (26) and offers a real-time rendering by precalculation. CT and MRI deliver the data cube for 3-D rendering, but other image formats are possible. The main idea of VSR is that a virtual sphere is placed around the data cube. The sphere consists of 5000 views: 100 views along the degree of latitude and 50 along the longitude (27). This sphere allows quasi-continuous views of the dataset from all view points.

5.9.2.3 Through-the-Window 3-D Visualization. The VSR algorithm has been used for planning purposes. Input data are currently in a CT dataset. The surgeon can view the 3-D stereoscopic images using the CrystalEyes glasses. The CT data are rendered in the following ways: surface rendering based on a threshold algorithm (Fig. 15.19), rendering showing transparencies based on Levoy (Fig. 15.20), maximum projection (Fig. 15.21), sum projection (Fig. 15.22), and definition of a region of interest (ROI) and display of the original slices in the ROI (Fig. 15.23).

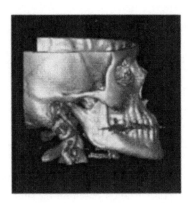

Figure 5.19. Opaque image with threshold for skull.

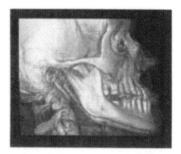

Figure 5.20. Transparent display of the skin with the underlying bone structure.

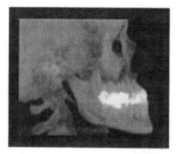

Figure 5.21. Visualization owing to maximum projection.

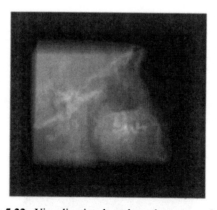

Figure 5.22. Visualization based on the sum projection.

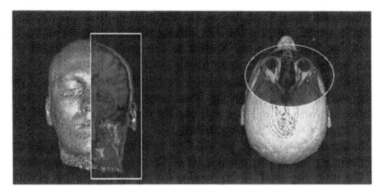

Figure 5.23. ROI as a rectangle and circle, showing the original data in the ROI.

The output is created by a simple surface rendering that is based on a pure threshold for detecting the surface, as shown in Figure 15.19. After it is detected, the surface is shaded. The user has the choice of selecting between one and four thresholds for segmentation. If more than one threshold is selected, the detected surfaces of the different ranges are displayed in different colors.

The transparent rendering of Levoy has also been implemented (28). This procedure gives each voxel not only a color c_{local} but also an opacity value α_{local}, which determines the amount of light transmission. The opacity value is determined in relation to the density of the tissue and the local gradient of the voxel gray values. This ensures that the border areas of a certain tissue could be used as reflection areas. The color and opacity value of one voxel along the viewing ray are calculated by:

$$\alpha_{out} \cdot c_{out} = \alpha_{in} \cdot c_{in} + (1 - \alpha_{in}) \cdot \alpha_{local} \cdot c_{local}$$

where c_{in} and α_{in} are the calculated values up to this point. The maximum projection algorithm finds the maximum value of the voxels lying on the viewing ray, which is projected in direction z. The sum projection algorithm adds all gray values of the voxels lying on the viewing ray, which is projected in the z direction.

The 3-D visualization can be combined with the visualization of the original data, which are displayed only in the defined ROI. The definition of the size and shape of the ROI is performed interactively. The user can scan through the dataset in any depth to see specific original data. The various visualization modes can be precalculated using VSR and then shown as alternating among the different rendering procedures, e.g., Levoy and surface, but with the same viewing perspective.

5.9.2.4 Interactive Articulator. The Interactive Articulator is based on VSR, so a new approach has been taken. The planning tool is not based on a wire frame model using FEM, but tackles the problem from the visualization of a volumetric model, keeping the 3-D volume model as the database. This has the advantage that one is not limited to the surfaces of selected anatomic structures but can view inside every object.

To obtain a realistic 3-D impression during the computer-based planning, my group used stereoscopic viewing. Two images were created for one view of the dataset: one for the right eye and one for the left. The CrystalEyes glasses served as the stereoscopic viewing device.

For intraoperative viewing, we will first used an ordinary display and then the see-through glasses. The advantages of the see-through glasses are that we can use the planning result as an overlay on top of the patient and that currently invisible structures (i.e., they are hidden underneath other body parts) can be made visible. To achieve the overlay, the actual position and orientation of the patient have to be registered. We use the magnetic 3-D sensor Polhemus 3Space Fasttrack for that task. The matching of the different imaging sources is performed by the Virtual Patient System. The registration of the patient data has to be performed with high accuracy. Therefore, a specific splint has been designed at the UKBF. The splint includes measurement points (four on the right and eight on the left side as well as one on the front side) that serve as external fiducial markers.

5.9.2.5 Integration of the Virtual Patient System. The Virtual Patient System was chosen for the intraoperative control of the surgical operation by comparison with the preoperative planning (http://www.artma.com/html_files/products.html). The final installation at the UKBF will consist of the following components: Power Macintosh 8600/300, network access using TCP/IP, Fasttrack 3-D sensor, head-up display, video camera, Headcam, stereoscopic video cameras, Indigo 2, CrystalEyes stereoscopic glasses, and Virtual Patient software.

5.9.2.6 Intraoperative Navigation Aid. The intraoperative assistance of the navigation is planned to be performed by the overlay of the actual patient together with the planning result at the accurate position and location of the patient's anatomy. In the first step, we want to use a normal display for the visualization of the planning results. In the next step, we aim at using a head-up display (HUD), which gives the surgeon the see-through possibility and allows a free view of the patient synchronously with the planning results. It is aimed at moving parts of the patient's anatomy freely in space during the operation. Therefore, we designed and built a splint that carries the 3-D Polhemus sensor (Fig. 5.24). On the splint, the dissected part of the anatomy, such as a bone, is fixed. Owing to registration performed ahead of time, it is possible to see the bone's position and orientation on the preoperatively taken scans in correlation to the actual patient's position in the operating theater.

Currently, we are installing the software and hardware in the operating theater and are faced with problems such as interferences and the typical problems one faces when transferring the setup from the laboratory into the

Figure 5.24. Splint for intraoperative use.

real environment. This big step should never be underestimated, because each real medical environment is unique.

5.10 COST–BENEFIT ANALYSIS

To determine if a VR environment is worth the effort, one must take into account the costs. This includes the cost of equipment, the necessary space, the development expenditure in the form of people and time, the teaching and training in the form of the trainer and students, the maintenance and the fixed cost of the running the application.

On the benefits side, one should consider that better training can lead to improved treatment and rehabilitation, which can result in a shorter stay in hospital and a better healing process. The nonmonetary benefits for the patient are difficult to measure, because only a long-term study with two control groups can show if the new techniques have an improving effect on the health of the patient. As a further benefit, an artificial training object can reduce the number of required living test subjects.

If one calculates the benefits of VR in numbers, one will see that a profit cannot be made as long as the planning process is not paid for by health insurance as an individual item.

5.11 CONCLUSION

This chapter described the components of VR systems. Special emphasis was given to the variety of 3-D interaction devices, their technical realizations, and the advantages and drawbacks. The medical field requires special attention because of its restricting environment with severe consequences for the health of the patient. The implementation of a VR system for assisting the navigation during maxillofacial surgery is currently under way at the University Hospital Benjamin Franklin in Berlin under my supervision.

VR has been published all too often under the heading of the new "magic tool," adding to the hype surrounding VR. Unfortunately, there has not been enough serious research up until now. Questions such as the following need to be addressed: Why aren't there more self-developed devices from the universities? Why do most universities buy equipment, apply them within VR, and call that research? Does this mean that the devices and equipment are already optimal?

I believe that presently there is no sufficiently adequate 3-D input or output device. Although a considerable amount of research has been done, further research is required. There continues to be a lack of computing power to enable the developer to use detailed information to create a VR environment and still have the required response time. Therefore, the designer must find a compromise between realism and the technically possible state of the art.

The technical descriptions given here should help one compare existing devices, hardware, and software systems, assisting with setting up a VR laboratory while keeping in mind all technical problems and human factors. The effort of setting up a VR laboratory in medicine should not be underestimated, nor should one overestimate the possible outcome. Be warned!

Despite the difficulties involved in establishing a VR laboratory, there are still many interesting research topics that will be challenging to solve. It seems promising to use VR to create an appropriate interaction, because it enables the doctor to improve the spatial understanding of the patient data. This technology offers a natural way of human–computer interaction for multidimensional medical data. The major advantage is that VR offers the ability to look inside a patient without making any incisions.

ACKNOWLEDGEMENTS

The Intra-operative Navigation Assistance project is funded by the German Research Council (DFG-To 108/6-1) and began on January 1, 1997; the first stage finished on December 31, 1998. The project team is grateful for this support. I should also like to thank Manfred Krauss and Johann Weingartner for their productive cooperation and the developments created at our laboratory. My special thanks goes to Lyn Faulkner for the proofreading; Metin Akay for his encouragement with this chapter; and to my husband, Duncan Faulkner, for all his support.

REFERENCES

1. K. Pimentel and K. Teixeira. Virtual Reality: through the new looking glass. Intel/Winderest/McGraw-Hill, New York, 1993.

2. D. Scott. Human-Computer Interaction, A Cognitive Ergonomics Approach. Ellis Horwood, New York, 1991.

3. E. B. Goldstein. Sensation and Perception. Wadsworth Publishing Company, Belmont, 1989.

4. M. L. Heilig. El Cine del Futuro: The Cinema of the Future. Presence 1:279–294, 1992.

5. R. S. Kennedy, M. G. Lilienthal, K. S. Berbaum, and L. J. Hettinger. Profile Analysis of Simulator Sickness Symptoms: Application to Virtual Environment Systems. Presence 1:295–301, 1992.

6. G. Allison, B. Catterall, M. Galer, M. Maguire, and B. Taylor. Tools for User Centred Design, Proc. of HUFIT Seminar, Loughborough University of Technology, October 10–13, 1989.

7. G. Faulkner and M. Krauss. Guidelines for Establishing a Virtual Reality Laboratory for Medical Applications, IEEE-EMBS Special Issue on "Virtual Reality and Multimedia in Medicine", Vol. 15, No. 2, March/April 1996, 86–93.

8. R. Kalawsky. From visually coupled systems to virtual reality: an aerospace perspective. Proc. of Computer Graphics, London: 121–130, 1991.

9. R. Kalawsky. The Science of Virtual Reality and Virtual Environments. Addison Wesley Publishing Company, Wokingham, 1993.

10. G. Burdea and P. Coiffet. Virtual Reality Technology. John Wiley & Sons, New York, 1994.

11. A. Watt. Fundamentals of Three-Dimensional Computer Graphics. Addison-Wesley Publishing Company, Wokingham, 1989.

12. S. Aukstakalnis and D. Blatner. Silicon Mirage The Art and Science of Virtual Reality, Berkley: Peachpit Press, 1992.

13. G. Hirzinger. Space Robot Activities—A Survey, Deutsche Forschungsanstalt für Luft- und Raumfahrt, Institute for Robotics and System Dynamics, Oberpfaffenhofen, Scientific Report, December, 1992.

14. Logitech Inc: 2D/6D Mouse Technical Refernce Manual, Document 620402-00 Rev A, Fremont, CA, 1991.

15. G. Smith. Call it Palpable Progress in: Business Week, October 9, 1995, 93–94.

16. J. Weingartner. Spezifikation und Implementation eines multimedialen Informationssystems für die Neurochirurgie unter Integration von stereoskopischem Video und Entwicklung einer Head Mounted Stereokamera, Diplomarbeit, Institut für Medizinische Statistik, Epidemiologie und Informatik, Freie Universität Berlin, 1997.

17. Brown, Slater 1991.

18. Fake Space Labs: Extreme Resolution Stereoscopic Display, Binocular Omni-Orientation Monitor (BOOM) 2C, Data Sheet, June 1992.

19. W. Krueger and B. Froehlich. The Responsive Workbench in: IEEE Computer Graphics and Applications, Vol. 14, No. 3, May 1994, 12–15.

20. http://evlweb.eecs.uic.edu/EVL/VR/

21. http://www.cre.com/acoust.html

22. M. Bajura, H. Fuchs, and R. Ohbuchi. Merging Virtual Objects with the Real World: Seeing Ultrasound Imagery within the Patient. ACM Computer Graphics 26: 203–210, 1992.

23. W. E. Lorensen, H. Cline, C. Nafis, R. Kikinis, and D. Altobelli, et al. Enhancing Reality in the Operating Room. SIGGRAPH 94, Course Notes, Course 03, Orlando, July 24–29:331–336, 1994.

24. H. E. Cline, W. E. Lorensen, S. Ludke, C. R. Crawford, and B. C. Teeter. Two Algorithms for Three-Dimensional Reconstructions of Tomograms, Medical Physics, May/June: 320–327, 1988.

25. J. A. Adam. Virtual Reality is for real. IEEE Spectrum 30 (10):22–29, 1993.

26. M. Truppe. Artma Virtual Patient^{TM}. Proceedings of Medicine Meets Virtual Reality II, Interactive Technology & Healthcare: Visionary Applications for Simulation Visualisation Robotics, San Diego, January 27–30:221, 1994.

27. D. Warner, T. Anderson, and J. Johanson. BIO-CYBERNETICS A Biologically Responsive Interactive Interface, The Next Paradigm of Human Computer Interaction—Biosignal Processing. Proceedings of Medicine Meets Virtual Reality II, Interactive Technology & Healthcare: Visionary Applications for Simulation Visualisation Robotics, San Diego, January 27–30:237–241, 1994.

28. A. C. M. Dumay. Cybersurgery. Proceedings of Medicine Meets Virtual Reality II, Interactive Technology & Healthcare: Visionary Applications for Simulation Visualisation Robotics, San Diego, January 27–30:42–44, 1994.

29. P. Neumann. Interaktive dreidimensionale Visualisierung von medizinischen Volumendaten durch Vorberechnung von Ansichten. Diplomarbeit, Technische Universität Berlin, Fachgebiet Computer Graphics, Dezember 1996.

30. P. Neumann, G. Faulkner, M. Krauss, K. Haarbeck, and T. Tolxdorff. MeVisTo-Jaw: A Visualisation-based Maxillofacial Surgical Planning Tool, Proc. of SPIE's Int. Symposium Medical Imaging 1998, San Diego, February 21–27, to be published.

31. M. Levoy. Display of Surfaces from Volume Data, IEEE Computer Graphics & Applications, Vol. 8, Nr. 3, Mai 1988, 29–37.

32. http://www.artma.com/html_files/products.html

CHAPTER 6

Medical Applications of Virtual Reality in Japan

MAKOTO YOSHIZAWA and KEN-ICHI ABE

Graduate School of Engineering
Tohoku University Aoba-yama 05, Sendai 980-8579, Japan

TOMOYUKI YAMBE and SHIN-ICHI NITTA

Institute of Development, Aging, and Cancer
Tohoku University Seiryo-machi, Sendai 980-8575, Japan

Japan is famous as a major power of video games and as an electronically developed industrial country. However, the present Japanese situation of academic research on virtual reality (VR) is not well known because of the linguistic barrier. In this chapter, VR research in Japan and its medical applications is surveyed and the future view of Japanese activities in these fields is discussed.

Information Technologies in Medicine, Volume I: Medical Simulation and Education, Edited by Metin Akay and Andy Marsh.
ISBN 0-471-38863-7   © 2001 John Wiley & Sons, Inc.

6.1 CURRENT VR RESEARCH

In the 1990s in Japan, VR was not sufficiently regarded as an important theme of research but a kind of strange human interface or extended video game. Currently, however, noone has any doubt that VR has a potential for extensive further development. Moreover, VR research in Japan is shifting from the fundamental stage to the application stage (1). It was supported by Grant in Aid for Scientific Research from the Japanese Ministry of Science, Culture and Sports. This project began in 1995 and lasted for 3 years. It involved about 60 representative researchers in a variety of fields, such as engineering, psychology, sociology, pedagogy, brain physiology, and medicine. The purpose of the project was to investigate the interaction between humans and a virtual environment (VE) composed by computers from an interdisciplinary viewpoint. The project consisted of four research groups:

- Elucidation of the human recognition process of VR (spatial recognition, sensory integration, psychological evaluation, etc.).
- Sensory display and sensory–motor interaction (visual, tactile, force, vestibular, etc.) in VR.
- Methods for composition of VR.
- Evaluation from the viewpoint of the internal world (or medical field) and external world (or sociological field).

The first and second reports of 500 pages were published in 1996 and 1997, respectively (2, 3). The final report in Japanese (partly in English) will be published soon.

Taking advantage of this research, the Virtual Reality Society of Japan (VRSJ) was established on May 27, 1996 (4). The focus of VRSJ is to regard VR as synthetic science aiming at fusion among engineering, science, art, and entertainment. The first president was Tachi. Currently, the society has about 650 members. The VRSJ holds annual conferences.

As shown, general VR research in Japan is popular and active in a variety of fields. However, note that there are few actually useful applications for industry besides video games or entertainment machines.

6.2 TRENDS IN MEDICAL APPLICATIONS

In Japan, the medical field has been attracting attention as one of the most typical fields to which VR should be applied. For 2 years, academic sessions for the medical application of VR have been included in a few medical conferences, such as the annual conference of the Japan Society of Medical Electronics and Biological Engineering (JSMEBE) (5) and the Symposium on Biological and

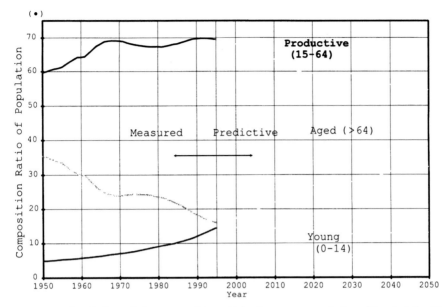

Figure 6.1. Prediction of the composition of the Japanese population. (Reprinted with permission from Ref. 7.)

Physiological Engineering of the Society of Instrument and Control Engineers (SICE) (6). In August 1997 about 10 papers on computer surgery were published in a special issue of JSMEBE's journal. Five presentations on the medical application of VR were given at a recent annual conference of VRSJ.

Currently, computer surgery using VR is being studied by many researchers, as in other countries. However, the focus of Japanese VR research for medicine is influenced by the population problem. Most of Japanese VR research is oriented toward the super-aging society of Japan as shown in Figure 6.1 (7). This is because the Japanese population is concentrated in their 50s, comparet to other generations, and the birth rate is decreasing. Hence, different kinds of research related to VR in consideration of the super-aging society as well as computer surgery have begun in many medical fields.

6.3 SPECIFIC RESEARCH

6.3.1 Computer Surgery, Training, and Education

Oyama at the National Cancer Center Japan is promoting Medical Virtual Reality (MedVR) Projects begun in 1993 as supercomputer studies approved by the Ministry of Health and Welfare (8). This research project aims at using VR technology to advance cancer treatment and support patients who are fighting

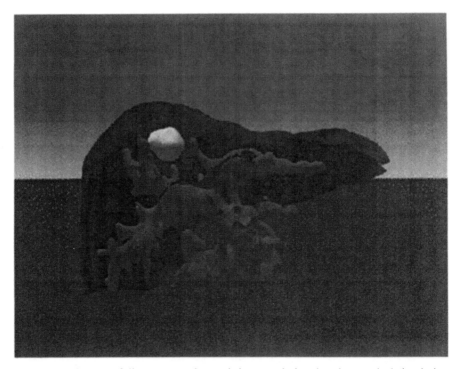

Figure 6.2. Image of liver cancer by real-time rendering by the surgical-simulation support project of MedVR. (Reprinted with permission from Ref. 8.)

cancer. Six virtual reality projects are currently under way: the surgical simulation support project, the psycho-oncological therapy project (in collaboration with Mitsubishi Co. LTD.), the medical education support project, the medical image diagnosis support project, the informed-consent support project (cancer information, VR theater), and the virtual medical communication project (medical VRML). Powerful but orthodox supercomputer systems have been employed to simulate internal organs as a virtual body for surgical operation, medical education, and computerized diagnosis (Fig. 6.2) (9).

Augmented reality for fusing a real world with the imaginary world has the potential to innovate surgical operations. If the patient's body were transparent, surgical operations would become much easier. Iseki (10) at Tokyo Womens' Medical College has developed such a three-dimensional (3-D) image-guide navigation (Volumegraph) for brain surgery as an augmented reality. Volumegraph is an integrated photography-based optical recording system, with multiple microlens and display, that enables us to observe truly 3-D images by means of a beamed light without any special eyeglasses (Fig. 6.3) (11). The images based on the data obtained from CT and MRI before the operation are superimposed on the patient's head and body via a semitransparent mirror. Such image data are applied for preoperative investigation for recognizing the 3-D structure of organs and the tumor.

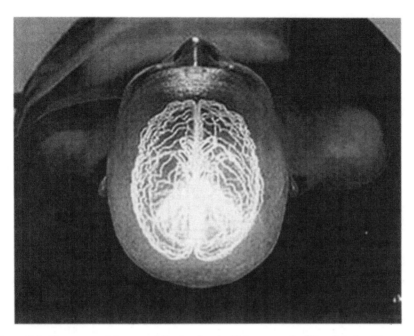

Figure 6.3. Transparent image of the brain via Volumegraph. (Reprinted with permission from Ref. 10)

At present, the projected image of Volumegraph is based on preoperatively obtained data and then static data. Hence, online calibration or correction of the intraoperative distortion during the surgical procedure is quite difficult. On the other hand, ultrasound CT is not balky and is cheaper than x-ray CT and MRI; thus ultrasound CT is useful for VR navigation in operations of soft and moving internal organs.

6.3.2 Remote Medicine

Ymaguchi at Nagoya Institute of Technology developed a prototype tele-medicine system using VR (Hyper Hospital) (12–14). Hyper Hospital aims at restoring the humane interactions between patients and medical caretakers by making a much closer contact between them in the satellite-based communication network and VR environment (Fig. 6.4) (15). He insists that Hyper Hospital can improve such irrational Japanese medical situations as allowing only 2 min for the patient who has been waiting for at least 2 h in the hospital waiting room. Special, aged, or handicapped patients who cannot go to hospitals in the real world will be able to find healing treatment in the Hyper Hospital if the quality and speed of the VR environment increase (Fig. 6.5) (15).

In response to the trend of academic research, the Japanese Ministry of Health and Welfare has recently begun to consider amending related old laws so that remote medicine can be spread all the more in Japan.

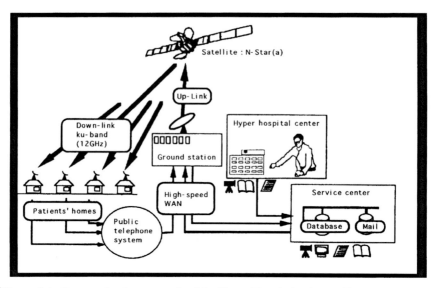

Figure 6.4. Communication network of the Hyper Hospital. The satellite-based network using IP over ATM technology was used to build a high-speed, yet inexpensive, communication system that connects patients' homes to the Hyper Hospital Center. (Reprinted with permission from Ref. 14.)

Figure 6.5. A sample screen from the original local-area network (LAN) version of the Hyper Hospital. This is a simulated outpatient office with consultants, a nurse, and some user-modifiable objects. (Reprinted with permission from Ref. 14.)

Figure 6.6. One scene of Pokemon, which was considered to cause epilepsy-like seizures in Japanese young viewers.

6.3.3 Evaluation of Mental and Physical Influences of VR

At 18:51 on December 16, 1997, a Japanese popular TV cartoon "Pocket Monsters" (Pokemon) caused a serious problem (16). The blight flashing lights used in *Pokemon* triggered epilepsy-like seizures in more than 700 young viewers (Fig. 6.6). As they were rushed to hospitals after watching the programs, further broadcasts of the show were cancelled and video copies were pulled from rental store shelves. Japanese Ministry of Health and Welfare called in doctors, psychologists, and animation experts and asked them to investigate the cause and make a guideline for protecting TV viewers. On April 14, 1998, the research commission announced the first temporary report (17). In it, statistical results and a simple guideline were given, but scientific and substantial causes were not sufficiently clarified.

The report indicated that the blight flashing lights that alternatively change between red and blue at a period of about 10 Hz used in Pokemon may have induced light epilepsy. Because Pokemon is based on a video game produced by a big manufacturer, it is important to ascertain whether video game machines or VR equipment may have bad effects on humans.

In particular, VR forces one to watch a virtual space with unnatural stereo vision, which human beings don't naturally experienc. Hence, the mental and physical effects of VR on the human must be fully investigated from various viewpoints, such as medicine, physiology, psychology, and ergonomics. The fourth purpose of the Important-Territorial Research Project Fundamental Studies on Virtual Reality was introduced to cope with such anxiety.

Independent of this project, the "Feasibility Study on Development of Synthetic Systems for Evaluating Effects of Three Dimensional Image on the Human" was begun on September 18, 1996, by Electronic Industries Association of Japan (18) entrusted by the Japan Society for the Promotion of Machine Industry. The project team consists of about 40 researchers from universities, hospitals, and companies and aims at developing new measurement systems for examining and evaluating bioeffects of 3-D images found in VR, stereo TV, video game machines, etc. The group published an interim report (19) and will give public guidelines for industrial products using 3-D images in the final report. Unfortunately, there may not be an English version of the report.

Yoshizawa et al. (20) at Tohoku University have been studying the biomedical evaluation of head-mounted displays (HMDs) using a physiologic index. They measured heart rate variability, blood pressure variability, and sympathetic nerve activity of healthy test subjects who watched a video tape of a roller coaster scene or calm scene with the HMD or on an ordinary TV set. The ratio of the low-frequency component to the high-frequency component included in the power spectrum density, Lyapunov exponent, and fractal dimensions were extracted from these data. On the basis of these physiologic indexes, the effect of long-term wearing of HMD and differences among the kinds of watching devices and content of the videotape were discussed (Fig. 6.7) (20).

However, it has not yet been concluded that these physiologic indexes are useful enough to give an exact guideline for protecting the human health, because the problems of individual differences and reappearance have not yet been solved. For example, it could be ascertained that Pokemon produced 700 patients with serious convulsions. However, its occurrence is probability only 1/5,000 because the number of viewers who were watching Pokemon simultaneously was no less than 3,500,000. To cope with such problems, it is urgently necessary to find or develop novel and effective measurements, methods of analysis, or experimental protocols. This is because it will be utterly unacceptable to gather test subjects beyond 5,000 if the occurrence probability of the corresponding phenomenon is similar to Pokemon.

6.3.4 Psychotherapy and Rehabilitation

As well as undesirable influences, VR has the potential to give good effects on the human, especially for bed-ridden patients. Ohsuga at Mitsubishi and Oyama at the National Cancer Center have developed a new machine for psychotherapy using VR in the hospital (the Bedside Wellness System) (21, 22) (Fig. 6.8). The purpose of the psychotherapeutic machine is to provide patients with emotional support and to encourage them to enjoy an active life in a virtual space when facing a serious disease such as cancer. This is because patients with an active lifestyle survive longer than those with a passive lifestyle.

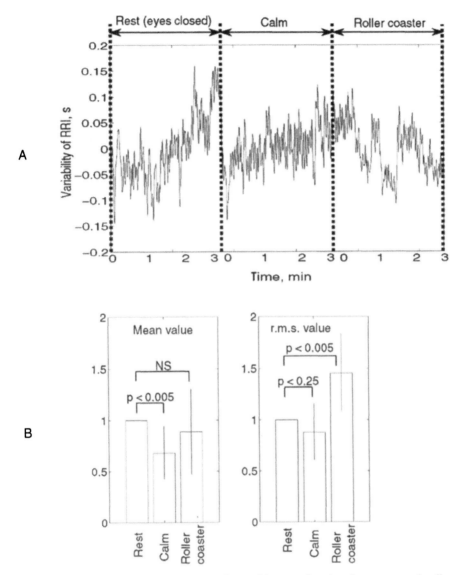

Figurg 6.7. Effects of different contents (rest with eyes closed, calm scene, and roller coaster scene) of videotape watched with a HMD by 15 healthy volunteer subjects (20). A, An example of variability of R-R interval (*RRI*) of heart rate vs. time. B, Mean and root mean square (*r.m.s.*) values over 3 min different ratios of the low-frequency component to the high-frequency component (LF/HF ratio) included in RRI variability (rest = 1). Note that the roller coaster scene caused a significantly higher r.m.s. value of the LF/HF ratio that rest and the calm scene. This implies that mental excitement induced by the roller coaster scene may have been represented as larger time variance of the LF/HF ratio reflected by autonomic nerve activity.

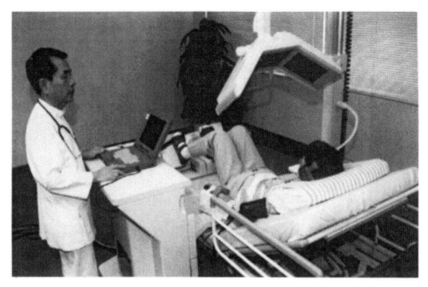

Figure 6.8. The Bedside Wellness System. (Reprinted with permission Ref. 22.)

To provide the mental care for the patient subjected to long-term hospital-ization, this system offers a simulated experience of basking in a forest, the virtual stimulation providing the senses of sight, sound, touch, and smell. The system uses interactive VR technology to provide mental stimulation and rehabilitation at the patient's bedside. The patient can walk through the forest by working a pair of pedals set in the machine and watch photographs synchronized with his or her walking pace. The photographs are displayed on three liquid-crystal screens with a wide visual field of 100°. The presentation includes not only a visual scene but also a fresh wind carrying the smell of the forest and the sounds of small birds, a brook, and trees.

Patients' vital signs (electrocardiogram, blood pressure, and breathing) were measured to evaluate the effect of this treatment and to prevent them from over stimulation. In the future, it is expected that the system will be expanded for use over a network so that two or more people can meet and chat while basking in a forest.

Takeda at the Nagasaki Institute of Applied Science developed a virtual training environment using VR technology with audiovisual images and force-feedback capability (Fig. 6.9) (23). In this system, the trainee wears a HMD and a force display used to apply force to the upper extremity. The force display is a kind of robot arm driven by pneumatically controlled rubber actua-tors; thus it can provide the patient with an appropriate and comfortable force. In the virtual space, the trainee can see a virtual arm and a virtual ball. The virtual arm moves in the same manner as the real arm but a virtual ball moves according to artificial physical laws that can be changed by the trainer as

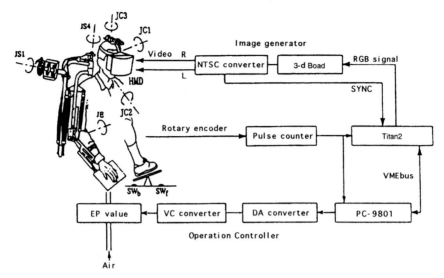

Figure 6.9. Virtual training environment using VR technology with audiovisual images and force-feedback capability. The system enables the trainee to experience virtual ball dribbling. (Reprinted with permission from Ref. 23.)

needed. For example, the trainer can abruptly change the gravity constant or the elasticity rate of the ball to, say, half of its original value.

To increase the effect of the rehabilitation, the element of joyful entertainment was introduced into the system (the Virtual Arm Wrestling Machine) as shown in Figure 6.10 (24). The virtual wrestler can automatically change his behavioral patterns to behave in as similar manner to the real human fighter as possible, because the virtual wrestler's behavior is produced by an adaptive algorithm based on a combination of the classifier algorithm and the genetic algorithm.

6.3.5 Motor Functional Examination

VR also has the potential to be applied to the neurologic examination of the human motor function. This is because VR presupposes a real-time intercommunication between the human and a computer with two kinds of 3-D quantitative information: motor information from the human and sensory information from the computer in the 3-D space. Hence, VR can provide quantitative, objective, and statistical time-series data derived from the motion of the human limbs, head, or trunk. Such data play an important role in neurologic diagnosis or evaluation of the effect of drugs. In addition, clinicians can freely compose the virtual space as they want, and then they can make alterations to the real world and artificial inconsistencies among sensory feedbacks. This leads to studies on effects of diseases on the integrated function of multisensory infor-

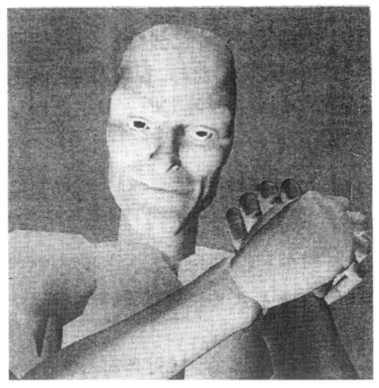

Figure 6.10. Triumphant virtual wrestler shown through the HMD of the Virtual Arm Wrestling Machine. He shows a depressed face when he loses. (Reprinted with permission from Ref. 24.)

mation in the brain with this in mind, Yoshizawa et al. at the Tohoku University developed a neurologic examination system for motor ataxia using VR (Fig. 6.11).

Motor ataxia is a symptom of spinocerebellar degeneration (SCD). In general, patients with SCD have disorders of motor function of the limbs and lack of smoothness and accuracy. For example, dysmetria is one of symptoms of SCD, which is a disorder of the servomechanism of the limbs. When a patient with dysmetria tries to reach out the hand for a target, the hand sometimes goes beyond the target (hypermetria) and sometimes stops before the target (hypometria) contrary to the intention. In addition, the patient with SCD may have intention tremor, which is a tremor that increases in intensity as the limb gets closer to the target.

Traditionally, such patients have been tested with simple methods, without complex tools. For example, the nose-finger-nose test is typical; patients are told to reach their fingertip to the doctor's fingertip and return it to their nose while the doctor is moving his or her fingertip randomly. Of course, such methods lack quantitative, objective, and statistical evaluation.

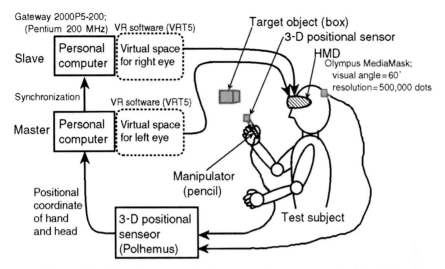

Figure 6.11. Neurologic examination system for motor ataxia using VR.

On the other hand, the system shown in Figure 6.11 aims at making the patient carry out tracking tasks similar to the traditional nose-finger-nose test but in a virtual space. It is an improverment over the traditional one. For example, as shown in Figure 6.12, the patient is told to move the manipulator with Polhemus sensor by hand so that the tip of the virtual pencil may go and return between the patient's nose and the virtual target box. When the tip of the pencil reaches the target, the target disappears and immediately after that, it reappears at another random place. The virtual space was intentionally altered and then became different from the real space to emphasize symptoms of motor ataxia and to induce new symptoms. Two kind of alterations were used:

1. Reversed polarity of the lateral direction. When the manipulator is moved, for example, to the right, the virtual pencil moves to the left, and vice versa.
2. Extended display gain of the depth direction. When the manipulator is moved by the unit distance in the depth direction, the virtual pencil moves, for example, by twice the unit distance.

Figure 6.13 shows an example of time trajectories of the 3-D position of the tip of the virtual pencil (follower) with that of the virtual box (target), which was controlled by a 54-year-old patient with SCD. In this case, only the polarity of the lateral direction was reversed, and the target box appeared randomly only on the sagittal plane. It can be seen that the lateral position of the follower moved to and fro although the lateral position of the target was invariant. Moreover, it is suggested that this disorder in the lateral direction affects the depth direction and causes oscillatory movement in the depth direction.

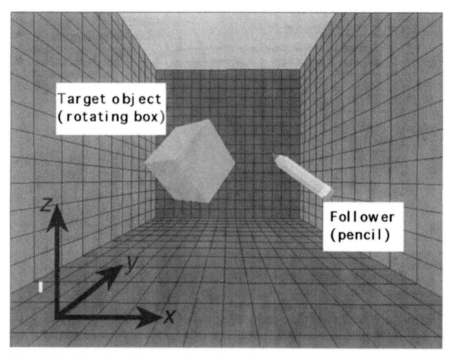

Figure 6.12. Virtual working space in which the patient moves the follower (pencil) with the manipulator to reach the target (box).

In Panel B, note that the time taken from the patient's nose to the target is much longer than the time taken from the target to the nose. This means that the task of tracking to the target, relying on visual feedback (visually closed loop), is difficult but the task of returning to the nose, using only the proprioceptive feedback (visually open loop), is quite easy. The OC-ratio may be an important index for evaluating the patient's motor function because it is possible to use it to classify patients. For example, the OC ratio may be close to unity in patients with a low-level disorder of motor function, whereas it may be much larger in patients with a high-level disorder, such as the integrated function of multisensory information. Of course, the OC ratio may also increase when the visual space is artificially changed.

Figure 6.14 shows the mean value of the OC ratio averaged over five (aged 54 to 78 years) patients with SCD in three stituations with respect to the alteration of appearance of the domain of the target. It can be seen that the OC ratio in the case of laterally reversed polarity is large despite the narrow domain of the target appearance (limited in the sagittal plane), whereas the OC ratio in the case of doubly extended display gain was almost the same as that in the unchanged space. This indicates that it is important to find an appropriate alteration to the virtual space to emphasize symptoms of motor ataxia.

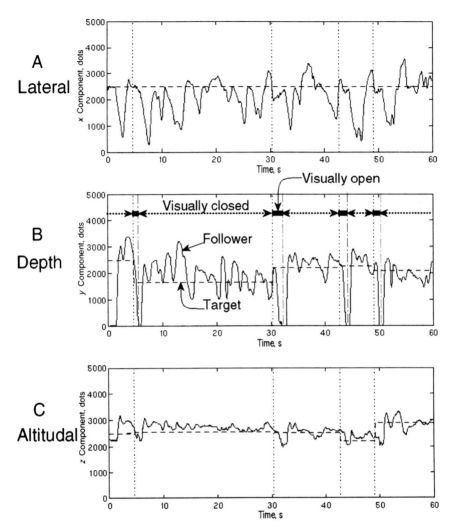

Figure 6.13. An example of time-series data of the 3-D coordinates of the target (*broken line*) and follower (*solid line*) of a patient with SCD. The appearance domain of the target was the sagittal plane, and the polarity of the lateral direction was reversed.

On the other hand, VR can also be used to test human equilibrium function when examining disorders in the vestibular organ or equilibrium center in the brain. The first such approach was done by Yoshizawa's group at Tohoku University in 1985 (25–27). They employed the electronic view finder of a videocamera as a HMD and a CCD camera set on a test subject's head to analyze the human postural control characteristics. By altering the visual feedback information with frequency filtering, it was estimated that the visual information plays different roles in the corresponding different frequency do-

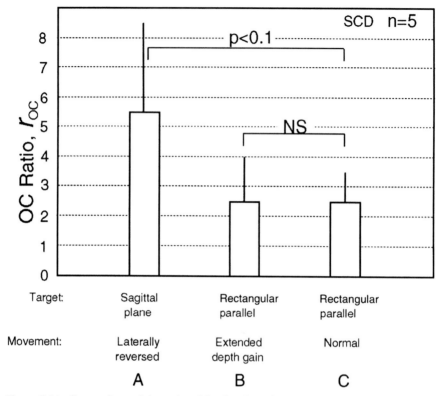

Figure 6.14. Comparison of the ratio of the time in a visually closed loop to the time in a visually open loop (OC ratio) among different combinations of the appearance domain and the alteration (average of 15 patients with SCD).

mains for stabilizing the upright standing. Taking into account that the control of human posture depends strongly on marginal vision, Ifukube et al. (28) tried to analyze the postural control characteristics by use of a HMD or a projector with a wide visual field (29).

6.4 CONCLUSION

As mentioned, applications of VR in medicine in Japan have been progressive and innovative in a variety of fields. To promote such activities, all researchers must solve the following problems:

- Medical, psychological, and social effects of VR on the human beings, especially on children, must be investigated further, urgently, and seriously.
- The price of VR equipment should be decreased for extensive diffusion of VR products for medicine.

- Performance of 3-D sensors, tactile or force displays, and HMDs must be improved further lest VR be misunderstood as just a toy, which is, of course, not limited to medical applications.
- More tools using VR for supporting aged and handicapped people in daily life must be developed.
- To encourage medical doctors to actively work in cyberspace consisting of computer networks and VR, researchers must prepare informative, social, and legal environments and create a new style of medical education.

As for the costs of a VR system, Japanese manufactures are quite suited for developing low-cost VR systems, because it may be easy for them to use video game computers or amusement machines for VR systems. Even after the Product Liability Law was enacted July 1, 1995, in Japan, however, manufactures are still conservative, worried that they would be accused if their products caused a medical accident. Of course, it is also possible that they will change their mind, depending on the results of research into the effects of VR on humans.

REFERENCES

1. http://www.star.rcast.u-tokyo.ac.jp/VRjuten/.
2. S. Tachi, ed. Research report of the Important-Territorial Research Project 'Fundamental Studies on Virtual Reality' (#265) in 1995. Mar 1996.
3. S. Tachi, ed. Research report of the Important-Territorial Research Project 'Fundamental Studies on Virtual Reality' (#265) in 1996. Mar 1997.
4. http://www.vsl.gifu-u.ac.jp/vrsj/.
5. http://www.bcasj.or.jp/me/.
6. http://www.sice.or.jp/.
7. http://www.ipss.go.jp/English/info-e/information-e.html.
8. http://medvr.res.ncc.go.jp/.
9. http://medvr.res.ncc.go.jp/vrip.html.
10. H. Iseki, N. Hata, Y. Masutani, et al., Three dimensional image-guided navigation with overlaid three-dimensional image (Volumegraph) and volumetric ultrasonogram (V-US).
11. http://www.sankei.co.jp/databox/paper/9607/paper/0718/miraisi.html.
12. http://pfsl.mech.nitech.ac.jp/.
13. http://fh.u-tokai.ac.jp/cgi-bin/genpage-e.cgi.
14. http://fh.u-tokai.ac.jp/Articles/MedicalAsahi/medical_asahi-e.html.
15. T. Yamaguchi, Performance tests of a satellite-based asymmetric communication network for the 'Hyper Hospital.' Telemed Telecare 1997;3:78–82.
16. http://headlines.yahoo.com/Full_Coverage/World/Japanese_Cartoon_Triggers_Convulsions/.

17. http://www.mhw.go.jp/houdou/1004/h0414-2.html.
18. http://www.eiaj.or.jp/english/.
19. Japan Society for the Promotion of Machine Industry. Research report of 'Feasibility Study on Development of Synthetic Systems for Evaluating Effects of Three Dimensional Image on the Human.' Mar 1998.
20. M. Yoshizawa, N. Yoshizumi, K. Abe, et al. Evaluation of head mounted display by means of heart rate and blood pressure analysis. Paper presented at the 10th Symposium on Biological and Physiological Engineering.
21. http://www.melco.co.jp/news/1997/0207-f.htm.
22. http://www.melco.co.jp/news/1997/image/0207-f.jpg.
23. T. Takeda, Y. Tsutsui, M. Sato, et al. Computer simulation of basket ball dribble using force display. Hum Interface News Rep 1994;9:241–246.
24. S. Kamohara and T. Takeda, et al. An virtual reality approach to the arm wrestling by CS & GA. Hum Interface News Rep 1995;10:295–300.
25. M. Yoshizawa, N. Yanai, H. Tanaka, et al. Alteration to the visual feedback information and measurement of body sway. Jpn J Hum Posture 1985;5:39–46.
26. M. Yoshizawa, H. Takeda, H. S. Lin, et al. A constrained feedback model of the human postural control system. Paper presented at the 9th Annual Conference of IEEE/EMBS, 1987.
27. M. Yoshizawa, M. Ozawa, and H. Takeda. A frequency domain hypothesis for human postural control characteristics. IEEE EMBS Mag 1992;11:59–63.
28. http://133.50.28.75/eng/english.htm.
29. H. Nara, T. Ifukube, S. Ino, et al. Effects of moving visual stimulation produced from a wide view head mounted display. Trans Virtual Reality Soc Jpn 1996;1:33–39.

CHAPTER 7

Perceptualization of Biomedical Data

EMIL JOVANOV

University of Alabama in Huntsville
Huntsville, Alabama

DUSAN STARCEVIC

Faculty of Organizational Sciences
University of Belgrade
Belgrade, Yugoslavia

VLADA RADIVOJEVIC

Institute of Mental Health
Belgrade, Yugoslavia

Virtual reality technology (VRT) enabled a new environment for biomedical applications (1–6). Increased computing performance emphasizes the importance of human–computer interface, bound by characteristics of human perception. VR technologies shift the human–computer interaction paradigm from a graphical user interface (GUI) to a VR-based user interface (VRUI) (7,8). The main characteristic of VRUI is extension of visualization with acoustic and haptic rendering (1). New interface technology and natural interaction make possible perceptual data presentation. Immersive environments are particularly

Information Technologies in Medicine, Volume I: Medical Simulation and Education, Edited by
Metin Akay and Andy Marsh.
ISBN 0-471-38863-7 © 2001 John Wiley & Sons, Inc.

appropriate for improving insight into complex biomedical phenomena, which are naturally multidimensional (9,10).

The technique of data presentation using variable sound features is called sonification (11–14). We employed sonification to improve insight into spatio-temporal patterns of brain electrical activity (15). Animation on three-dimensional (3-D) models gives insight into spatiotemporal patterns of activity. Visualization is based on topographic maps projected on the scalp of a 3-D head model. We present here the use of sonification for refining temporal cues or introducing new information channels in the human–computer interface. In addition to visualization, which gives predominantly spatial distribution, acoustic rendering improves temporal cues. A novel method of sonification implements modulation of natural sound patterns to reflect certain features of processed data, and creates a pleasant acoustic environment. We used the global vigilance index as a warning signal for drowsiness during EEG analysis. This feature is particularly important for prolonged system use.

Our multimodal interactive environment for biomedical data presentation is based on a VRML head model with sonification used to emphasize temporal dimension of selected visualized scores. We applied VRML language as a standard tool for VR applications in the Internet environment (16). The Virtual Reality Modeling Language (VRML) is a file format for describing interactive 3-D objects and worlds, applicable on the Internet, intranets, and local client systems. VRML is also intended to be a universal interchange format for integrated 3-D graphics and multimedia. VRML is capable of representing static and animated dynamic 3-D and multimedia objects with hyperlinks to other media such as text, sounds, movies, and images. VRML browsers, as well as authoring tools for the creation of VRML files, are widely available for many different platforms. Therefore, we picked VRML as the platform for Internet-based information systems. In our system, the VRML world is controlled by Java applets.

7.1 PERCEPTUALIZATION

Perceptualization is an emerging trend in biomedical data presentation. VR systems already employ efficacy of auditory and tactile techniques for extending visualization and creating immersive environments. The main design issue of VR applications is the user interface. Bernsen (17) proposed a model of human–computer interface with the following layers: Physical representation, input/Output representation, and internal computer representation. A two-step transformation process is required for human–computer interaction. For the input, it is abstraction and interpretation, and for the output representation and rendering.

The physical input media are kinaesthetics (body movement input), acoustics (voice input), and graphics (video capture). The output media are graphics, acoustics, and haptics. In addition, some VR and multimedia systems involve smell output (18).

For example, movement of the finger generated on an input device (keyboard) is a physical representation, pressed character keys. During the abstraction phase, larger symbolic forms, like words and numbers, are recognized. To retrieve the concept behind the representation, the computer uses an interpretation. On the output side, the first transformation process is the representation of the information using some representation modality. Bernsen (19) recognized 20 representational output modalities. For instance, it is possible to present text using different modalities: narration, written text, moving text, moving lips (possibility to lip-reading), and haptic text such as Braille. The second transformation output process is rendering to the representation that the output device can handle.

Technology and tools for multimodal presentation are commercially available owing to the progress of multimedia and VR hardware and software. The success of VR applications mostly depends on the interaction paradigm of the user interface design space (8). Unfortunately, multimedia and VR technology applied in the human–computer interface does not guarantee a successful presentation.

Limited resources of previous-generation information systems established the concept of optimal resource use, which implies nonredundancy. As a consequence, conventional applications still rely on the principle of using minimal resources to mediate the information. Therefore, the presentation modality is mostly unimodal. Simultaneous presentation of the same information in different modalities creates a seamless loss of resources. However, our natural perception is based on redundancy. For example, using mouse as pointing device we are not aware of additional sensory modalities used as feedback: We see the cursor movement, perceive the hand position, and hear the mouse click.

Redundancy of the human–computer interface should be realized using a multimodal presentation. The main issue in the design of multimodal presentation is the level of redundancy. Low-level redundancy increases the cognitive workload, whereas a high redundancy irritates the user. There is an appropriate measure of the multimodal redundancy for a given application.

7.2 SONIFICATION

Early sonification applications mostly used the so-called orchestra paradigm, in which every data stream had an assigned instrument (flute, violin, etc.) (12, 20). Data values were then represented by notes of different pitch. The main advantage of this approach is possibility to apply standard MIDI support, using the system application programming interface (API). Unfortunately, the proposed approach often lead to a cacophony of dissonant sounds, which made it hard to discern prominent features of the observed data streams.

Multimodal data presentation is a complex problem, because of the nature of cognitive information processing (21). Efficiency of sonification, as acoustic presentation modality, depends on other presentation modalities. The most important advantages of acoustic data presentation are faster processing than visual presentation; easier to focus and localize attention in space, which is appropriate for sound alarms; good temporal resolution (almost an order of magnitude better than visual); additional information channel, releasing the visual sense for other tasks; possibility of presenting multiple data streams.

However, all modes of data presentation are not perceptually acceptable. When applying sonification, one must be aware of the following difficulties of acoustic rendering: difficult perception of precise quantities and absolute values, limited spatial distribution, Dependent sound parameters (pitch depends on loudness), Interference with other sound sources (like speech), Absence of persistence, dependent on individual user perception. It can be seen that some characteristics of visual and aural perception complement each other. Therefore, sonification naturally extends visualization toward a more holistic presentation.

There are many possible ways of presentation, so the system must provide the ability to extract the relevant diagnostic information features. The most important sound characteristics affected by sonification procedures are as follows.

- *Pitch* is the subjective perception of frequency. For pure tones, it is basic frequency; and for sounds, it is determined by the mean of all frequencies weighted by intensity. Logarithmic changes in frequency are perceived as a linear pitch change. Most people cannot estimate the exact frequency of the sound.
- *Timbre* is the characteristic of the instrument generating sounds that distinguishes it from other sounds of the same pitch and volume. The same tone played on different instruments will be perceived differently. It could be used to represent multiple data streams using different instruments.
- *Loudness* or subjective volume is proportional to physical sound intensity.
- *Location* of the sound source may represent information spatially. A simple presentation modality may use balance of stereo sound to convey information.

Although mostly used as a complementary modality (22), sound could serve as a major human–computer interface modality (23). Aural renderings of pictures and visual scenes represent important and promising extensions of natural language processing for visually handicapped users. The same technology is directly applicable in a range of hands-free, eyes-free computer systems.

7.2.1 VRML Audio

The VRML specification allows creation of virtual worlds with spatialized, 3-D localized audio sources for achieving a sense of immersion and realism in a virtual environment. Perception of the sound source position is implemented using head-related transfer function (HRTF) algorithms (2,16). The sound node specifies the spatial presentation of a sound source in a VRML scene as follows:

```
Sound {
    exposedField SFVec3f   direction    0 0 1    # (-,)
    exposedField SFFloat   intensity    1        # [0,1]
    exposedField SFVec3f   location     0 0 0    # (-,)
    exposedField SFFloat   maxBack      10       # [0,)
    exposedField SFFloat   maxFront     10       # [0,)
    exposedField SFFloat   minBack      1        # [0,)
    exposedField SFFloat   minFront     1        # [0,)
    exposedField SFFloat   priority     0        # [0,1]
    exposedField SFNode    source       NULL
    field        SFBool    spatialize   TRUE
}
```

The sound is located at a point in the local coordinate system and emits sound in an elliptical pattern. Two ellipsoids are defined with *minFront, minBack, maxFront*, and *maxBack* parameters. The ellipsoids are oriented in a direction specified by the direction field. The shape of the ellipsoids may be modified to provide more or less directional focus from the location of the sound. The *source* field specifies the sound source for the sound node. If the source field is not specified, the sound node will not emit audio. The source field must specify either an *AudioClip* node or a *MovieTexture* node.

The intensity field adjusts the loudness of the sound emitted by the sound node. The intensity field has a value that ranges from 0.0 to 1.0 and specifies a factor that is used to scale the normalized sample data of the sound source during playback. The *priority* field provides a prompt for the browser to choose which sounds to play when there are more active sound nodes than can be played at once owing to either limited system resources or system load. The *location field* determines the location of the sound emitter in the local coordinate system.

7.3 MULTIMODAL VIEWER

We implemented the environment for monitoring brain electrical activity consisting of 3-D visualization synchronized with data sonification of EEG data. Visualization is based on topographic maps projected on the scalp of 3-D head model. Sonification implements modulations of natural sound patterns to reflect certain features of processed data, and create pleasant acoustic environment. This feature is particularly important for prolonged system use.

Principally, there are two possible multimodal data presentations. The simplest one signals state transitions or indicates certain states and is often implemented as a sound alarm. The second one presents current values in a data stream. Additional modes of presentation may be employed as redundant modes of presentation to emphasize certain data features or to introduce new data channels. Redundant presentation creates artificial synesthetic perception of the observed phenomena (24). Artificial synesthesia (Greek, *syn*, "together" and *aisthesis*, "perception") generate sensory joining in which the real information of one sense is accompanied by a perception in another sense. Multisensory perception could improve the understanding of complex phenomena by giving other clues or triggering different associations. In addition, an acoustic channel could facilitate new information channels without information overloading. Audio channels could be also used as feedback for positional control, which could be a significant aid for surgeons in the operating room. Just as musicians use aural feedback to position their hands, surgeons could position instruments according to a preplanned trajectory, preplaced tags or cues, or anatomical models. In a DARPA-financed project, Wegner et al. (25) developed a training surgical simulator. Multiple parallel voices provide independent channels of positional information, used as a feedback during simulation or surgical operation.

Sonification of EEG sequences was also applied to detect short-time synchronization during cognitive events and perception (26). Each electrode was assigned a different MIDI instrument, and EEG synchronization was perceived as synchronous play during data sonification.

7.3.1   Visualization and Sonification of Brain Electrical Activity

Visualization provides significant support for understanding of complex processes. Possible insight into brain functions could be facilitated using visualization of brain electromagnetic activity, observing either its electric component recorded on the scalp (EEG) or magnetic field in the vicinity of the head (MEG). EEG has been routinely used as a diagnostic tool for decades. The more recent MEG has been used to complete the picture of underlying processes, because the head is almost transparent for magnetic fields, but its inhomogenities (caused by liquid, bone, and skin) considerably influence EEG recordings.

Topographic maps of different parameters of brain electrical activity have commonly been used in research and clinical practice to represent spatial distribution of activity (27). The first applications used topographic maps that represented the activity on two-dimensional (2-D) scalp projections. They usually represented a static picture from the top view. EEG brain topography is gradually becoming clinical tool. Its main indication is to facilitate determination of brain tumors, other focal diseases of the brain (including epilepsy, cerebrovascular disorders, and trauma), disturbances of consciousness (narcolepsy and other sleep disorders), vigilance (anesthesia, of coma, intraoperative brain activity). It is a valuable tool in neuropsychopharmacology to estimate the effects of drugs acting on nervous system (hypnotic, psychoactive drugs, antiepileptics, etc.). In psychiatry, EEG brain topography has been used to identify biologic traits of certain disorders, such as depression and schizophrenia, early onset of Alzheimer disease, hyperactivity with or without attention deficit disorders in children, and autism, (27–29). EEG is used also as a therapeutical tool: Apart from its use in various biofeedback techniques in therapy of tension headaches and stress disorders, there have been attempts to use it in more serious diseases such as epilepsy (30).

Recent advances in computer graphics and increased processing power provided the means for implementing 3-D topographic maps with real-time animation. 3-D visualization resolves one of the most important problems in topographic mapping: projection of the scalp surface onto a plane. The other problems of topographic mapping are interpolation methods, number and location of electrodes, and score to color mapping.

Whereas in CT and PET images every pixel represents actual data values, brain topographic maps contain observed values only on electrode positions. Consequently, all the other points must be spatially interpolated using known score values calculated on electrode positions. Therefore, a higher number of electrodes makes possible more reliable topographic mapping. Electrode setting is usually predefined (like the International 10–20 standard), although for some experiments custom electrode settings could be used to increase spatial resolution of specific brain regions. Finally, color representation of data values may follow different paradigms such as *spectrum* (using colors of visible spectrum, from blue to red) and heat (from black through yellow to white) (27).

Isochronous representation of observed processes preserves genuine process dynamics and facilitates perception of intrinsic spatiotemporal patterns of brain electrical activity. However, animation speed depends on perceptual and computational issues. Commercially available computer platforms can create an animation rate in the order of tens of frames per second, depending of image size and score calculation complexity (31). Although animation rates can go up to 25 frames/s, the actual rate must be matched with the information-processing capabilities of the human observer. Otherwise, problems such as temporal summation and visual masking may arise (32). Both effects occur if the frame rate is too high, when details on adjacent maps interfere, creating false percepts. The most important computational issues for real-time execution are complexity of score calculations, image size, and animation rate.

7.3.2 System Organization

Our first visualization prototypes have clearly shown the necessity of the experimental environment in which different perceptual features could be easily set and their diagnostic value explored. We developed *Tempo* in Visual C^{++} for the Windows 95/NT operating system (33). The program was developed to test the user interface and the most important perceptual features of visualization, e.g., animation control and speed, evaluation of scores, color mapping (look-up tables), background properties, scene lighting, and model evaluation.

The system consists of three parallel execution threads: data acquisition, score calculation, and score visualization. They are synchronized by means of the critical sections, and could be executed in parallel on different processors. Even in a single processor system, data acquisition is usually supervised by an intelligent controller on a A/D board; score calculation could be performed by add-on DSP processor, and the graphic coprocessor could handle visualization tasks.

EEG data could be retrieved either on-line (from the A/D converter board) or off-line (from the file). We implemented an input filter standard EEG files generated by *Rhythm* 8.0 (Stellate System) and then implemented the ASTM EEG file format standard (34). Sound processing relied on Microsoft *DirectX* concept, intended to provide faster access to system resources and lower processing latency. *DirectSound* facilitates low-latency mixing, access to accelerated sound hardware, and real-time control of reproduction parameters. We developed software support for sonification as a library, which uses standard *DirectSound* procedures. Custom procedures make possible the use of natural sound patterns, stored as WAV files. For instance, we found the sounds of a creek or bees to be a naturally pleasant basis for sonification. Application modulates pitch, volume, and balance of the selected sound pattern according to the values of data stream to be sonified. The VRML-based application *mmViewer* was developed for distributed Web-based information systems. The only requirement for the target system is a VRML browser, supported by most Web browsers. The user interface of *mmViewer* is given in Figure 7.1.

7.4 EXPERIMENT AND RESULTS

EEG signals vary as a function of the state and of the area of the brain. These signals reflect spatiotemporal patterns of brain electrical fields that consist of a series of short-lasting quasi-stationary epochs corresponding to brain functional microstates (35).

The state of drowsiness is classically associated with the disappearance of the occipital α rhythm and the appearance of some rhythmic and semirhythmic θ activity (36). It has been shown that there may exist several variations of this pattern, including persistence of the occipital α waves into the drowsy state or the emergence of other EEG patterns that are more complex and variable than the wakeful EEG patterns (37). Recognition of these patterns is critical to the interpretation of the EEG both in clinical practice and in psychophysiological studies, because episodes of drowsiness may reveal abnormal rhythms and discharges not otherwise manifest. On the other hand, some normal patterns of drowsiness are a common hazard for misinterpretation. Transition form full wakefulness to sleep involves complex functional changes in the brain cortical

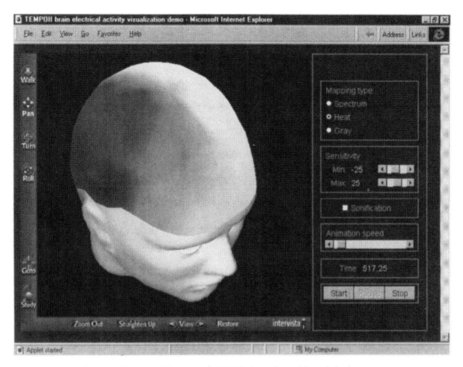

Figure 7.1. mmViewer, a VRML-based multimodal viewer.

activity, which produces diverse EEG patterns. These patterns may contain important information concerning brain physiologic and patophysiologic processes, such as epilepsy, disorders of sleep and cognition, and aberrations of aging process (36).

We estimated vigilance in humans solely from EEG recordings, by means of power spectrum analysis and its indexes (38). This research showed that automatic detection of fast fluctuations (on the order of a few seconds) of the vigilance is possible. The state space created by the variables used enabled a successful separation of the states of alertness and drowsy wakefulness.

In this example we focused on changes in the distribution and amplitude of α and θ activity in healthy adult subjects. We used topographic mapping (16 recording sites) to examine EEG changes during the transition from wakefulness to drowsiness to reveal how the brain as a whole changes its activity and to define regional and hemispheric differences.

Electroencephalograms were recorded in an electromagnetically shielded room on a Medelec 1A97 EEG machine (Medilog BV, Nieuwkoop, The Netherlands). Band-pass filter limits were set at 0.5 Hz and 30 Hz; Ag/AgCl electrodes, with impedance of <5 kΩ were placed at 16 locations (F7, F8, T3, T4, T5, T6, Fp1, Fp2, F3, F4, C3, C4, P3, P4, O1, O2) according to the inter-

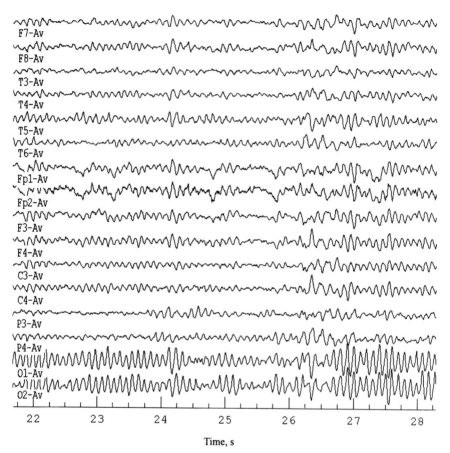

Figure 7.2. EEG wave forms during onset of drowsiness. Awake state, 22 to 24 s; drowsy state, 25 to 27 s.

national 10-20 system as an average reference. The EEG output was digitized with 12-bit precision at a sampling rate of 256 Hz per channel using the A/D converter Data Translation 2801. Records were analyzed off line on artifact-free segments.

Figure 7.2 shows EEG waveform during onset of drowsiness. The first 2 s of the recording belong to the fully awake state, and the rest of the signal belongs to the drowsy period. Topographic maps of changes in α (7.5 to 13 Hz) and θ rhythm power (4 to 7 Hz) are given in Figure 7.3. Our research showed the strength of the index θ/α power ratio (ITA) for identification of drowsy EEG periods (38). Figure 7.3 shows the ITA during a short period of drowsiness. We present the change in the spatiotemporal pattern of electrocortical activity as series of topographic maps, taken in 0.25-s steps.

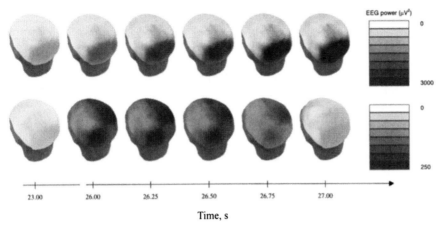

Figure 7.3. Spatial change in α (*top*) and θ (*bottom*) powers from the awake ($t = 23$ s) to the drowsy ($t = 26$ to 27 s) states.

In the fully awake state, there is characteristic posterior (parieto-occipital) maximum of α power, and scarcity of θ power. With the transition to the drowsiness, α power gradually increases symmetrically over the posterior regions and retains its normal distribution. In the same period, θ power shows a huge increase over both hemispheres, accentuated over the right hemisphere. Apparently, this pattern is stable during whole period of drowsiness, showing a gradual decrease toward the end of the period. However, power changes are not so uniform in the spatial and temporal domains during drowsiness. There is another pattern of subtle regional changes in power spectrum that can be revealed only by further analysis.

We used ITA as derived parameter to expose those subtle EEG changes. Figure 7.4 shows the evolution of changes from the initial period with a broad increase of θ over both the frontal and the central regions, followed by prominent increment over the right parietal region, spreading to the left hemisphere with a maximum over the left temporal region. The next step is a diffuse increase in θ over the same regions, with the maximum over the right central-parietal region, followed by a further bilateral increase with a clear accentuation over the right hemisphere, sparing the occipital regions. A return to the awake state is accompanied by a decrease of ITA, retaining its local maximum over the left temporal-parietal and right temporal region. It is obvious that there are many subtle and fast changes during this short period of drowsiness, starting as one pattern and finishing as a completely different one. The ITA index much better qualifies this spatiotemporal pattern, but the overall pattern of changes is too fast and complicated for visual interpretation only. Therefore, we calculated an average ITA index over the hemispheres (Fig. 7.5), as data reduction and generalization of brain electrical activity. The essence of the

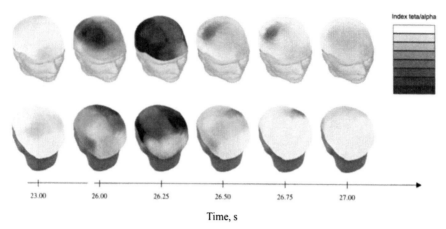

Figure 7.4. Spatial ITA corresponding to Figure 7.2. View from the right (*top*) and left (*bottom*) sides.

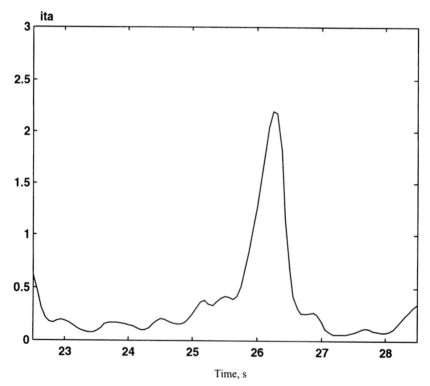

Figure 7.5. Normalized average ITA values for the right hemisphere from the drowsy period (25 to 27 s).

analysis was detection of the drowsy period, which is easily evident from the average ITA index.

We used the sonification of the average ITA index as an additional information channel for the human observer, to draw attention to the short periods of drowsiness. Human attention is decreased during prolonged mental effort, such as the analysis of a long-term EEG recording in outpatient clinical practice or intensive care units (39). During examination of long EEG records, physicians need to sustain a high level of concentration, sometimes for more than 1 h. Monotonous repetition of visual information induces mental fatigue, so that some short or subtle changes the in EEG signal may be overlooked. This requires attention to on target events (spikes, drowsiness, etc.) by another information channel. The auditory channel is the most suitable, because it has a much better temporal resolution and prevents the information overload of the visual channel. We have found that the most suitable sonification is mapping ITA to a continuous and natural sound pattern.

7.5 DISCUSSION

Our positive experience from this experiment was that the performance of commercially available systems was good enough to support real-time visualization for most calculated scores, so that human perceptual bandwidth became a major bottleneck. For example, on a PC PentiumPro 166 MHz machine, with 64 MB RAM/512 KB L2 cache and Windows NT operating system, the animation speed for 320×240 pixel 3-D maps is 10 frames/s (31). Therefore, visualization of EEG/MEG scores could be executed even on standard PC platforms. It is particularly important in a distributed environment to allow multiple site evaluation of stored recordings.

Unfortunately, there are no obvious design solutions to a given problem. It is hard to find the most appropriate paradigm or sound parameter mapping for a given application (40). Therefore it is advisable to evaluate different visualization and sonification methods and find out perceptually the most admissible presentation. Moreover, creation of user-specific templates is highly advisable, as perception of audiovisual patterns is personal.

The selection of scores for a multimodal presentation is another delicate issue relying on human perception. Scores selected for an acoustic rendering may be used either as a new information channel (sonification of symmetry in addition to visualization of EEG power) or a redundant channel of visualized information. When introducing additional channels, one should be careful to avoid information overloading. Redundant multimodal presentation offers the possibility to choose the presentation modality for a given data stream or to emphasize the temporal dimension for a selected stream. In our example, the sonification method proved valuable in the dynamic following of some parameters of brain electrical activity that would be otherwise hard to perceive.

Finally, the new generation of programming environments significantly reduce implementation efforts, providing support for the most frequently used functions. For example, there is no need to support a change of viewpoint in a VRML-based model, because it is supported directly by the VRML viewer. A proposed VRML-based visualization and sonification environment requires only a standard Web and VRML browser; therefore, it is applicable both to standalone workstations and to distributed telemedical applications. Further development of our environment shall incorporate real head models derived from MRI recordings, which will enable functional mapping of brain activity to anatomic regions.

7.6 CONCLUSION

Complex biomedical processes require sophisticated analysis environment. However, physiological characteristics of human perception limit the number of perceived parameters and their dynamics. Multimodal data presentation could increase throughput, introduce new data streams, and improve temporal resolution. In our environment, graphics remains the primary physical media; acoustics sound is an extended information channel. Owing to the lack of general insights into VRUI design space, the art of designing multimodal parameters is still required. For every application, multimodal parameters must be chosen to maximize the separation of changes in the perceptual domain.

In our 3-D EEG visualization environment, sonification has two functions. Acoustic rendering could create synesthetic extension of a selected data channel or present a new parameter. In the presented environment, visualization is used to show animated 3-D topographic maps of brain electrical activity. Sonification is employed either as a synesthetic presentation of a selected visualized score or to render complex biomedical data derived from an input dataset. Sonification improved the possibility of assessing the genuine dynamics and perceiving the inherent spatiotemporal patterns of brain electrical activity.

REFERENCES

1. G. C. Burdea. Force and touch feedback for virtual reality. New York: Wiley, 1996.
2. D. R. Begault. 3-D sound for virtual reality and multimedia. Boston: Academic Press, 1994.
3. J. M. Rosen, H. Solanian, R. J. Redett, and D. R. Laub. Evolution of virtual reality. IEEE/EMBS 1996;15:16–22.
4. W. J. Greenleaf. Developing the tools for practical VR applications. IEEE/EMBS 1996;15:23–30.
5. M. Akay. The VRT revolution. IEEE/EMBS 1996;15:31–40.
6. C. Cruz-Neira, D. J. Sandin, T. A. DeFanti, et al. The CAVE: audio visual experience automatic virtual environment. Commun ACM 1992;35:65–72.

7. M. K. D. Coomans and H. J. P. Timmermans. Towards a taxonomy of virtual reality user interfaces. Paper presented at the International Conference on Information Visualization. 1997.

8. R. A. Earnshow, J. A. Vince, and H. Jones, eds. Virtual reality applications. London: Academic Press, 1995.

9. N. Akkiraju, H. Edelsbrunner, P. Fu, and J. Qian. Viewing geometric protein structures from inside a CAVE. IEEE Comput Graph Appl, 1996;16:58–61.

10. C. Cruz-Neira, T. A. DeFanti, R. Stevens, and P. Bash. Integrating virtual reality and high performance computing and communications for real-time molecular modeling. Paper presented at High Performance Computing 95. Apr 1995.

11. G. Kramer, ed. Auditory display, sonification, audification and auditory interfaces. Addison Wesley, 1994.

12. T. M. Madhyastha and D. A. Reed. Data sonification: do you see what I hear? IEEE Software 1995;12:45–56.

13. R. Minghim and A. R. Forrest. An illustrated analysis of sonification for scientific visualization. Paper presented at the 6th IEEE Visualization Conference VISUAL 95. 1995.

14. G. Grinstein and M. O. Ward. Introduction to visualization: '96 Tutorial #2. Data Visualization. http://www.cs.uml.edu/~grinstei/tut/v96 tut2.html.

15. E. Jovanov and V. Radivojevic. Software support for monitoring EEG changes in altered states of Consciousness. In D. Rakovic, et al., eds. Brain and consciousness, Workshop on Scientific Bases of Consciousness. Belgrade: ECPD, 1997.

16. The Virtual Reality Modeling Language, http://www.vrml.org/Specifications/VRML97.

17. N. O. Bernsen. Foundations of multimodal representations: a taxonomy of representational modalities. Interacting Comput 6, 1994:347–371.

18. M. Pavic. Dictionary of the Khazars [CD-ROM]. Belgrade: Multimedia, 1998.

19. N. O. Bernsen. A toolbox of output modalities. http://www.mrc-apu.cam.ac.uk/amodeus/.

20. R. Brady, R. Bargar, I. Choi, and J. Reitzer. Auditory bread crumbs for navigating volumetric data. Paper presented at IEEE Visualization '96. San Francisco, 1996.

21. P. J. Barnard and J. May, eds. Computers, communication and usability: design issues, research and methods for integrated services. Amsterdam: Elsevier, 1993.

22. S. Noah, R. G. Loeb, and R. Watt. Audible display of patient respiratory data [Technical report]. University of Arizona, 1996.

23. T. V. Raman. Auditory user interfaces: toward the speaking computer. Boston: Kluwer, 1997.

24. R. E. Cytowic. Synesthesia: phenomenology and neuropsychology a review of current knowledge. Psyche. 1995.

25. C. Wegner, D. B. Karron, and A. Flisser. Navigation using audio feedback. Paper presented at Medicine Meets Virtual Reality. 1997.

26. G. Mayer-Kress. Sonification of multiple electrode human scalp electro-encephalogram (EEG). http://www.ccsr.uiuc.edu/People/gmk/Projects/EEGSound/.

27. F. H. Duffy, ed. Topographic mapping of brain electrical activity. Butterworth, 1986.

28. F. H. Lopes da Silva. A critical review of clinical applications of topographic mapping of brain potentials. J Clin Neurophysiol 1990;7:535–551.
29. A. C. Tsoi, D. S. C. So, and A. Sergejew. Classification of electroencephalogram using artificial neural networks. Adv Neural infor Processing sys 1994;6:1151–1158.
30. B. Rockstroh, T. Elbert, N. Birmbauer, et al. Cortical self-regulation in patients with epilepsies. Epilepsy Res 1993;14:63–72.
31. A. Samardzic. 3D visualisation of brain electrical activity. M. S. Thesis, University of Belgrade, 1996.
32. V. Klymenko and J. M. Coggins. Visual information processing of computed topographic electrical activity brain maps. J Clin Neurophysiol 1990;7:484–497.
33. A. Samardzic, E. Jovanov, and D. Starcevic. 3D Visualisation of brain electrical activity. Paper presented at the 18th Annual International Conference IEEE/EMBS. Amsterdam, 1996.
34. ASTM E1467–94.
35. F. H. Lopes da Silva. Neural mechanisms underlying brain waves: from neural membranes to networks. Electroenceph Clin Neurophysiol 1991;79:81–93.
36. D. D. Daly and T. A. Pedley. Current practice of clinical electroencephalography. 2nd ed. New York: Raven Press, 1990.
37. J. Santamaria and K. H. Chiappa. The EEG of drowsiness in normal adults. J Clin Neurophysiol 1987;4:327–382.
38. P. Sukovic, V. Radivojevic, D. Rakovic, et al. Neural network based classification of vigilance from the EEG Power spectrum. Unpublished manuscript.
39. M. van Gils, A. Rosenfalck, S. White, et al. Signal processing in prolonged EEG recordings during intensive care. IEEE EMBS 1997;16:56–63.
40. J. Coutaz, D. Salber, and S. Balbo. Towards automatic evaluation of multimodal user interfaces. Know Based Sys, 1994:267–274.

CHAPTER 8

Anatomic VisualizeR: Teaching and Learning Anatomy with Virtual Reality

HELENE HOFFMAN, MARGARET MURRAY, ROBERT CURLEE, and
ALICIA FRITCHLE

San Diego School of Medicine
La Jolla California, USA

8.1 BACKGROUND

The University of California San Diego (UCSD) School of Medicine's Learning Resources Center (LRC) has been actively engaged in the development and implementation of a virtual reality (VR) based application for education and training (1, 2). The resultant product, *VisualizeR*, is a virtual environment (VE) designed to support the teaching and learning of any subject that requires an understanding of three-dimensional (3-D) structures and complex spatial relationships. *VisualizeR*'s multimodal application interface approach, named vir-

Information Technologies in Medicine, Volume I: Medical Simulation and Education, Edited by
Metin Akay and Andy Marsh.
ISBN 0-471-38863-7 © 2001 John Wiley & Sons, Inc.

tual reality–multimedia synthesis (VR-MMS), enables interaction with 3-D models and concurrent access to multimedia resources, including text, images, animations, video, and sound (3). Moreover, the flexible and extensible *Visualizer* architecture accommodates the needs of a wide variety of different teaching approaches and provides the capability for dynamic and unstructured student exploration (4, 5).

The scientific domain selected for UCSD's first *VisualizeR* lessons was human anatomy, because it represented one context in which a VR-MMS-based strategy was both achievable and apropos (6). While still considered the gold standard against which alternatives are judged, current educational methods—a combination of lectures and laboratory dissections—fall short of instilling the requisite 3-D conceptualization, retention, and application of anatomic knowledge to clinical-problem solving (7). These pedagogical challenges are further complicated by shortened anatomy curricula owing to competition from other courses (8, 9); the desirability of less dependence on human cadavers because of scarcity, costs, aesthetics, and environmental concerns (10); and reductions in hours and resources (including faculty) available for wet laboratory coursework (11). At the same time, many curricula are including greater amounts of anatomic information, including conceptually challenging 3-D relationships (8, 12), a need that could be well met by VR-based anatomy resources.

8.2   PROJECT DESCRIPTION

Efforts to develop *Anatomic VisualizeR* began with an assessment of faculty and student needs for anatomy training at UCSD and a consideration of current best practices for anatomy education in a wide variety of contexts. The resulting information was neither new nor surprising to individuals who have spent significant time teaching human anatomy to medical students. However, organizing the findings and articulating them as educational and developmental goals was an important first step in the development process. It also established that once developed, *Anatomic VisualizeR*-based anatomy lessons could be used either as adjuncts to or as replacements for the current practices in anatomy education.

Anatomic VisualizeR provides a virtual dissecting room in which students and faculty can directly interact with 3-D models (anatomic, schematic, etc.) and concurrently access supporting curricular materials (text, images, sound, video, etc.) (Fig. 8.1). Instructional activities, organized into learning modules, can be selected from a collection of previously developed learning modules or can be specially developed using the associated lesson authoring environment. Modules can be created for individual instruction, for presentation in large group settings, and for other curricular contexts.

The instructional design of *Anatomic VisualizeR* addresses needs identified during the initial assessment phase, recognizes current standards and practices for adult education (13, 14), and capitalizes on the unique opportunities afforded

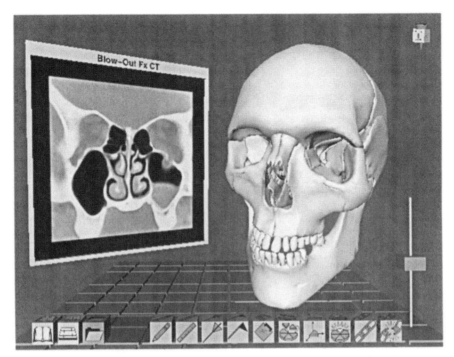

Figure 8.1. A scene from the *Anatomic VisualizeR* learning module "Clinical Anatomy of the Skull." This portion of the lesson provides students with access to both the 3-D models of the skull and the diagnostic images that demonstrate the effect of trauma to the head. The small object in the upper right corner of the screen, is a 3-D reference tool that indicates the anatomic position of the model. The menu bars at the bottom of the screen provide tools for interacting with the anatomic models (right) and environmental controls (left).

by the *VisualizeR* architecture. The *Anatomic VisualizeR* paradigm was created to encourage exploration, discovery, and active learning by enabling students to creatively construct individualized and self-paced experiments. The learning modules are also designed to help students create a symbolic framework for anatomic knowledge and to establish a context in which to integrate clinical skills and reasoning.

At the heart of each *Anatomic VisualizeR* learning module is a study guide that supplies descriptive text and an organized presentation of key concepts, suggested exercises, exploratory actions, and flexible nonsequential access to a variety of lesson materials (Fig. 8.2). The study guide and the menu bars provide the syntax for users to navigate, manipulate, and interact with the application and its resources. A broad range of virtual exploratory tools and options are available that enable users to investigate structures in ways not possible in the real world (Fig. 8.3). Students are able to repeatedly "dissect" structures and regions or to reconstruct any area from its component parts. The options

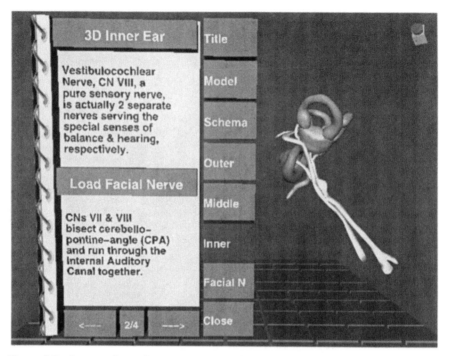

Figure 8.2. A scene from the *Anatomic Visualizer* learning module "Anatomy of the Ear," highlighting the study guide portion of the application. The tabs on the right side of the study guide provide ready access to each segment of the lesson. The forward and back arrows and the numeric indicator provide navigation within the tab sections. Study guide pages, such as the one shown, can include descriptive text and links to additional resources.

available to users include link/unlink models, change opacity or size, dynamically create cross-sectional views using a clipping plane, measure sizes and distances with a virtual ruler, mark structures with a flag, identify structures using a probe, and draw lines and simple objects using a SpaceDraw tool. Anatomic orientation can be maintained regardless of view or magnification, and anatomic position can be re-established through other menu-bar options. Moreover, within any lesson and at any time, a student may choose to access additional information resources (e.g., correlative histology or pathology images, surgical videos, diagnostic studies) using *Anatomic VisualizeR*'s search tool.

8.3   3-D ANATOMIC MODELS

The 3-D polygonal models that constitute the nucleus of *Anatomic VisualizeR* can be derived from a wide variety of sources. Current lessons are based in large part, on anatomic polygonal models derived from the National Library of

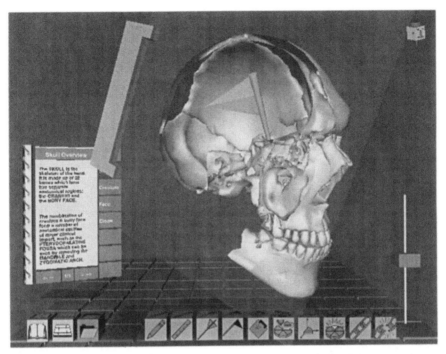

Figure 8.3. A scene from the *Anatomic Visualizer* learning module "Clinical Anatomy of the Skull" includes the study guide and array of virtual tools. It depicts the use of the clipping plane to create dynamic cross-sections of the skull. Also seen is the flag tool, marking a structure in the skull's interior. The menu bar in the lower right side of the screen has the following tools (right to left) scaling, unlink, link, highlight, orient part, orient whole, clipping plane, flag, probe, ruler, and space draw. The smaller menu bar at the lower left side has (right to left) search, grid on/off, study guide on/off.

Medicine's (NLM) Visible Human Project dataset. These models were produced and supplied by Visible Productions (Fort Collins, CO). Other models have been created by our in-house 3-D modeler/medical illustrator.

Although the models supplied by Visible Productions were of high quality, implementation issues quickly emerged that had to be addressed with the end user in mind. To elucidate particular learning objectives, careful consideration was given to determining the necessary level of anatomic accuracy of each model and the most appropriate model groupings. Faculty often requested specific modifications to change certain idiosyncratic structures to represent those seen in a higher percentage of the general population. The impact of learning objective-driven choices on application performance was also an important consideration. For example, there is a finite practical limit to the number of polygons that can be displayed at one time, depending on technical limits such as a particular machine's graphics hardware capability or whether its display is monoscopic or stereoscopic. Taking both accuracy and perfor-

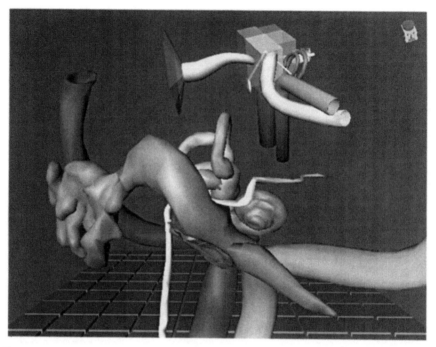

Figure 8.4. A scene from the *Anatomic Visualizer* learning module "Anatomy of the Ear" demonstrating the use of 3-D anatomic models (foreground) in combination with 3-D schematic models (background) to teach visually complex subjects.

mance issues into account, the combined polygonal count in each VR scene was reduced as much as practical without interfering with curricular objectives. Several approaches to decimation have been tried; and even after reductions of 70 to 90%, plausible results were approved by expert anatomists. In addition to decimation, careful editing of facets and adjusting of polygonal patterns were required to optimize application performance.

The need to create both new anatomic structures as well as 3-D conceptual schematics led to the use of alternative methods and approaches to 3-D modeling (Fig. 8.4). Template Graphic Softwares *Amapi 3D* was employed in these efforts. For example, missing palatine and lacrimal bones had to be created for the skull. In other cases, new models created in *Amapi* were substituted for graphically problematic models. The original models were used as a 3-D spatial templates so that when problems were fixed, the replacement model retained proper spatial relationships. In addition, 3-D conceptual schematics needed for a lesson on the ear were designed by a clinical anatomist and developed by our in-house 3-D modeler/medical illustrator. *Amapi 3D* was also used to scale and spatially register models from another source to make them work with existing models. Other tools were employed to differentiate models from each other according to their color, shininess, and transparency attributes. More recently, texture mapping solutions were explored as a computationally cost-effective means to enhance visual realism.

8.4 APPLICATION ARCHITECTURE

Anatomic VisualizeR's architecture includes specially constructed media display and user interface capabilities designed to enhance the VR learning experience (4). The encapsulation of individual graphical components into "blocks" enables efficient management and concurrent presentation of curricular resources, exploratory VR tools, and organized textual materials. All blocks have the same core functionalities, including the ability to be loaded or unloaded within the VE, selected or de-selected, iconicized or de-iconicized, grouped or ungrouped, and moved around the VE in 6 degrees of freedom (dof). In this way the user has complete control of how to arrange the 3-D real estate of the VE.

Blocks may contain any number of 3-D anatomic models that have additional, type-specific characteristics relevant to their use within the lesson. For example, models can be examined individually or in any combination. A particular model's transparency can be changed from opaque (Fig. 8.5) to trans-

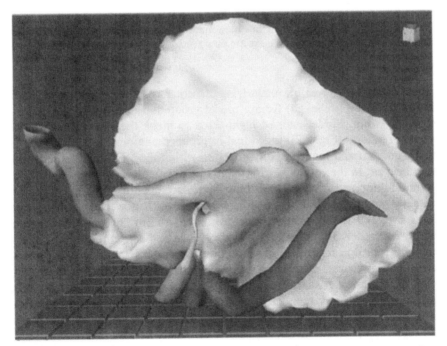

Figure 8.5. A scene from the *Anatomic Visualizer* learning module "Anatomy of the Ear" showing the right temporal bone with portions of several blood vessels and nerves associated with the ear.

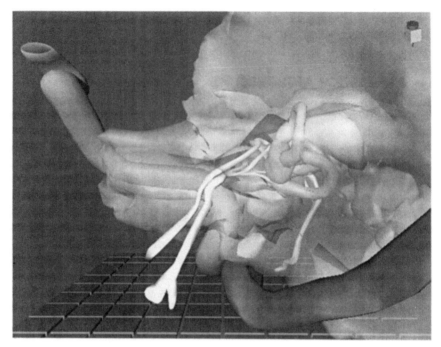

Figure 8.6. A scene from the *Anatomic Visualizer* learning module "Anatomy of the Ear," in which the temporal bone has been made transparent. Many of the underlying structures of the inner and middle ear are now apparent.

parent (Fig. 8.6), revealing underlying structures and relationships. A model can be removed (unlinked) from a model group and then added (linked) to a different group. Models can be highlighted to make them stand out within a group of models (Fig. 8.7). Individual or grouped anatomic models can be virtually grasped and moved in any direction within the VE, and then reoriented to proper or, in the case of organs, anatomic position on request.

In addition, a variety of tools have been developed to work in conjunction with the anatomic models, providing the user with powerful interface capabilities. A 3-D spatial reference tool, displayed within the lesson environment whenever models are present, provides a simple and constant reminder of anatomic orientation regardless of view. One exploratory tool is a clip plane, or cross-section viewer, capable of making coronal, sagittal, or any other planar view of structures. A structure identification tool is provided that can be placed to intersect with any number of models and then queried to list the models it intersects. Another tool, a 3-D space draw utility, allows the user to create a 3-D line in the VE that can be used in a variety of ways within the lesson. Learning modules can include flag markers, used to ask students to identify particular structures as part of a practical examination. A virtual ruler is also provided, enabling students to measure and compare model sizes (Fig. 8.8).

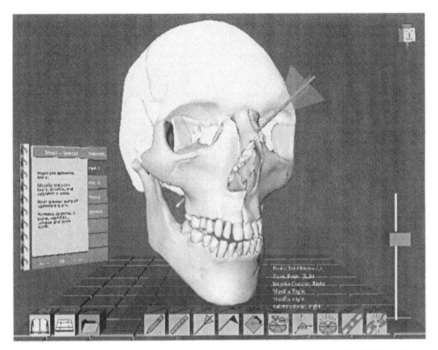

Figure 8.7. A scene from the *Anatomic Visualizer* learning module *"Sphenoid and Autonomic Cranial Nerves."* The cranial portion of the skull has been highlighted to distinguish those bones from the face. Also, the probe tool has been placed in the skull and the structures it intersects are listed in the lower right hand portion of the screen.

Textual material is organized within a study guide designed to resemble a laboratory notebook. Tabs organize lesson sections. Pages can be turned forward and back. When a page is selected, resources within the VE are added or removed to match the requirements of the lesson objective that it addresses. Each page may specify which models will be loaded and where they will be placed. In addition, the level of transparency and the initial orientation of the of the models can be set as desired. Multimedia resources such as clinical images, video clips, or sounds can also be loaded and placed. User interface tools may also be loaded and placed in the VE as required by the lesson objectives. Pages may contain didactic material and instructions for the student as well as student-selectable buttons to call up related multimedia resources.

The student may at any time choose to break away from the structure of the study guide and look up resources in the LRC's curricular resource database, search the Medline database, or connect to any remote computer using a telnet session. This allows student-driven comparison and correlation across modalities, enhancing the ability to explore ideas, generalize situations, and integrate concepts.

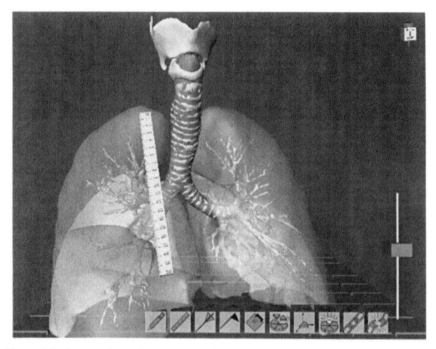

Figure 8.8. A scene from the *Anatomic Visualizer* learning module "Pulmonary Anatomy" illustrating the use of the virtual ruler to measure sizes and distances. In this *Anatomic VisualizeR* learning module, users are asked to investigate the dimensions of each lobe of the human lung.

8.5 3-D USER-INTERFACE DEVELOPMENT

The overall goal of the *VisualizeR* user-interface design is to minimize the "cost of knowledge" (16) and enable the user to integrate previously compartmented knowledge using an intuitive, visually compelling, and kinesthetic interface. Because few paradigms for 3-D interface design exist, flexibility to quickly try different combinations of hardware devices and software design layout features has also been a design requirement.

VisualizeR's software architecture offers several levels of features and controls. Core functionality is provided by Facet, which concurrently manages 3-D manipulatable components (blocks) that enable different modalities of resource display or user interaction. Facet manages events and implements messaging between blocks. In this way, blocks can be combined by faculty to build mentored lessons or by students in real-time within the VE. Blocks can also be constructed by a system architect to extend the core features of Facet and build new user-interface tools. Facet can manage newly created 3-D user-interface widgets inserted within any block. These 3-D widgets are similar to selectable lists, scrollbars, and buttons common to any Windows-based user interface, except they are designed and implemented specifically for 3-D presentation and interaction. For example, combination of 3-D widgets, such as text, images, and buttons, currently comprise the Study Guide Block, while the Video Block includes 3-D start, stop, and loop button widgets.

The Lesson Editor can be used to develop the learning module scripts. The sequence of pages or tabbed sections can be set, as can instructions as to which models to load or remove, where to place them, and whether or not to group them. Other multimedia blocks or tools can also be loaded or removed. Page headers and their text and link buttons with anchors for accessing any resources can be entered. The Lesson Editor generates an ASCII file that can also be further modified using any text editor.

Customization of the VE occurs at two different levels. An expanding list of Xresources can be used to specify changes to user interface characteristics such as color, size, position, device baud rate, and communications port without the need to recompile the application. Facet can also be extended to support any type of input/output (I/O) devices and their associated device drivers via shared objects loaded at run time. Events for a particular device are named and associated with command actions. Named events are passed to Facet for handling. A central I/O configuration file is used to define any valid command actions. This simple ASCII file specifies user-interface commands as event definitions associated with command-to-action mappings. Commands global to the application may therefore be implemented equivalently by several distinct device drivers. Commands relevant only to a particular I/O device may also be defined. Device drivers are well encapsulated so that the addition of new devices as well as modifications to existing device commands are easily made. Another means of extending Facet is through the addition of customized blocks and tools, which inherit core Block and tool functionality as prescribed by Facet. These new blocks and tools are also created as dynamically shared objects that are loaded into the application at run time, freeing the need to recompile the application when any changes or additions are made.

Using blocks with events allows *VisualizeR* to flexibly associate contextually appropriate interaction, display characteristics, and behaviors with extensible lesson content, while letting Facet maintain control of the visual display. This approach has been successful in providing core capabilities while allowing the application to evolve both functional capabilities and layout organization.

8.6 PLATFORM, HARDWARE, AND CONFIGURATION

Anatomic VisualizeR is currently written in C^{++} using Silicon Graphics's *Open Inventor* application programming interface (API). It has been run on Silicon Graphics's Onyx2, Onyx REII, Octane, High Impact, and O2 workstations. Faster hardware configurations support higher frame rates and greater numbers of concurrently loaded 3-D models. Dual processors available on some of these configurations have been found to significantly enhance performance by enabling the separate device I/O and graphics rendering threads to be processed in parallel. Specific frame rates depend on multiple factors, including the number of polygons in models and model sets and the choice of monoscopic or stereoscopic display. Currently, three visual display configurations are supported: monoscopic CRT, stereoscopic CRT using StereoGraphics CrystalEyes eyewear, and stereoscopic Virtual Research V6 or nVision Datavisor VGA headmounted displays (HMDs). Hand- and head-motion tracking is provided using Ascension Flock of Birds trackers. Hand position information from the Ascension trackers, when combined with hand pinches or gestures allow the user to grab any block and move it within the VE. Fakespace Pinch Gloves and 5DT's 5th Gloves are two such hand gesture devices that have been integrated so far. Immersion Corporation's MicroScribe-3D and SpaceTec IMC's Spaceball 3003 trackball are examples of other 6 dof devices implemented within *VisualizeR*. Application menu bars that appear in the VE organize interface options for user interaction. Location of menu bars as well as different gestures and motions are being evaluated for their ease of use. Development of a force-feedback haptic interface with collision detection is also being explored using SensAble Technologies' PHANToM device.

8.7 CURRICULAR IMPLEMENTATION

Anatomic VisualizeR is still an experimental application, SGI-based, and available on a limited number of workstations. Consequently its primary curricular use has been as a teaching/visualization tool in lecture. At UCSD, *Anatomic VisualizeR* has been a part of the School of Medicine's human anatomy course since 1998 for the teaching of the sphenoid bone and the autonomic cranial nerves. In 1999, a lecture on the anatomy of the human ear was also delivered to the UCSD medical students using this application. On each of these occasions, the corresponding *Anatomic VisualizeR*–based learning module was made available for individual and small group sessions on a voluntary basis and was used by more than 50% of the class.

    Anatomic VisualizeR made its curricular debut outside UCSD in fall 1999 when it was used for the teaching of two graduate-level nursing anatomy lectures at the Uniformed Services University of the Health Sciences (USUHS), in Bethesda, Maryland. USUHS is currently running the only α version of *VisualizeR* outside of the LRC and will be jointly developing other VR-based anatomy lessons. *Anatomic VisualizeR* has also been used to develop anatomy learning modules aimed at a high school student population. This pilot project, undertaken in 1998–1999, brought more than 30 senior high school students to the LRC for two half-day sessions using a lesson co-authored by their anatomy teacher. Both the USUHS and high school experiences have reinforced the necessity of porting the *VisualizeR* application to a platform (e.g., Linux or WindowsNT) that will make distribution to a wider student audience more feasible.

8.8 FUTURE PLANS

The primary research activities are now being directed at creating a version of *Anatomic VisualizeR* that will run on WindowsNT or Linux-based computers. This is a necessary next step in the evolution of *VisualizeR* from a research project to application capable of running on student workstations. To do so, the issues that are being addressed include the development environment, the 3-D graphics API, the Unix operating behaviors (e.g., multitasking, parallel processing), and the graphical user interface. Other near-term efforts are being directed at the development of new VR-based learning modules for use at USUHS and UCSD. In addition, UCSD is also working with the USUHS faculty to explore the pedagogical issues pertaining to teaching and learning with virtual environments. It is anticipated that a number of important research questions will arise from these efforts.

ACKNOWLEDGMENTS

This work was sponsored in part by a grant from the Defense Advanced Research Projects Agency (DAMD 17-94-J-4487) and a grant from the Office of Naval Research (ONRN00014-97-0356). The authors also wish to acknowledge the faculty at UCSD and USUHS for their invaluable contributions to lesson development and multimedia resource acquisition.

REFERENCES

1. H. Hoffman, A. Irwin, R. Ligon, M. Murray, and C. Tohsaku. Virtual Reality-Multimedia Synthesis: Next Generation Learning Environments for Medical Education, J. Biocommunications, 22:2–7, 1995.
2. H. M. Hoffman and M. Murray. Anatomic VisualizeR: Realizing the Vision of a VR-based Learning Environment. Studies in Health Technology & Information, 62: Westwood J et al. Eds, IOS Press, 134–140, 1999.
3. H. M. Hoffman, M. Murray, A. E. Irwin, and T. McCracken. Developing a Virtual Reality-Multimedia System for Anatomy Training. Health Care in the Information Age, Sieberg H, et al. Eds, IOS Press, 204–210, 1996.
4. H. Hoffman, M. Murray, M. Danks, R. Prayaga, A. Irwin, and D. Vu. A Flexible & Extensible Object-Oriented 3D Architecture: Application in the Development of Virtual Anatomy Lessons. Studies in Health Technology and Information, 39: Morgan K, et al. Eds, IOS Press, 461–466, 1997.
5. H. Hoffman and M. Murray. Anatomic VisualizeR—Virtual Anatomy for Education. Virtual Worlds & Simulation Conference, Landauer C & Bellman K Eds, Simulation Series, SCS, 30:25–28, 1998.
6. H. M. Hoffman, M. Murray, A. E. Irwin, and T. McCracken. Developing a Virtual Reality-Multimedia System for Anatomy Training. Health Care in the Information Age, Sieberg H, et al. Eds, IOS Press, 204–210, 1996.

7. C. Rosse. The potential of computerized representations of anatomy in the training of health care providers. Acad Med 1995;70:499–505.

8. D. Hubble, P. Byers, and P. McKeown. Clinical anatomy instruction in the operating room. Clin Anat 1996;9:405–407.

9. V. Yeager. Learning gross anatomy: dissection and prosection. Clin Anat 1996;9:57–59.

10. D. Jones. Reassessing the importance of dissection: a critique and elaboration. Clin Anat 1997;10:123–127.

11. K. Satyapal and M. Henneberg. Anatomy into the next millennium: quo vadis, or simply where to go. Clin Anat 1997;10:41–43.

12. E. Smoot and D. DaRosa. Effective teaching in the operating room. Plastic Reconstr Surg 1993;92:133–135.

13. S. B. Merriam and R. S. Caffarella. Learning in adulthood: a comprehensive guide. San Francisco: Jossey-Bass, 1991.

14. Association of American Medical Colleges. Educating medical students: assessing change in medical education—the road to implementation [ACME-TRI Report]. Acad Med 1993;68(suppl).

15. M. J. Ackerman, V. M. Spitzer, A. L. Scherzinger, and D. G. Whitlock. The Visible Human dataset: an image resource for anatomical visualization. Medinfo 1995;8:1195–1198.

16. S. Card, J. Mackinlay, and G. Robertson. A morphological analysis of the design space of input devices. ACM Trans Info Sys 1991;9:99–122.

CHAPTER 9

Future Technologies for Medical Applications

RICHARD M. SATAVA, MD FACS

Yale University School of Medicine
New Haven, Connecticut

The modern age of surgery began at the end of the nineteenth century because medicine discovered the Industrial Age, with its wealth of revolutionary technologies such as anesthesia, asepsis, microscopy, and new materials. At the close of the twentieth century, the Information Age diffused into medicine, and a revolution of even greater magnitude occurred. To understand the change it is necessary to look outside of medicine to society as a whole and find the underlying principles, and then apply them within our discipline. Futurists have been hawking the coming era; however, it took a pragmatist like Negroponte of the Massachusetts Institute of Technology (MIT) Media Laboratory in his book *Being Digital* to focus our attention on the critical element. Negroponte introduced the concept of "bits instead of atoms" to describe how we can represent the real world and the objects within it by a computer or information representation, which are referred to as information equivalents. The example that he used to illustrate his concept is that of the facsimile machine. For over 4000 years, messages have been sent from one person to another by sending the actual atoms, such as clay tablets, papyrus, or paper. With the facsimile

Information Technologies in Medicine, Volume I: Medical Simulation and Education, Edited by Metin Akay and Andy Marsh.
ISBN 0-471-38863-7 © 2001 John Wiley & Sons, Inc.

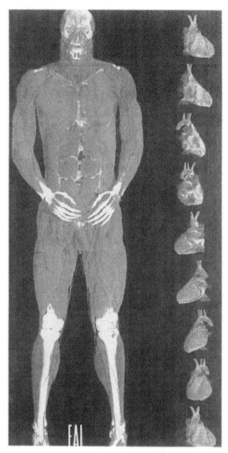

Figure 9.1. The Visible Human Project. The first representation of an individual human being in complete digital form (bits) (Courtesy V. Sptizer, University of Colorado Health Sciences Center, Denver.)

machine, the same messages can be sent nearly instantly (and at a greatly reduced cost) by sending the bits (data) over telephone lines rather than the atoms (letters). Within our profession, the object of attention is the patient, or more specifically the human body. Fortunately, in 1994 the information equivalent of the human body became available from the National Library of Medicine as the Visible Human (2) (Fig. 9.1). At the same time, robotic- and computer-assisted surgical technologies were beginning to emerge; they were trying to convert our hand motions and sense of touch into information by using sensors, effectors, and a computer. It was also at that time that a National Science Foundation workshop on virtual reality (VR) in 1995 informally asked the question, How much of what a physician does can be represented by information (3)? During laparoscopic surgery or interventional radiology, the surgeon or radiologist does not look at the patient's organs but at a video monitor with an image of the organs (information equivalent of the organs). When the procedure is finished and the patient is in the recovery room, the physician looks at the vital signs' monitor for the heart rate and blood pressure (an electronic equivalent of taking the pulse and touching). The medical record is now becoming electronic and nearly all of our imaging has changed from film (atoms) to digital images (bits). Medical education is using computer-aided instructions, CD-ROM, and VR to simulate and supplement cadaver and animal models. With the new research in robotics, even our hand motions are being changed in to electronic signals and being sent from one place to another. The future of medicine is no longer blood and guts, but bits and bytes.

The relevance is that the Information Age technologies are based on this metaphor, with technologies such as diagnostic imaging for visualization, sensors for vital signs and physiologic parameters, microelectronic machine systems (MEMS) for new instruments, computers and telecommunications for database and record keeping, and artificial intelligence for decision support, quality assurance, and outcomes analysis. These are the engines of empowerment, not only for the physician but for the patient as well. While the vast field of medical applications of biotechnology and genetic engineering will not be addressed here, it is pertinent to point out that DNA is, in its very essence, information—a fancy set of bits and bytes represented by the base pairs instead of zeros and ones. It is this commonality of information that enables us to tie together a whole new concept of how medicine could evolve, like an entire medical ecosystem, whereby discoveries in micro-sensors permits new imaging devices, which in turn enable new forms of image-based surgery. It is an upward spiral, one discovery providing a giant step forward toward the next technology and escalating the whole changing system logarithmically. This could help explain why we are all so overwhelmed by the rapidity of our changing profession.

Yet the younger generation of physicians-to-be are not so uncomfortable with the rapidly changing technologies. They surf the Internet, get instant news from CNN, watch MTV, and conquer video games with ease. They are the *Nintendo* surgeons who were born, raised, and educated and now are being trained with Information Age tools. They absorb information by osmosis, just as they learn a language with all the intuitive ability of a native. Their ability to cope with, and even demand, these newer technologies confirms that this is a major direction for the future. And one of their fundamental tools is the ability to understand the world in the form of three-dimensional (3-D) visualization (once again, replacing atoms with bits). There is a speculative scenario that can be used as a framework to illuminate the integrating power of this concept. It is referred to as the "doorway to the future" and extrapolates to 20, 50 or perhaps 100 years into the future.

As a patient visits her surgeon for a consult, she passes through the office door and, just as scanning is performed today by airport security, she has multiple imaging modalities scanning her (perhaps CT, MRI, ultrasound, and infrared). Placing her hand on a pad on the desk, both physiologic vital signs and biochemical parameters are instantly acquired noninvasively with hyperspectral analysis, as is done with noninvasive acquisition of oxygen saturation, pulse, etc. by pulse oximeters today. The data are all collected and then displayed as a 3-D image of her (looking like the Visible Human) but with not only correct anatomic structure but also all the biochemical and other data added to the correct organ systems. If she complains of right upper quadrant pain, the surgeon can rotate the image, tap or click on the liver, and have the relevant data displayed (e.g., bilirubin, lactate dehydrogenase, and alkaline phosphatase). If an abnormality is seen, such as a colon mass, a virtual colonoscopy can be done on the image by flying through the colon with the same view as an actual colonoscopy. If a lesion is found, the image can be used for patient education, illustrating to the patient exactly what her specific problem is. Should colon resection require a complicated procedure, the image can be used for preoperative surgical planning or imported into a surgical simulator to practice resection on the patient's actual anatomy for the optimal procedure. At the time of surgery, the image can be imported onto the video monitor of laparoscopic colon resection, and with data fusion the two images displayed simultaneously as an intraoperative navigation tool (stereotactic navigation). At the postoperative follow up visit, the patient is scanned again, by comparing the postoperative with the preoperative datasets and using digital subtraction techniques, the difference between the two datasets is automatic outcomes analysis. Because the record is a dataset, it can be stored on a credit card (the U.S. military is using a prototype card called the MARC card) or kept on a Web server to be distributed worldwide over the Internet for consultation. Thus by considering the medical record as a 3-D image of the patient, the entire spectrum of patient care can be integrated and continuously updated.

The purpose of the this scenario is to provide an explanation of and rationale for why it is so important to understand how information can empower us, to show the looking glass through which the next-generation surgeon will be viewing the world. To bring the scenario out of the speculative and rhetorical and into the real world, the technologies that these views are presented in this chapter must be held accountable to the scrutiny of science. Only when these new discoveries are properly evaluated with rigorous testing and clinical trials can they take their place in the framework of the future. It is the postulate that these technologies are based on proven scientific principles but have significant challenges for development, clinical trials, and commercialization before they can become the standard of practice for medical applications. The following three areas are an arbitrary division of medical applications for the new technologies: diagnostics, therapeutics, and education and training.

9.1   DIAGNOSTICS

In the area of diagnostics, noninvasive microsensors for physiologic and biochemical data and portable 3-D imaging systems will obtain information for the physician (Fig. 9.2). A wearable vital signs monitoring system for soldiers (4) developed by Sarcos (Salt Lake City) called the Personnel Status Monitor (PSM) was field tested in 1996 (Fig. 9.3). This consists of a geolocation position

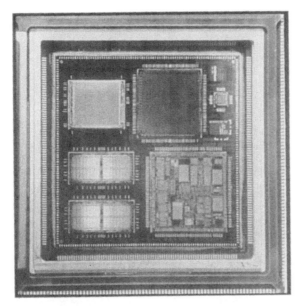

Figure 9.2. Microsensor system for temperature. An entire sensor, computer, radio transmitter, antenna, and power supply are on a single chip. (Courtesy T. Ferrell, Oak Ridge National Laboratories, Oak Ridge, TN.)

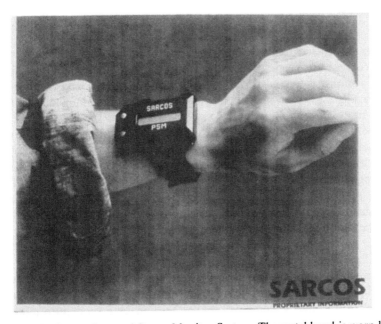

Figure 9.3. The Sarcos Personal Status Monitor System. The watchband is worn by the soldier. (Courtesy of S. Jacobsen, Sarcos, Inc., Salt Lake City.)

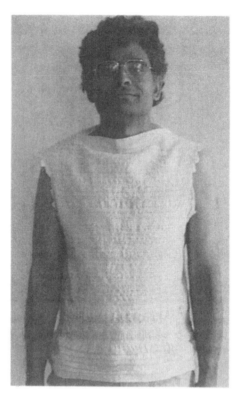

Figure 9.4. The Smart Tee-Shirt. showing fiberoptic and piezoelectric fibers woven into the garment. (Courtesy S. Jayaraman, Georgia Technology Institute, Atlanta.)

satellite (GPS) locator, telecommunications, and a suite of vital signs (pulse rate, temperature, respiration, etc.); the medic has a hand-held receiving unit. When a soldier is wounded, the medic is instantly alerted, and the unit displays the casualty's location and vital signs so the medic can immediately find and triage the wounded. To compliment this, the Smart Tee-Shirt is being developed jointly by the Naval Research Laboratory at San Diego and the Georgia Technology Institute, which has sensors woven into the fabric (fiberoptic and piezoelectric materials) or embroidered into strategic locations (ECG leads); their signals are read by the PSM system for remote transmission (Fig. 9.4) (5, 6). Although the initial application is for the battlefield, it is clear that such technologies, when produced as a consumer product, can be used equally well for health and fitness, for intensive care patients, in the operating theater, and for nursing homes invalids. These monitoring devices emphasize the trend toward point-of-service of health care.

There are a number of newer 3-D imaging modalities being developed, most with the intent of miniaturizing. Smaller, portable CT and MRI scanners and portable ultrasound systems will make these imaging modalities more affordable and available. Significant progress is occurring in the ultrasound field.

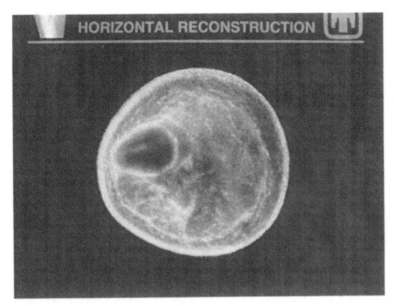

Figure 9.5. Cross-section of the lower leg, mid-calf level, using ultrasound. (Courtesy Morimoto, Sandia National Laboratories, Albequerque, NM.)

Taking sophisticated digital signal processing algorithms from the satellite image community, Sandia National Laboratories are refining the clarity of ultrasound to approach that of CT or MRI scans (Fig. 9.5). In addition, full 3-D representations can be made from serial slices. In September 1996, the U.S. military used a Battelle (Pacific Northwest Laboratories) prototype portable 3-D ultrasound system in Bosnia (Fig. 9.6). With this unit, full 3-D ultrasound images were acquired in the field hospitals (MASH) and sent back to a radiologist at Walter Reed Army Medical Center or Madigan Army Medical Center for interpretation and immediate reporting back to the field hospital. There were no radiologists in Bosnia, yet the combat surgeons had access to this information. There are also new miniaturization discoveries that have led to the next generation of hand-held ultrasound (Fig. 9.7), so that the physicians of the future will have both a stethoscope to hear inside the body and an ultrasound to see inside the body. In 1990, Troidl (7) of Cologne, Germany, stated in his presidential address to the European Association of Endoscopic Surgeons that "ultrasound will be the visual stethoscope of the future." Progress is such that this is no longer a technology issue, rather one of practicality and cost.

The acquisition of 3-D images permits the reconstruction of actual patient organs and tissues in a visual format similar to the images acquired from various endoscopic techniques (8–11). By taking the serial sections of CT, MRI, or ultrasound and segmenting (individually separating) the organs, the computer-generated organ can be flown around or through, which gives a computer

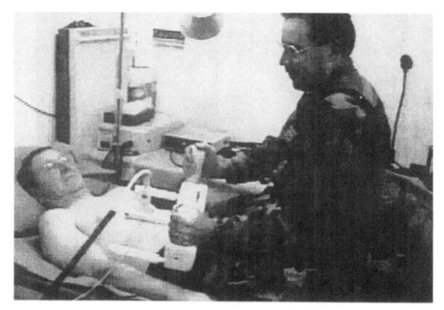

Figure 9.6. The portable 3-D tele-ultrasound system used in Bosnia. (Courtesy R. Littlefield, Battelle Pacific Northwest Laboratories, Hannaford WA.)

visualization that is the same as a video or fiberoptic image during the endoscopic procedure. Thus diagnosis can be made from a computer image rather than from inserting the actual instruments—the savings in complications, patient discomfort, and cost are evident. The procedure most investigated to date is that of virtual colonoscopy (Fig. 9.8), and one of the latest clinical trials by McFarland and Brink (11) show initial discovery of polyps by virtual colonoscopy in patients with proven polyps is 75% sensitivity and 91% specificity. The authors reviewed a number of new directions made possible by virtual endoscopy, including autonavigation through the colon, unraveling like a virtual gross pathology, or flattening out into a Mercator map-like projection. In addition computer-aided diagnosis can be used to automatically identify suspicious areas based on specific geometrics such as wall thickness. Today, virtual colonoscopy must first have a bowel cleansing and insufflation of air; the problem of adequate bowel prep is being addressed by investigations into eliminating the residual stool or liquid with various techniques of tagging of the stool or using contrast agents. These new directions should improve diagnostic accuracy over that stated above. More important, these initial successes are spreading to other areas, such as bronchoscopy, sinusoscopy, and cystoscopy. Not only does this make screening procedures more cost effective and patient compliance higher but also the images obtained form the fundamental building blocks of the virtual human (a representation of a patient by computer image).

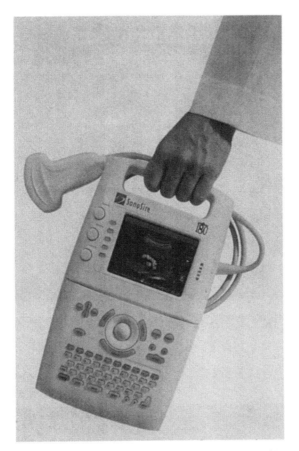

Figure 9.7. Small, handheld portable ultrasound unit by SonoSite. (Courtesy S. Carter, University of Washington, Seattle, WA.)

9.2 THERAPEUTICS

Along with the well-known benefits, laparoscopic surgery imposed significant difficulty for surgeons because of the loss of 3-D vision, dexterity, and the sense of touch. A number of systems have been devised to regain those lost qualities, using various computer-assisted, image-guided, and robotic systems. After Robodoc for hip replacement (12) (Fig. 9.9), the Green (SRI International) telepresence surgery system was developed (13) (Figs. 9.10 and 9.11). This system, like all current teleoperation systems, was devised to increase the dexterity for the surgeon. However, because it is mediated through a computer, it automatically has the capabilities of a remote surgical system as well. This system is currently being commercialized by Intuitive Surgical, Inc. and human use studies are being conducted in Belgium (14). This system, along with others

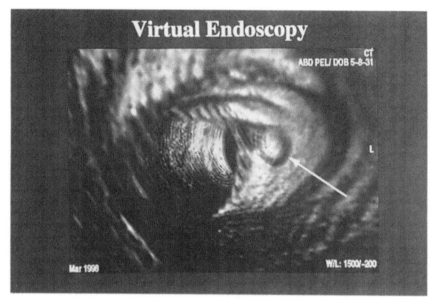

Figure 9.8. Virtual colonoscopy. (Courtesy J. Brink, Yale University School of Medicine, New Haven, CT.)

Figure 9.9. RoboDoc robotic surgery system for coring the femoral shaft in hip replacement. (Courtesy of H. Paul, University of California at Davis, Sacramento.)

Figure 9.10. The surgeon's console on the telepresence surgery system—first generation. (Courtesy P. Green, SRI International, Menlo Park, CA.)

such as Computer Motion Inc's. Zeus (15) (Fig. 9.12), Microdexterity Systems's Paradex (Fig. 9.13), and Ian Hunter's system at MIT (16) are adding sophisticated motion tracking, tremor filtration, and scalability for dexterity enhancement. Other laboratory researchers, such as Hannaford at the University of Washington, are experimenting with adding tactile sensation to the instruments (17). One of the target applications will be minimally invasive surgery on the beating heart. The goal is to produce a system with the same or greater dexterity than the human hand through a minimally invasive approach without the need for cardiopulmonary bypass. Today a significant part of the cost, operative time, and complications for coronary artery surgery are related strictly to placing the patient on cardiopulmonary bypass. The motion tracking, dexterity-enhancing capabilities of the systems under development are all aimed at elim-

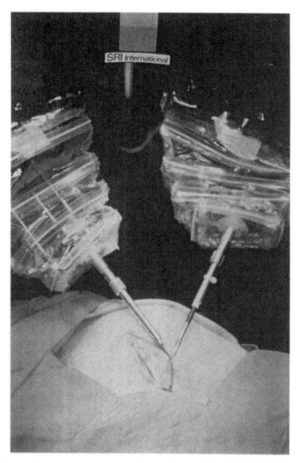

Figure 9.11. The remote manipulators of the telepresence surgery system—first generation. (Courtesy P. Green, SRI International, Menlo Park, CA.)

inating the need for cardiopulmonary bypass, thus gaining the advantages listed above. Interestingly enough, all systems work through a computer interface and, therefore, are inherently a remote telepresence surgical workstation. Although the cost–benefit analysis of the implementation of the cardiac application makes the technique appear viable, there are questions about the need for remote surgery. Thus early acceptance of these newly emerging technologies may well be first seen in the cardiovascular surgery arena, and only later migrate to other areas of surgery. We must remember that other robotic systems have been used for neurosurgery (stereotactic neurosurgery) (18), urology (prostate) (19), orthopedics (hip, knee) (20), and ophthalmology but have gained less-than-universal acceptance. The prolonged period of clinical trials and FDA approval is currently under way. Eventually these methods will

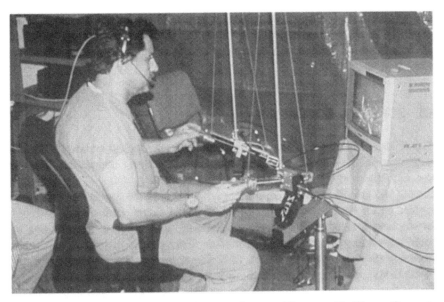

Figure 9.12. The Zeus Telepresence Surgery System. (Courtesy Y. Wang, Computer Motion, Inc., Goleta, CA.)

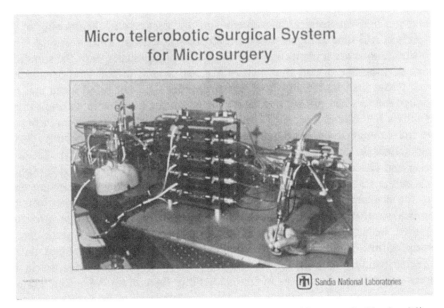

Figure 9.13. The Paradex System for laser retinal surgery. (Courtesy S. Charles, Micro-dexterity Systems Inc., Nashville, TN.)

merge into the mainstream of clinical surgery. The value to the average surgeon will be the chance to enhance his or her skills beyond human limits and the benefit to the patient will be greater access to a higher quality of surgical care.

9.3 SURGICAL EDUCATION

One of the advantages of the laparoscopic and telesurgical systems is that the surgeon looks into a video image rather than directly at the patient. Thus, by replacing the real-time video image with a computer model of the patient or disease, the system automatically becomes a VR surgical simulator. This can be applied in an enormous number of fields, in medicine (endoscopy), radiology (angioplasty), nursing (IV needle placement), and surgery. Simulations can occur with many different levels of models, from simple graphic objects to representing various organs or tissues to highly complex environments portraying multiple systems. The simple simulators are used to teach a task, such as an IV needle insertion, and more complex models can be used for procedures such as angioplasty or complete operations such as laparoscopic cholecystectomy. However, the more complicated the environment that is being simulated, the less realistic appearing the images will be. Even with current high-performance computers, there is not enough computational power to display all the needed aspects of the simulation. These requirements include the visual fidelity of the tissues, the properties of tissues, the dynamic changes to tissues, the contact detection between surgical instruments and the tissues, and the drawing of the objects in real time in high-resolution full color at least 40 times a second. Thus all simulations are a compromise of the above components. Will the simulator have cartoon-like organs that behave like real organs in real time or will they look photo realistic but not have any properties (i.e., not bleed when cut, not change shape when poked) and be displayed on the monitor in jerking motion at only a few frames a second? Until we have massively more computer power, we must match the educational need with the technological capability. Simulators such as the MusculoGraphics's Limb Trauma Simulator (21, 22) (Fig. 9.14) and Boston Dynamics's. Anastomosis Simulator (23) (Fig. 9.15) provide not only a training opportunity but also a skills performance assessment tool. As the instrument handles of the simulator are manipulated to perform the surgical simulation, the system can also be tracking the hand motions, pressures applied, accuracy and precision of needle placement, etc. These data can be compiled into a full analysis of individual skills for objective feedback on enhancing training or even for credentialing. Early implementations are in the areas noted above as well as in complementing the current Advanced Trauma and Life Saving (ATLS) course. The key elements in all of these simulators will be the educational content, curriculum, and assessment tools more that the technical capabilities (24–28). To improve surgical training, efforts must be focused as much on these nontechnical areas as on the simulator capabilities.

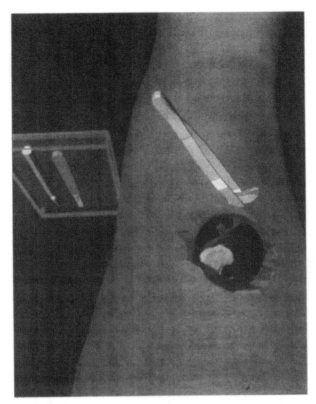

Figure 9.14. Limb Trauma Simulator demonstrating the level of fidelity possible when all properties and surgical instruments are included. (Courtesy S. Delp, Stanford University, Palo Alto, CA.)

9.4 CURRENT STATUS

All the technologies are in the laboratory prototype stage or early clinical evaluation. They must be completely validated in clinical trials, reduced to commercial product, and obtain FDA approval. Throughout this stringent process, some of the technologies will fail to meet the standards of clinical efficacy, cost effectiveness, or practicality. However, there are some overall trends that will probably persist. The diagnostic biosensor systems will continue to become miniaturized, with sensors becoming embedded (into clothing or even possibly the patient) wireless, nonencumbering, noninvasive, ubiquitous, and transparent to the patient. The imaging devices will be portable or hand held and, eventually, ubiquitous and embedded. The therapeutic systems will soon prove their efficacy for dexterity enhancement for surgical procedures; however, there are significant technical barriers that must be overcome to prove clinically relevance for remote surgery. At this time, the approximate limit for using the telesurgery systems for remote surgery is determined by the delay or lag time

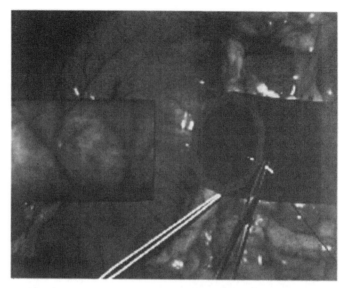

Figure 9.15. The Anastomosis Simulator demonstrating the use of measurement of hand motions to objectively quantify manual skills. (Courtesy M. Raibert, Boston Dynamics Inc., Boston, MA.)

between the movement of the hand and the movement of the remote instrument; this is because of the time needed for the signal to travel from the central to the remote area, which has an approximate maximum of 200 miles by direct terrestrial cable or 35 miles by wireless communication. Even when the technical problems are solved, the question of practical need must be answered. It is attractive to postulate that providing surgical expertise in remote areas through telepresence surgery will greatly improve access to health care, but the slow acceptance of telemedicine in general has shown that barriers of reimbursement, licensure, legal, social, and behavioral issues will frequently impede if not prevent the implementation of what appears a priori to be a great benefit. The area of surgical education will begin to follow the 40-year proven record of flight simulators. As simulators improve in quality and are reduced in cost, medicine can realize the value of training, skill assessment, and ultimately credentialing that has been the mainstay of the aviation industry and the basis for their incredible safety record. While the challenge of employing VR for medical simulation of the human body is orders of magnitude more complex than flight simulators, it is not insurmountable.

9.5 CONCLUSION

This chapter gave a survey of emerging medical devices and technologies that support a fundamentally different view of the future of medicine and surgery in which the information equivalent of the human body plays a central role. Many of the devices acquire information (though sensors or imagers) to build a virtual representation. Powerful informatics tools will process the information, and then therapeutic devices will receive the processed information and provide the results, whether as an enhanced surgical procedure or virtual endoscopy or an entirely new way to display information. The same images will become the centerpiece for the education and training of the future. But we must not be so enamored by the technology that we ignore the reason for these advances—the patient. There is a sacred trust embodied in the Hippocratic oath that must be the final measure of any of these concepts or devices. Every surgeon has accepted personal stewardship for the safety and interest of his or her patients, and to that end we must not rush to embrace or reject, but carefully and prudently evaluate the advances that are of greatest benefit to the patient.

REFERENCES

1. N. Negroponte. Being digital. Cambridge, MA: MIT Press, 1995.

2. J. M. Ackerman. The Visible Human Project. Proc IEEE 1988;86:504–511.

3. N. I. Durlach and A. S. Mavor. Virtual reality: scientific and technological challenges. Washington, DC: National Academy Press, 1995.

4. R. M. Satava. Virtual reality and telepresence for military medicine. Ann Acad Med Singapore 1997;26:118–120.

5. E. J. Lind, S. Jayaraman, S. Park, et al. A sensate liner for biomedical monitoring applications. In: J. D. Westwood, H. M. Hoffman, D. Strendney, S. J. Weghorst, eds. Medicine meets virtual reality: art, science, technology: health care revolution. Amsterdam: IOS Press, 1998:258–264.

6. S. Park, C. Gopalsamy, R. Rajasanickam, and S. Jayaraman. The wearable motherboard: a flexible information infrastructure or sensate liner for medical applications. In: J. D. Westwood, H. M. Hoffman, R. A. Robb, D. Stredney, eds. Medicine meets virtual reality: the convergence of physical and informational technologies: options for a new era in healthcare. Vol. 62. IOS Press: Amsterdam, 1999:252–258.

7. Troidl. 1990.

8. R. A. Robb. Visualization and analysis of biomedical images. Paper presented at the 13th annual international conference of the IEEE Engineering in Medicine and Biology Society. Piscataway, NJ, 1991.

9. D. J. Vining. Virtual colonoscopy. Gastrointest Endosc Clin North Am 1997;7:285–291.

10. D. S. Paik, C. F. Beaulieu, R. B. Jeffrey, et al. Automatied flight path planning for virtual endoscopy. Med Phys 1998;25:629–637.

11. E. G. McFarland and J. A. Brink. Helical CT colonography (virtual colonoscopy): the challenge that exists between advancing technology and generalizability. AJR 1999;173:549–559.

12. H. A. Paul, W. L. Bargar, B. Mittlestadt, et al. Development of a surgical robot for cementless total hip arthroplasty. Clin Orthop 1992;285:57–66.

13. P. S. Green, J. H. Hill, and R. M. Satava. Telepresence: dextrous procedures in a virtual operating field [Abstract]. Surg Endosc 1991;57:192.

14. J. Himpens, G. Leman, and G. B. Cardiere. Telesurgical laparoscopic cholecystectomy. Surg Endosc 1998;12:1091.

15. E. R. Stephenson, S. Sankolkar, C. T. Ducko, and R. J. Damiano. Robotically assisted microsurgery for endoscopic coronary artery bypass grafting. Ann Thorac Surg 1998;66:1064–1067.

16. I. W. Hunter, T. D. Doukoglou, S. R. Lafontaine, et al. A teleoperated microsurgical robot and associated virtual environment for eye surgery. Presence 1993;4:265–280.

17. G. Burdea and P. Coifett. touch and force feedback. In: Burdea and Coifett. Virtual reality technology. New York: Wiley, 1994:81–116.

18. R. D. Bucholz and D. J. Greco. Image-guided surgical techniques for infections and trauma of the central nervous system. Neurosurg Clin North Am 1996;7:187–200.

19. J. E. A. Wickhamn. Future developments of minimally invasive therapy. Brit Med J 1995;308:193–196.

20. A. M. DiGioia, J. Branislav, R. V. O'Toole, et al. Medical robotics and computer assisted surgery in orthopedics: an integrated approach In: R. M. Satava, K. Morgan, H. Sieburg, R. Matthews, and J. P. Christen. Interactive technology and the new paradigm for healthcare. Washington, DC: IOS Press, 1995:88–90.

21. C. Kaufmann, P. Rhee, and D. Burris. Telepresence surgery system enhances medical student surgery training. In: J. D. Westwood, H. M. Hoffman, R. A. Robb and D. Stredney. Medicine meets virtual reality: the convergence of physical and informational technologies: options for a new era in healthcare. Vol. 62. Amsterdam: IOS Press, 1999:174–179.

22. H. Hoffman and M. Murray. Anatomic Visualizer: realizing a vision of VR based learning environment. In: J. D. Westwood, H. M. Hoffman, R. A. Robb, and D. Stredney. Medicine meets virtual reality: the convergence of physical and informational technologies: options for a new eva in healthcare. Vol. 62. Amsterdam: IOS Press, 1999:134–40.

23. M. Raibert, R. Playter, and T. M. Krummel. The use of a virtual reality haptic device in surgical training Acad Med 1998;73:596–597.

24. A. M. Derossis, G. M. Fried, M. Abrahamowicz, et al. Development of a model of evaluation and training of laparoscopic skills Am J Surg 1998;175:482–487.

25. R. Resnick, G. Regehr, H. MacRae, et al. Testing technical skill via an innovative bench station examination. Am J Surg 1997;173:226–230.

26. J. A. Martin, G. Regehr, R. Reznick, et al. Objective structured assessment of technical skill (OSATS) for surgical residents. Br J Surg 1997;84:273–278.

27. H. Faulkner, G. Regehr, J. Martin, and R. Reznick. Validation of an objective structured assessment of technical skills for surgical residents Acad Med 1996;71:1363–1365.

28. J. C. Rosser, L. C. Rosser, and R. S. Salvagi. Skill acquisition and assessment for laparoscopic surgery. Arch Surg 1997;132:200–204.

Lightning Source UK Ltd.
Milton Keynes UK
UKOW03n2109030114

223944UK00001B/75/P